The Christian Mama's
Guide to Having a Baby

Everything You Need to Know

to Survive (and Love)

Your Pregnancy

by Erin MacPherson

Guideposts
New York, New York

The Christian Mama's Guide to Having a Baby

ISBN-10: 0-8249-4858-0
ISBN-13: 978-0-8249-4858-0

Published by Guideposts
16 East 34th Street
New York, New York 10016
www.guideposts.org

Distributed by Ideals Publications, a Guideposts company
2630 Elm Hill Pike, Suite 100
Nashville, TN 37214

Guideposts and *Ideals* are registered trademarks of Guideposts.

Acknowledgments

The author of this book is not a physician, and the ideas, procedures, opinions and suggestions in this book are not intended as a substitute for the medical advice of a trained health professional. All matters regarding your health and the health of your baby require medical supervision. Consult your physician before adopting the suggestions in this book, as well as about any condition that may require diagnosis or medical attention. The ideas, procedures, opinions and suggestions in this book are those of the author and not of the publisher or its editors.

Every attempt has been made to credit the sources of copyrighted material used in this book. If any such acknowledgment has been inadvertently omitted or miscredited, receipt of such information would be appreciated.

"Praise the Father, Praise the Son" by Chris Tomlin and Ed Cash. Copyright © 2008 worshiptogether.com Songs (ASCAP) sixsteps Music (ASCAP) Vamos Publishing (ASCAP) (adm. at EMICMGPublishing.com) / Alletrop Music (BMI) All rights reserved. Used by permission.

Library of Congress Cataloging-in-Publication Data

MacPherson, Erin.
  The Christian mama's guide to having a baby : everything you need to survive (and love) your pregnancy / by Erin MacPherson.
     p. cm.
  ISBN 978-0-8249-4858-0
  1. Pregnant women--Religious life. 2. Pregnancy--Religious aspects--Christianity. 3. Pregnant women--Health and hygiene. 4. Pregnancy--Popular works. I. Title.
  BV4529.18.M33 2010
  649'.10242--dc22
                              2010029228

Cover design by Georgia Morrissey
Cover and interior illustrations by Monica Lee
Interior design and typesetting by Gretchen Schuler-Dandridge

Printed and bound in the United States of America
10 9 8 7 6 5 4 3 2 1

To Alisa and Stevi:

my sisters in pregnancy and life

• contents •

• a c k n o w l e d g m e n t s •

$\mathcal{S}$oli Deo Gloria. To God alone be the glory. That's my prayer for this book. And I am acutely aware of the fact that every good gift comes from the Lord and I am eternally grateful for everything that He has given me—I am so blessed.

I want to acknowledge Rachelle Gardner, my agent from Word-Serve Literary, who believed in my project from day one and worked tirelessly to make sure it came to fruition. And to Rebecca Maker at Guideposts who not only took a chance on a first-time author, but also gave me invaluable insight into my book. Thank you.

I also want to thank my husband Cameron—who took the kids on countless "adventures" to Barnes & Noble so that I could write, who cooked dinner (and did the dishes) faithfully while I edited this book and (perhaps most importantly) is the best daddy my kids could ever ask for. Thank you for paving the way—and making sure that I had every opportunity to follow my dream.

Also, my parents. Mom, thank you for stepping in to babysit every single time I had the urge to put some words onto paper. Thank you for always thinking my work is great no matter what and for always having ideas, suggestions and insight. And Daddy, thank you for being my number one fan. Thanks for always wanting to talk about my book, for always asking questions and for always showing me that you truly care. I love you both so much. And to my mother-in-law Nanette, thank you for always (always) stopping whatever you were doing—even if you were in the middle of a superimportant meeting—to pick up the phone and listen to me ramble about my book.

To my de facto editorial team: Alisa, Hildi, Jessica, Mom and Stevi. Thank you for your hilarious ideas, your brilliant suggestions and most of all, for catching every single typo. I'm sure there were a lot of them. And to Hildi, thanks for holding my hand through the entire querying and book-writing process and for being willing to read and reread and reread my work again and again.

Thank you to Alisa Dusan (enjoyrealfood.com) who served as my official consultant on the eating chapter. Thanks for your ideas and your expertise. And thank you to Nicole Cruz from Stroller Mommies Bootcamps (strollermommiesbootcamps.com) for your ideas, suggestions and, most of all, for inspiring me to get off the couch and actually exercise.

Also, thanks to my mommy girlfriends—Alisa, Anna, Annie, Beth, Brooke, Carrie, Jessica, Karen, Katie, Michelle, Mollie, Nicole, Rachel, Rebecca, Staci, Stevi and Teresa, to name a few— who were completely honest and open with me about all of their pregnancy woes, even when it meant that I was going to share (potentially embarrassing) stories with the entire world. And thanks to the guys—Cameron, Troy, Michael and Peter—who shared their hard-earned pregnancy lessons with other dads-to-be so that they wouldn't have to learn the hard way.

Finally, I want to thank my two adorable kids: Josiah and Kate. Joey, my four-year-old, is always telling everyone that his mommy is a superhero. I'm far from it—but it's so wonderful to know that someone believes in me. And Kate, thank you for the hugs, the kisses and the general sweetness. You make me a better person.

· i n t r o d u c t i o n ·

You're Havin' a Baby!

The fact that you're reading this probably means you're pregnant. Yep. YOU are pregnant. Has a nice ring to it, doesn't it? If you thought your graduation day or your last birthday or even your wedding day was exciting and exhilarating and amazing, just wait until you hold your little bundle in your arms for the first time. The feeling is breathtaking. I get misty-eyed just thinking about it. That said, you have eight months (give or take) to wait before that misty-eyed moment, so don't start packing your hospital bag yet.

I've always wondered how God created the heavens and the earth in seven short days and yet it takes nine long months to create a baby. Nine months. Seems like an eternity, doesn't it? I remember getting so irritated when people told me that my pregnancies would pass in the twinkle of an eye. They swore that I'd be holding my baby before I knew it. That's kind of hard to believe when you're carrying around twenty (*er,* thirty) extra pounds and gagging every time you catch a whiff of someone else's dinner.

But, really, your pregnancy *will* be over before you know it. In the meantime, you're probably going to need some girlfriend-to-girlfriend advice to get you from point A—the miserable, exhausted, growing-by-the-minute, gagging, vomiting and sweating point that you're most likely at right now—to point B—the glowing, ecstatic, sleep-deprived-but-you-don't-care-at-all point that you'll be at in less than forty weeks. And that's why I wrote this book.

I remember during my first pregnancy, the first thing I did after peeing on a stick was head to the bookstore to find a book that would keep me informed about what to expect (nausea, bloating and night waking) and what not to expect (a glorious time where I could eat unlimited amounts of ice cream while my husband massaged my feet). Not surprisingly, there were oodles of choices. There were pregnancy guides for new moms-to-be, old moms-to-be, young moms-to-be and tall moms-to-be. There were pregnancy guides for dads-to-be and grandparents-to-be and second-cousins-to-be. But there was nothing for Christian moms-to-be. So I did what any somewhat sane mother-of-two would do. I wrote my own Christian pregnancy guide.

The good news is that I'm not going to bore you with medical jargon. It's not that I don't like medical jargon (when I was pregnant, I loved reading books that told me all about the medical feats that my body was performing while growing a baby), but simply that I'm not a doctor. In fact, I don't have any medical training at all (unless you count the fact that I took—and *passed*—health education in high school). So if you're looking for medical rhetoric and big-word–laden advice for a magical medical breakthrough that will quell your ever-present nausea and keep your weight gain to a minimum, this probably isn't the place.

But while my medical expertise stops at "take some Tylenol and go lie down," I do have some pregnancy expertise. I've been pregnant twice. My sisters have all been pregnant. My friends have all been pregnant. Heck, a few months ago, my dog got pregnant. I've been surrounded by pregnancy nonstop for the past six years, and as I dealt with morning sickness and weight gain and decorating a nursery, I gleaned some pregnancy knowledge.

I also had horrible pregnancies. I know. I shouldn't be saying that to new moms-to-be, but for the sake of honesty, I'm going to throw it out there. I went through the ringer during my first pregnancy and swore up and down that I would never, *ever* survive and that if by some miracle I did survive, I would never, ever, ever get pregnant again. Well, I survived. I fell in love with my baby and promptly got pregnant again. And you know what? I survived the second awful pregnancy too. And if we're being honest, I'd take another pregnancy (or two), God willing. In an instant.

You probably don't want to hear this right now, but it *is* worth it. Every time you gag. Every time you throw up into your mouth. Every pound you gain. Every sleepless night. All of it. It's worth it. Just wait. I promise that nine months from now, you're going to be e-mailing me and telling me I was right.

I won't say I told you so.

You figured out how to actually *get* pregnant (go, you!); now you have to figure out how to *be* pregnant. And contrary to popular belief, being pregnant isn't as simple as remembering to take your prenatal vitamins, which is a feat unto itself. Pregnancy is exhausting, exciting, exhilarating and stressful all at once, which means that you're going to be exhausted, excited, exhilarated and stressed for the next few months. Not an easy thing to be—especially when you're gaining weight at a rate of three pounds per week.

I hate to even say this to a pregnant woman, but the next few months might not be the best months of your life. (Sorry!) I think my biggest misconception about pregnancy was that I expected it to be easy. I thought I'd be bubbling with baby-growing joy for the entire nine months. Maybe that's true for some people, but it wasn't the case for me. Pregnancy was hard. And stressful. And super-annoying at times. And I wrestled with emotions that I'm embarrassed to even admit. (But we'll get to that later.)

Interestingly, while I was trying to get a handle on the stress and emotions of pregnancy, I felt an overwhelming urge to draw closer to God. There's something about impending motherhood that makes a girl really reflect on who she is and who she wants to be. I knew that my future children needed a godly mother, and I knew that I fell (far) short of the mark. This caused me to spend a lot of time reflecting on the characteristics of godly mothers and how I could become one.

As Christian women, we have to live up to a pretty high standard. The legendary Proverbs 31 woman is gracious and kind and long-suffering and probably never snapped at her husband for leaving dirty clothes on the floor. I'm not even close. I find myself in a daily battle to live up to God's standard for my life. I wake up praying that I'll live with patience and integrity throughout the day... and find myself losing my cool before breakfast.

Yet, at one of the most stressful, emotional and trying times of my life (my first pregnancy), God drew me closer to Him. I actually felt His presence as I spent time praying and reflecting on my baby and my future as a mother. It's comforting to hear His voice in a time of need and feel His presence when you're feeling your worst. And hearing God's voice (and knowing He's there) is great motivation to have a godly attitude throughout pregnancy.

Of course, I was still the same old girl who couldn't seem to make it to breakfast without losing patience about something. (Have I mentioned the dirty laundry that is always left on the bathroom floor?) Still, God did show me that purposefully choosing to have a godly attitude resulted in my feeling closer to Him. That, in turn, allowed me to have a more gracious attitude about my pregnancies.

Sounds a bit trite, doesn't it? I mean, if it was all about choosing to smile through any situation, every day would be gumdrops and preggo-pops, right? Not exactly. But God does call us to be content in any circumstance (even morning sickness!), which means choosing to focus on the reasons we have to be grateful, even when it's tempting to be grumpy.

And trust me, when I was pregnant, I had lots of reasons to be grumpy. But I did strive to have an attitude of gratitude about my pregnancy. Here's how I did (and didn't) do it.

How to Get into the Pregnancy Groove

1. Get Yourself Pumped Up

When I first got pregnant, I was giddy with excitement. And who wouldn't be? I was going to have a *baby*. I couldn't stop thinking (or talking) about it. But then I got tired. And sick. And bloated. And suddenly I wasn't so giddy anymore. In fact, once those pregnancy symptoms kicked in, I turned into a whiney, moaning, self-pitying mess. I resented my baby for making me feel so bad and resented everyone else because they didn't feel as bad as I did. I resented my job because I had to go to it. I resented my husband because he could sleep and I couldn't. I even resented my dog because she could spend the entire day basking in the sunshine while I had to actually get up and function.

So how exactly do you start thinking about rainbows and baby booties when you've spent weeks hugging the toilet bowl? One thing I did was immerse myself in babyland. I bought books about pregnancies and babies. I hung out with friends who had babies. I ogled over baby gear on the Internet and rented funny movies about babies and watched them over and over. The only thing I didn't do was volunteer to babysit because that would've taken way more energy than I had at that point. But if you're feeling up to dirty diapers and peekaboo, go for it.

The point is, the more time you spend around babies (and other mothers), the more excited you will be about your own baby. And believe me, the only thing in the world that is worth nine months of pregnancy is a baby. And you're getting one. So hop on board the baby train (I don't have to tell you twice, do I?), and start living baby.

2. Turn That Mommy Guilt into Glee (or at Least Contentment)

That resentment that I felt because I was sick, tired and fat quickly turned to guilt. I felt guilty for resenting my baby who was supposed to be my pride and joy. I felt guilty for resenting my husband, who was honestly trying to help me as much as he could. Mostly I felt guilty that I wasn't thrilled to be pregnant.

I started to wonder if God didn't approve of my pregnancy and my baby. Crazy talk, right? I know that now, but at the time, I felt so awful and so confused that I started to doubt God's providence. Of course, once I realized—*duh!*—that God blessed me with the pregnancy, I wanted to be grateful to Him regardless of how I was feeling. God wants us to be content in our pregnancies, even when we're not feeling good. Tough job, huh?

It was a long, uphill battle for me. I had to constantly remind myself of God's grace and mercy. But in the midst of the battle, God taught me many lessons that I wouldn't have otherwise learned: how to accept help from others, how to trust and what it means to truly depend on God for strength.

3. Pray for Your Baby

Another way to get into the pregnancy groove is to start praying for your baby in utero. Sounds obvious, right? Well, it wasn't for me. (I was tired *and* sick, okay?) It took me several weeks of pregnancy to start praying for my son. I was so stunned and overwhelmed by the idea of being pregnant that the idea of praying for my baby didn't cross my mind. One day, one of the girls in my small-group Bible study mentioned that she had prayed for her baby throughout her pregnancy, and suddenly the light went on. I wanted to pray for my unborn child too!

I could go into the mushy details about how my husband and I lay in bed and put our hands on my slightly protruding tummy and prayed for our son, but I'm sure you get it. In fact, you've probably been praying for your baby since the moment you found out you were pregnant. But just in case there's another woman out there like me who didn't think of it, I thought I'd mention it.

4. Think about the Pros of Pregnancy

There are some (okay, lots of) wonderful things about pregnancy. What other time in your life do you have free license to eat extra calories, sleep late and buy baby clothes without reservation?

Plus, when you're pregnant, everyone—and I mean *everyone*—gushes over you. I remember walking into church just as I was starting to show. Two of the guys in our Sunday school class ran to grab me a chair. My husband got me water, and my girlfriend brought me muffins from the class next door. They had blueberry crumble! Everyone *oohed* and *aahed*. Part of me hated all of the fuss—uh, who am I kidding? I loved the attention! Who wouldn't?

But aside from the minor benefits, when you're pregnant it's easy to dwell on all of the things you're missing out on. You can't eat sushi. You can't wear your favorite pencil skirt. Your bras are all too small. And you're too tired to stay up late watching chick flicks with your hubby (as if *that* happened before). I remember bursting into tears in the middle of our church group's Christmas party because the eggnog was made from raw eggs, and I was a little uneasy about exposing my unborn child to salmonella. I actually sobbed. Totally irrational, I know—especially considering the fact that there were a million other drink options at the party—but I felt so deprived.

The thing is that pregnancy isn't about deprivation. Sure, there are things you shouldn't and can't do, but there is also one huge thing that you can do: Nurture your own child inside of you. What an incredible privilege. I'm sure some of our husbands are secretly envious of us that we get to do it and they don't! How else can we account for their sympathy weight gain?

The best way to get out of a pregnancy funk is to think about the reason for the pregnancy. I know that sounds obvious, but focus on your baby. Focus on the privilege. It'll help you to forget the pain. And if that doesn't work, think of all of the things that you can get away with during this brief period of your life.

Things You Can Do While Pregnant (That You Would Never Get Away with Otherwise)

- Wear flip-flops or clogs every day. Even to church.
- Leave the toilet unscrubbed for the entire nine months (might as well make it an even ten).
- Order dessert (and eat it all by yourself).
- Wear sweats to the grocery store, to work and to dinner at your mother-in-law's.
- Skip your morning shower. Three days in a row.
- Add half and half to your decaf (or half-caf).
- Send your hubby to Sonic for a foot-long hot dog at eleven o'clock at night.
- Eat a foot-long hot dog at eleven and wash it down with Chunky Monkey.
- Go to bed at seven on a Friday night.
- Spend your entire Saturday camped out on the couch watching *A Baby Story*.
- Borrow your husband's T-shirts.
- Chat about baby names on a baby names message board.

- Go to BabiesRUs and camp out in one of their rockers for an entire afternoon. (You probably need to test it out, so go ahead and take a nap if you'd like.)

Pregnancy Rocks (Even Though It Sometimes Stinks)

The fact is, in spite of all of the nausea, bloating and constant peeing, there's also an ecstatic, blissful, giddy joy that comes from the fact that you have a baby growing inside of you. It's amazing. And no matter how bad you feel, you can still cling to that. I remember being hunched over the toilet puking up my guts and thinking to myself how amazing it was that there was a tiny life growing inside of me.

The truth is, it's okay to be a little ambivalent, depressed, scared, worried, nervous, angry, irritated or annoyed by your pregnancy. Feeling that way is natural. And feeling that way about your pregnancy has nothing to do with how you're feeling about your baby. Of course you love your baby. But you don't have to love pregnancy to love your baby! Just because you're thrilled to be pregnant, you don't have to ignore all the aches and pains and annoyances.

So enough pep talking. You're ready, right? Time to get down to the nitty-gritty. What are the next nine months *really* going to be like? What can you do to combat morning sickness? And bloating? And the rest of those icky pregnancy symptoms? And perhaps most importantly, how much longer (in minutes) are you going to be able to fit into your favorite prepregnancy jeans? Let's talk first trimesters.

chapter 2

Pregnancy 101

A Crash Course on
Your First Trimester

Let me guess: You're exhausted, you're nauseous, you're bloated and you have to pee every five minutes. Oh, and did I mention exhausted? First trimesters are like that. Sure, you could be one of the lucky girls who skates through her first trimester with nary an ache or pain, but most gals spend their first trimester waiting for their second trimester and their second trimester thanking God that they are no longer in their first.

In fact, I'm going to venture that you are probably lying on the couch in the same exact position that you've been in for three days wearing the same holey sweats you've been wearing for a week. The mere thought of getting up might just make you retch, so you're playing it safe by lying as still as possible and watching your husband flit around while asking if there is anything *(anything)* that will make you feel better.

The fact that you picked up this book was an accomplishment unto itself. Now that you've actually started reading, you're probably thinking that it is already a little too cheery for you. I know that you probably want to stand up and beat it against the wall and scream in agony and frustration, but that would require (a) getting up off the couch, and (b) using energy—two things that probably aren't going to happen right now. So you're stuck. And while you're sitting there wallowing, you might as well have something to do. So read on.

There is some good news: First trimesters are much shorter than second or third trimesters. Technically, your first trimester encompasses the first twelve weeks of your pregnancy, but by the time you know you're pregnant, you're already five weeks along, and by the time your pregnancy symptoms kick in (usually around six or seven weeks), you're over halfway through. Still, the fact that it's short doesn't make it sweet.

When you get preggers, your body's hormones suddenly go into overdrive. Fortunately, these hyperactive hormones are what help your baby grow, thrive and survive, so they're pretty important. Unfortunately, these misbehaving hormones also cause all sorts of crazy symptoms—and during the first trimester, while your body is adjusting to the changes, these symptoms are at their worst.

So if you're feeling tired and sick and bloated and grumpy, blame it on the hormones, and realize that you won't be in your first trimester for long. In the meantime, here's how to cope.

Waiting on the Lord

A few months ago, my husband and I planned a trip to the beach. We told our son (he's four) about the trip a few days before we left. He got superexcited. He sprinted off to his room where he filled his suitcase full of stuffed animals, books and toys and then stood by the door, suitcase in hand, and waited. And waited. And waited. I finally asked him what he was doing and he said he was waiting to go to the beach. When I told him we weren't leaving for four more days, he looked at me teary-eyed and said "Four whole days? I'll be *old* by then!"

That's how my first trimester felt to me. I felt like I was standing at the door with my bag packed…and waiting and waiting and waiting. I felt God telling me to be patient and wait on Him. All the while, my heart was whimpering: "Nine whole months? I'll be *old* by then!"

Pregnancy involves a lot of waiting. Waiting for the doctor, waiting for your ultrasound, waiting for your nursery rocker to arrive and (of course) waiting for your baby to be born. And if you're anything like me, you're going to feel impatient—especially during your first trimester. It's a time when delivery is still months away, you're hardly showing, most people don't even know you're pregnant, yet you're feeling the symptoms of pregnancy in full force. For me, the wait felt excruciating.

Jude 1:21 tells us to "Keep ourselves in God's love as we wait for the mercy of our Lord Jesus Christ." It's interesting to me that God not only calls us to wait for Christ's mercy—and to be patient while we're doing it—but also tells us to keep ourselves wrapped in His love while we're waiting. Yes, it can be agonizing to wait through a long first trimester (or a long pregnancy), but it feels a bit more doable when you know you'll be wrapped in God's love while you wait.

While it sounds all warm and fuzzy to imagine yourself wrapped in God's love as you wait, what exactly does that mean? And how exactly do you keep yourself in God's love? We're told to remain in Him (John 15:5). That means even as you stagger through your first trimester, waiting for your second trimester and more importantly, your baby to arrive, your job is to cling to Christ: to pray, to trust and to steadfastly remain in Him.

Keeping your focus on Christ isn't easy (we already talked about that), but it is something we must purposefully train our minds to do. It doesn't come naturally. It takes practice and perseverance—and a bit of personal accountability. I'm not telling you to kick yourself in the shin every time you start to feel impatient (although that might be a good start), but I am saying that striving to constantly refocus your mind on Him is a good first trimester goal.

One of my favorite songs is "Praise the Father, Praise the Son" by Chris Tomlin. In it, he says "These sufferings, this passing tide, under Your wings I will abide, and every enemy shall flee, You are my hope and victory." That was one of my favorite songs to listen to during my pregnancy as it reminded me exactly what it meant to remain in Him—and to wait on Him. And while you wait, here are a few first trimester factoids to keep your mind busy. See? The wait is getting easier already!

Midwife or Doctor?

One thing you're going to have to decide pretty early on in your pregnancy is who you're going to see for your prenatal care. There are midwives and certified nurse-midwives and nurse practitioners and obstetricians (OBs) and even good ole family doctors. Whoever you choose (and really, there are lots of benefits to each type of practitioner, so I'm not going to make a recommendation), make sure you're comfortable with the person you choose, because you're going to be seeing a lot of each other.

I chose to stay with the same OB/GYN who had been doing my yearly checkups for the past few years. I was comfortable with him (yes, he's a man) because he had done a major, difficult surgery on my mom years before and seemed to really know his stuff. Plus, his office staff was friendly and appointments were easy to get. For me, that was the best choice, and I'm glad I made it because I ended up having complicated pregnancies and my doctor's knowledge and support was a lifesaver.

Lots of women choose to go to a midwife or certified nurse midwife instead of an OB/GYN to deliver their baby. There are lots of advantages to midwives. First of all, midwives tend to have fairly small practices, meaning you'll probably get a lot of one-on-one time with your midwife. Also, midwives tend to encourage natural childbirth, so if you're interested in a drug-free labor and delivery or a home birth, you may want to consider using a midwife. Of course, there are some disadvantages to midwives too. Midwives typically don't have the same medical expertise as an OB/GYN, so they may not be able to handle complicated pregnancies. Plus, midwives generally aren't as keen on using pain medication, which is a real disadvantage in my book.

Another thing to consider when choosing between an OB and a midwife is where you want to deliver your baby. An OB will deliver your baby in a hospital. Period. Midwives, on the other hand, have much more flexibility with where they deliver. A lot of midwives deliver babies at birthing centers (more on that later). Some will even assist you with a home birth. My friend Kathy said that her midwife did a rotation at a hospital near her, and while an OB helped with her actual delivery, her midwife was there the entire time to assist, coach and advocate for her. In fact, she swears that she would've ended up with a C-section had her midwife not been there.

Another thing to think about is the cost. Depending on where you live (and where your midwife delivers), using a midwife can be significantly less expensive. I have a friend who didn't have health insurance when she got pregnant. (*Eek!*) She found a midwife who was willing to work out a payment plan and was able to pay for her entire pregnancy out-of-pocket without taking out a second mortgage.

Speaking of health insurance, it doesn't matter how much you love a certain doctor or midwife, if your insurance isn't going to cover your visits, you're going to be spending a whole lot of out-of-pocket cash—thousands of dollars that you'd probably rather use to buy baby clothes and crib bedding. So call your insurance company and make sure that you're superclear on how your health insurance plan works.

Finally, don't stress about your decision. Yes, choosing your OB or midwife is a big decision, but it's not binding. You don't have to sign any nine-month contracts, so if things don't work out, you can always find another practitioner. I have another friend who chose an OB for her pregnancy and realized after a few visits that it just wasn't going to work. She decided to switch midpregnancy and it was fine! Her new doctor happily accepted a woman who was twenty weeks along (no questions asked!), and she finished her pregnancy without another problem. (For more information to help you make this decision, see page 52.)

Your First Appointment

After I found out I was pregnant, for the first time in my life, I was actually *excited* to go see my OB/GYN. I needed confirmation that the three (okay, seven) pregnancy tests that I peed on weren't lying. I needed assurance that I wasn't somehow inadvertently hurting my baby by smelling the fumes from someone else's double espresso. And I needed to know if the fact that I was already having trouble buttoning my jeans was normal or a sign of first trimester overeating.

I called my OB's office and proudly announced that I was pregnant. Stop the presses! I'm pregnant! Wasn't this big news at the OB/GYN's office? I don't know what I expected them to say. I mean, a little applause or an urgent page to the doctor would've been nice. Instead, the receptionist transferred me to the appointment desk (with little fanfare) where they scheduled me for an appointment FOUR weeks in the future. I was just another one of the fifty bazillion pregnant patients that they see every day. And apparently, OBs don't see the need to schedule appointments with nervous, apprehensive, first-time moms until they are eight weeks along. *Eight weeks? Isn't that like the fourth trimester or something?*

I couldn't believe my ears. I asked to be transferred to the nurse. The nurse explained to me that typically women don't need much prenatal care before eight weeks and that as long as I was taking my prenatal vitamins and eating healthfully, I was going to be fine.

I didn't feel fine. I had so many questions! What should I be eating? What should I be doing? And how was I supposed to know if I was really pregnant or if I had misread the instructions on the pregnancy test box eight times and this was really some cruel joke? (Now you're starting to see why I'm the least patient person in the world.)

When I finally did get to the OB, the visit was fairly uneventful. I heard my baby's heart, checked out my cute little jumping bean on an ultrasound and got a prescription for supermaximum strength prenatal vitamins (which were apparently an upgrade from the plain old ones I had been taking). I asked my questions (No, you cannot hurt your baby by simply sitting in Starbucks and breathing. Who knew?) and each was patiently answered. The best part was my doctor gave me the number to his nurse's line. He said I could call it with questions any day, any time. Suddenly, I had a pregnancy hotline. I was thrilled.

In the end, I guess it was okay that I had to wait eight weeks to see my doctor (it helped with that whole learning patience bit), but before I move on, I want to make sure you know that the eight-week rule isn't set in stone. If you're feeling there's a reason to see the doctor before that, GO! Camp out in the waiting room if you must. You know your body, and there is no reason to spend two weeks in constant anxiety.

Things You May Want to Know about Your First Medical Visit

- Store-bought pregnancy tests actually have an almost non-existent failure rate (especially when taken twelve at a time), so your OB will probably trust you when you say you're pregnant. You could ask to take a blood test "just to be sure," but I'm guessing your OB/midwife will just take your word for it.

- Your doctor or midwife can only see your baby through a trans-vaginal ultrasound until you're in your second trimester. And, yes, *vaginal* means what you think it means. (I'll get into this more in the next chapter, so if you're dying for more details, thumb ahead.)

- No matter how hard you try (and no matter how well it's explained to you), you will never be able to find your baby's legs, arms or face on a first trimester ultrasound picture.

- The nurse who weighs you is not judging you for eating an extra chocolate chip cookie last night. Her job is to chart your growth to make sure you're actually *gaining* weight. So resist the urge to regale her with a full account of your caloric intake for the last two days.

- The prescription for superstrength prenatal vitamins will give you great nails and lustrous hair. The catch? *All* of your hair will be lustrous. (Note to self: Don't forget to shave before your next appointment!)

- Despite what the old wives say, your doctor won't be able to tell your baby's gender by the speed of his/her heart rate or the way he/she is sitting in your uterus. He can try, but there's a 50 percent chance he'll be wrong.

Bleeding

Probably the scariest thing for a newly pregnant mama is bleeding. And it's no wonder why. Bleeding is the number one sign of miscarriage, which—sorry to be a Debbie Downer—is definitely a risk in your first trimester. Plus, lots of Web sites and books claim that first trimester bleeding is a sure sign of an imminent miscarriage, which causes most pregnant mamas to completely freak out at even the slightest sign of blood in their panties.

Let me reassure you: Bleeding does *not* mean that you're definitely having a miscarriage. In fact, first trimester bleeding is fairly common, and there are many, many things that can cause that bleeding—many of which are completely harmless to you and your baby. My sister Alisa noticed some spotting when she was about seven weeks along. After hours of crying, freaking out and tests in her OB's office, she found out that she was not miscarrying, but instead had a small tear in her uterus near the implantation site. This did not put her pregnancy at risk, and she went on to deliver a healthy baby girl.

With this in mind, if you notice any spotting or bleeding, the first thing you need to do is relax. I know it's hard to do when you are worried about your baby, but you stressing out isn't going to help. Call your doctor or midwife immediately. They will probably have you head to the clinic where they can formally assess the cause of your bleeding.

Worrying

Ever heard of *constantworryitis?* Well, probably not, because I made it up. It's my word for a very common, very annoying pregnancy ailment that often lasts well into motherhood (and even into grandmotherhood for some women). Most moms I know develop *constantworryitis* early in their first trimester and see a significant worsening of their symptoms as their pregnancies progress—often resulting in middle-of-the-night trips to the ER and husbands who spend large amounts of time massaging tense shoulders.

The symptoms of *constantworryitis* are pretty straightforward, although the disease affects every woman differently. Here are a few of the most common signs:

- Putting your doctor on speed dial so you can call at a moment's notice if you develop a strange twinge, pain or get the hiccups.
- Calling your best friend or mom at least twelve times a day to see if she felt the same way you do when she was six weeks along.
- Taking large numbers of pregnancy tests after the pregnancy has been confirmed just to make sure that you're "still pregnant."
- Waking up in the middle of the night to Google things like "feeling strange tingly sensation while pregnant" or "forgot to take prenatal vitamin for one day while pregnant."
- Being on a first-name basis with your doctor's nurse.
- Obsessing over everything that crosses your lips just in case it's on the pregnancy don't list.

If you think you might have *constantworryitis*, run—don't walk—to the nearest ER and demand that they check you over from head to toe just to make sure there's nothing wrong with you that you hadn't already thought of. Seriously though, it's natural to worry—just wait until your baby figures out how to climb onto the kitchen table and hang from the chandelier (yes, mine did that). And remember that God is very clear in the Bible that worry is futile. He tells us over and over again that He is in control and that our job is to trust Him completely. In Luke 21:14, Jesus even goes a step further and asks His disciples to make up their minds *not* to worry. So not only does God say that worrying is a waste of time, but He also tells us that we can (and should) choose not to worry. Interesting, right?

But knowing that we shouldn't worry and actually not worrying are different things. It's very clear to me that worry is useless, yet I have a really hard time trusting God with my kids. That's almost laughable considering the fact that He's the creator and ruler of the universe, but it's really easy for me to slip into an untrusting mind-set. Instead of relying on God to carry me and my children, I start trying to figure out how I can control things. And since I have very little ability to control the world (who knew?), I usually end up worrying more and more. It's a terrible spiral that ends with my feeling anxious, upset and stressed.

The only way to break out of this spiral is to turn to Him. Try replacing worry with Scripture: Memorize a verse that reminds you who is in control and recite it in your mind until the worry has passed. When I start to worry, I repeat Psalm 91:2 in my mind: *I will say of the Lord, "He is my refuge and my fortress, my God, in whom I trust." I will say of the Lord, "He is my refuge and my fortress, my God, in whom I trust." I will say of the Lord, "He is my refuge and my fortress, my God, in whom I trust."*

Let's (Not) Talk about Sex, Baby

You've probably spent a lot of time lately lamenting the fact that you ever consummated your marriage in the first place. After all, consummating is how you got into this pickle. It's no wonder that whenever your husband gives you *that look,* your gut reaction is to run and put on the ugliest flannel pajamas you can find and spend the rest of the night cowering on the couch behind a book entitled *Pope Gregory's Theology of Chastity.*

Take heart, ladies (and miserable husbands): By your second trimester, a sudden increase in progesterone (hormones again!) will make you forget all about Pope Gregory. In the meantime, your sex life doesn't have to disappear altogether just because you're in the middle of the first trimester woes.

You've probably realized by now that first trimester sex is a far cry from baby-making sex or even regular old sex. Pregnancy sex is usually slightly (okay, entirely) less frequent—mostly because you're contending with icky first trimester symptoms like bloating, exhaustion and morning sickness. It's a whole new learning curve, and you'll probably need some practice to master it. Just to get you started, here's a crash course on pregnancy sex.

Sex 101 for First Trimester Mamas

- **Don't worry.** One cool thing about pregnancy sex is that it's very unencumbered. You don't have to worry about ovulation calendars (joy killers) or birth control (too late for that). Be careful not to "reencumber" your sexual moments by fretting. No, sex won't hurt your baby, and no, you won't get pregnant again. You can just sit back and enjoy the, *ahem,* ride.
- **Protect your breasts.** Most guys love boobs, which means the first thing your hubby's going to reach for is the gals. Warn him ahead of time that they might be a *little* tender. This will help you avoid a midsex screaming session. And speaking of breasts—they *might* leak a little during sex. Sorry to be so graphic, but your boobs are preparing to breast-feed a baby, so it's totally normal for them to leak a bit of milk from time to time. You might want to warn your man about that as well.
- **Go for a nooner.** First trimester mamas have a tendency to go to bed early. Like at six o'clock. So try mixing things up and hav-

ing sex in the morning. Or at lunchtime. Or at three on a Sunday afternoon just because you'll probably be asleep by four.

- **Set the mood.** It's hard—but not impossible—to get that sexy feelin' when you're in your first trimester. Light some candles. Put on some music. Crack open a bottle of, *er,* fruit juice. Turn the lights down low. With a little effort—and a good massage from your hubby—you might realize that sex does sound like fun after all.

- **Don't worry about how you look (or smell).** You're probably feeling kind of gross right now. You're bloated and sweaty and you've thrown up fourteen times in the last fifteen days. And it's hard to imagine how your man could find a bloated, sweaty and constantly puking girl sexy. But he does. So quit worrying about whether your man thinks you're sexy and start showing him that you are. Really. I mean it. Go now. Just brush your teeth first.

Pregnancy *Grrrravings*

When you got pregnant, you expected to have first trimester food cravings. At least I did. I actually thought it would be kind of fun— midnight cartons of Ben & Jerry's and fat, juicy pickles for break-

fast. I looked forward to being able to eat whatever I wanted for no reason other than the fact that I wanted it. Sounds like a dream, huh?

The problem with pregnancy food cravings is that they're not the usual "I feel like pizza tonight." Instead, they're "If I don't get a slice of pizza in my belly in the next ten minutes I'm certain I'm going to die right here on the couch and you will be to blame." Since pregnancy cravings are nowhere near as calm as your typical food cravings, I think they deserve a whole new name. I'm proposing *grrrravings*.

That way your husband will know when you say, "I'm *grrrraving* a foot-long hot dog with all the fixin's right now," it means: "Get in the car and head to Sonic *stat*," not, "Look and see if there's something similar in the back of the fridge." Well-meaning husbands who have never had a *grrrraving* before don't always understand what it's like. They tend to get a bit frustrated at being sent to the grocery store in the middle of the night to fetch a pint of Chunky Monkey. Not that I know from experience or anything.

For me, *grrrravings* varied. Once, there was a two-week period where the only thing I wanted to eat was Chipotle chicken burritos. I literally dragged myself off the couch and drove to Chipotle every single day to order a burrito and then went home and sat on the couch relishing every morsel. My husband checked our bank statement and informed me that I'd spent $149 at Chipotle in the last month. He just didn't understand *grrrravings*. What did he want me to do? Starve?

Pregnancy Aversions

The problem with pregnancy *grrrravings* is that they usually turn into pregnancy aversions. It's a catch-22. Anything you want to eat while you're pregnant, you probably *will* eat, which in turn will make you never want to eat it again. Ever. This does not bode well for Costco-sized packages of crackers or buy-one-get-one-free frozen burritos.

Remember that Chipotle *grrrraving* I told you about? Well, now it's a Chipotle aversion. I won't set foot in that restaurant. Heck, I'll take a different (and longer) route to the mall just so I don't have to drive by Chipotle. It's not that I don't like Chipotle. I do. At least I used to. But there is no way I could manage to take a single bite of a Chipotle burrito ever again. Well, maybe not ever, but at least not for a long, long time. My point? Just because you're dying to devour an extra large bag of Tater Tots right now, don't do anything crazy like buy stock in the Tater Tot company. Chances are, you'll gag at the thought of Tater Tots tomorrow. The key to pregnancy grocery shopping is to buy small amounts of things. Wait. Strike that. The key to pregnancy grocery shopping is to remind your ever-doting husband to buy small amounts of everything. Just remind him that if he buys an industrial-sized box of Cheese Nips, he's the one who's going to be eating them for the next seven months.

The First Trimester Trifecta

Even with all of your first trimester food cravings, aversions, worrying and doctor's visits, probably the highlight (read: lowlight) of the first trimester for most pregnant gals is what I call the First Trimester Trifecta: utter exhaustion, bloating and morning sickness. If it rains, it pours, and when you're in your first trimester, it really pours. Constant exhaustion, 24-7 nausea and massive bloating are all formidable in their own right, but having to deal with them all at the same time for weeks on end is enough to drive a girl insane. No wonder I was so impatient waiting for my second trimester!

I'm dedicating an entire chapter to morning sickness (feel free to flip ahead to Chapter 4 if you want) because hands down, morning sickness is the worst of the three, but before we go on to those, let's talk exhaustion and bloating.

Utter Exhaustion

Utter exhaustion is a universal symptom of early pregnancy. I know women who have evaded bloating and even women who have dodged the morning sickness bullet. I even know one gal who didn't gain an ounce before she was twenty-five weeks along. But every woman I know was utterly exhausted during her first trimester.

For me, it started before I even knew I was pregnant. I was falling asleep on the couch at seven thirty while watching *American Idol* and still struggling to get up on time for work. The sleep button on my alarm clock was getting a lot of use. I couldn't seem to stay awake during sermons at church. (*Shhh!* Don't tell!) I started to worry that I had mono.

I mentioned my exhaustion to my mom and she just looked at me and smiled as if she knew something that I didn't. Apparently she did. I found out a week later that I was pregnant.

Ways to Deal with Constant Exhaustion

- **Take catnaps.** If you have to, take an alarm clock to work and catch a few winks in your car or office (if you're lucky enough to have a door) during your lunch break.
- **Let housework slide.** I know it's hard (trust me, I'm a bona fide neat freak!), but if your house doesn't get vacuumed for a few weeks (or months), it's not going to be the end of the world.
- **Try to get a little exercise.** Okay, so you hardly have energy to get off the couch and grab a glass of water (which, by the way, totally counts as exercise!), but getting moving can often make you feel more energized. I'm not recommending that you go out and run eight miles, but a twenty- (or even five-) minute walk will work wonders.
- **Add a little caf to your decaf.** I tried to cut out the caffeine when I first got pregnant and that lasted about twelve minutes. A little bit of caffeine is not going to hurt your baby (if you don't believe me, ask your doctor), and there is no reason to put yourself through the torture of caffeine withdrawal if you don't have to. I'm not

advocating going out and drinking a quadruple Americano every morning, but a cup of morning joe is just fine.

- **Drink up!** Water, that is. Let's face it—you're going to pee every ten minutes anyway and drinking water is good for you *and* your baby.
- **Go to bed earlier.** An eight o'clock bedtime is perfectly acceptable for a pregnant woman (and for new parents, just for future reference).
- **Take your prenatals.** Lots of pregnant mamas end up getting anemia from iron deficiency, which makes you even more tired. (Can you imagine?) So be diligent about taking your vitamins.
- **Cut back on your social life.** I know, it's a real bummer to miss out on movie night or a girl's shopping trip, but it's also a real bummer to be flat-out exhausted for weeks on end. Know when to say no (a skill that will serve you well when your kid is in preschool and the teacher asks you to be the room mom, PTA coordinator and class craft director all at the same time). You won't be pregnant forever.

Pregnancy Bloat

My jeans started to feel too tight about fifteen minutes after I took my pregnancy test. It was way too early for me to be showing (my baby was the size of a blueberry!), yet there was no way I was going to get my pants buttoned. Thank you, pregnancy bloat!

Apparently the same hormones that help your baby to grow big and strong also help you grow big and puffy. Technically, the increased progesterone in your system is slowing down your metabolism so that your body can more readily absorb nutrients for your baby. (God thought of *everything,* didn't He?) So while your body works extra hard to give your baby every vitamin and mineral she needs, you get to deal with extra gas floating around in there, which leads to bloating, burping and, yes, even farting. (Did I say that? Ahem, I meant *passing gas.*)

I remember going out to dinner with friends once early in my first pregnancy. The jeans I wore to dinner fit fine when we went in, but after a couple of fajitas, they were starting to feel a bit tight. I discreetly unbuttoned the top button of my pants (what a relief!) and continued eating. Of course, the pregnancy bloat set in and when I went to rebutton them before we walked out, I couldn't get them buttoned. They were a good inch too small! I had to pull down my shirt as far as I could and hope no one noticed that I was walking around in public with my pants unbuttoned.

Ways to Battle the Bloat

- **Drink water.** Being constipated will only make you more bloated. Just sayin'.
- **Eat minimeals.** If you down an entire pepperoni pizza in one sitting, you're probably going to feel bloated for the rest of the week. Try eating two slices now, two slices in an hour and the last few slices at midnight when you get up to pee.
- **Slow down.** Now I sound like your mom, don't I? But eating more slowly keeps you from swallowing air and gets those digestive juices flowing.
- **Put your legs up.** Grab a glass of water and a good book and put your legs up high for a half hour or so. Elevating your legs can get the blood pumping and those gastric juices flowing. Bonus: Get your hubby to rub your feet while you kick back and sip water from a straw.
- **Avoid gassy foods.** I know, you crave what you *grrrrave,* but if you are feeling superbloated, try to avoid things like broccoli, onions and beans.
- **Watch the salt.** Sorry if it sounds like I'm treating you like a heart

patient or something! But you and I both know too much sodium is the kiss of death when you're trying to avoid the bloat.

Nonmaternity Clothes for the Early Maternity Days

When I got pregnant, I was actually excited to start wearing maternity clothes. Pregnant girls are so cute: adorable bellies, supersoft belly-hugging shirts, cute boot-cut maternity jeans and a glowing smile to cap it all off. I wanted to look like that!

The bad news is that even if you're feeling bloated (and gaining weight) during your first trimester, your belly probably won't be big enough to fit into maternity clothes until you're eighteen or nineteen weeks along. In the meantime, you'll be in this weird space where your jeans are too tight, your shirts are too short and your cleavage is too big for every article of clothing you own. It's like you've gained thirteen pounds of bloat and not a single inch around your middle where you expect to gain weight.

Talk about frustrating. Every morning I'd try to find something to wear to work and strike out over and over again. My pants dug into my hips and my shirts showed off my backside. And don't even get me started on my ginormous boobs. My husband was ecstatic (which was great at home), but I couldn't find a single appropriate shirt to wear to work. I was popping out of every blouse I owned.

How do you deal with the in-between months? Here are a few ideas.

First Trimester Wardrobe Tricks

- Tie a long scarf around your neck to cover excessive cleavage or a bulging middle.
- Borrow your husband's basics. A white button-down work shirt can be feminized with bright jewelry and cute shoes.
- Buy a rocking pair of nonmaternity jeans that are one or two

sizes bigger than your normal size. You'll thank me on the flip side when you've been wearing elastic-waisted pants for six months because you still haven't lost the baby weight.

- Try the rubber band trick: Loop a hair tie through your button-hole on your pants and then hook the looped ends to your button. Bada bing. Your pants just grew two sizes in twelve seconds.
- Or, if you're not into wearing your pants unbuttoned like I was, pick up a BellaBand at Target or at ingridandisabel.com. It's a stretchy elastic band that holds up (and hides the button) on your jeans when you can't button them anymore.
- Wear leggings under a lightweight cotton dress. Leggings smooth out your legs and hips and give you some control, while dresses do a good job of showing off cute pregnancy bellies without showing off icky pregnancy bulges.
- You know how excited you get when your husband wears that awesome white wife-beater? Swipe it from him. Not only are wife-beaters superfashionable, they make great preggo under-shirts as they're long enough to cover a bulging midsection and high enough to hide excess cleavage.
- Make sweats look good. Even if you're the type of girl who wouldn't have been caught dead wearing sweats to the grocery store two months ago, sweats are a totally acceptable wardrobe staple for a pregnant gal. Pair them with a cute pair of flats and a sassy maternity T-shirt (blessencematernity.com has some cute ones with Christian messages).

Still Waiting

Still waiting? Probably. Actually, I'm guessing you're *still* on the couch and *still* wearing those sweats. That's to be expected. Have your husband run and get you a tall glass of lemonade. Kick back. Try to relax. You're probably going to be there for a while.

First trimesters are long and can really test the patience of even the most long-suffering of us. It's hard to wait…and especially hard when you're waiting on something as big and important as your baby. The best advice I can give you is the advice you've heard over and over: Abide in Him.

When you're feeling your worst and impatiently waiting for the end, when you're ready to throw the towel on this whole pregnancy thing, abide in Him. Fall down on your knees and ask the One who truly understands pain, suffering and impatience to give you mercy. And He will. It may not be relief, but He will show you mercy. And He will wrap you in His love. And that's all you need to make it through.

Speaking of making it through, we still have the biggest leg of the First Trimester Trifecta left to talk about: morning sickness. But before we do that, let's talk about your first big visit to the doctor (or midwife)—because I know you're dying to get to the nitty-gritty of ultrasounds, blood tests and genetic testing.

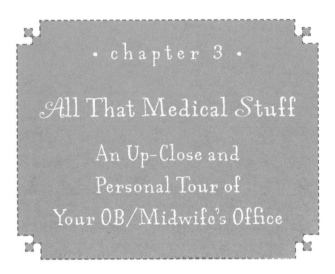

• chapter 3 •

All That Medical Stuff

An Up-Close and Personal Tour of Your OB/Midwife's Office

I'm not a doctor. I don't even watch *Grey's Anatomy*, so I can't fake it when it comes to medical stuff. And since it's generally frowned upon in the medical community to dole out medical advice when you don't know what you're talking about, I figure it's probably best that I avoid giving you medical counsel and leave that to your doctor or midwife.

I am, however, a waiting room veteran. I've spent a *lot* of time in one over the past few years. In fact, during my second pregnancy, I purposefully made my appointments during the busiest time of the day so I could drop my son off with my husband and spend an hour or two in the waiting room reading *Pregnancy Weekly*. It was my weekly indulgence.

Regardless of whether you look at time at the doctor's office as a relaxing getaway or an annoying necessity, you'd better get used to the idea of spending a lot of time there. In fact, you might want to buy yourself one of those butt cushions people sit on at ball games, or you're going to end up with hemorrhoids from all of that seat time. (Okay, so those are caused by the pregnancy, but you might as well blame the uncomfortable chairs).

Early in your pregnancy, they'll want you to visit at least once a month—which is manageable. At about twenty-six weeks, your doctor will probably increase you to every two weeks, which seems like a lot—but it's nothing compared to the end of your pregnancy. At about thirty-six weeks, they'll want you every week. At this point, it's a good idea to start praying that your baby will come early—just to save you some gas money or train fare. I won't even mention how often they'll want you to come once you've passed your due date. Let's just say that at that point, you might as well pack your bags and your bum cushion and move into the waiting room.

In the next few months you'll get more tests than you can count, be checked and rechecked and checked again and find yourself totally exposed with at least ten people in the room more than once. By the time your pregnancy is over, you'll be supercomfortable (okay, a little more comfortable than you would've been otherwise) with your feet in those awful stirrups. So for practice, prop your feet up on your coffee table and get ready for a chapter dedicated to the doctor's office. Consider it your own up-close and personal tour. After all, you'll probably spend almost as much time there as you do in the baby section at Target.

The Waiting Room Bathroom

Our first stop on your tour is the waiting room bathroom—the place you'll be sent first thing upon entering your doctor's office. Once inside, you'll notice that this is no ordinary restroom—yes, it has a toilet and a sink and (hopefully) some paper towels—but the entire layout of this restroom was designed for one purpose and one purpose only: to collect hundreds and hundreds of cups of pee from pregnant women like you.

Somewhere in the bathroom, you'll find a giant basket full of teeny, tiny plastic cups. Your task: Fill one of those tiny cups with pee. It doesn't matter how much pee you actually manage to get in there or how long it takes (although if you take too long, you'll have a hoard of angry cup-wielding pregnant women banging down the door). But you can*not* leave the bathroom until you have managed to squeeze something out. So look at your little cup as your golden ticket into the OB's office. Without it, you're not going any farther than the waiting room.

I'm not going to get into the details about how to pee in a cup because (a) I'm not really sure I want to get that graphic and (b) your OB has probably posted a step-by-step "Dummies' Guide to Peeing in a Cup" poster on the wall in the bathroom. There might even be pictures if you're a visual learner. I'm sure you'll figure it out.

Once you're done, your doctor will probably ask you to leave the cup in the bathroom or to bring it to the receptionist. Some fancy doctor's offices have little pee-deposit doors in the bathroom. Basically, this is a tiny two-way cabinet. You open a door, and put your pee cup on a shelf and a lab technician can open a door on the other side and take your pee out. Cool, right? One note: It's probably best to open and shut this door as quickly as possible—lab technicians tend to get a bit creeped out when they open the door and see you standing there staring at them. Just warning you.

And in case you're wondering, the lab techs aren't collecting all those cups of pee so that the lab looks sunny and colorful. They're testing your pee for all sorts of pregnancy health indicators. First, they'll check it to make sure you don't have a urinary tract infection or a kidney infection. Then, they'll dip a little paper chemical strip into your pee and see if it has high levels of sugar or protein, which can mean you might have gestational diabetes or preeclampsia. If you have lots of ketones in your urine, you're probably dehydrated, which means you need to get yourself a cherry limeade stat.

The Waiting Room

Once you've filled your cup, you'll be allowed back into the waiting room. From there, you can check in, grab a seat, order a latte (you wish!), grab a magazine and get comfortable. I mean it, put your feet up—you're going to be there awhile.

OBs and midwives are notorious for running behind schedule—but they have a really good excuse. You see, babies are born at all times of the day, which means your doctor probably spends a lot of time running back and forth between delivering babies and seeing patients. And since babies don't tend to wait just because the doctor has a packed schedule, your doctor will probably run to deliver a baby before worrying about a full waiting room. This is a good thing. Better to pay your dues now when you're comfy in the waiting room than when you're dilated to ten centimeters, right?

While you're waiting, you'll probably have plenty of time to read the magazines that are conveniently strewn about the waiting room. On a lucky day, you may be able to snag an intact copy of *Pregnancy Weekly* or *FitPregnancy*—but that'll be the day that your doctor happens to be running on-schedule and you end up only waiting for five minutes. On most days, you'll probably scour the room and find that most of the magazines are either (a) two years old, or (b) missing half their pages because other pregnant women have torn out all of the articles. That's when you'll end up thumbing through a special promotional magazine.

Promotional magazines are put together by companies that are trying to promote (read: sell) some special baby or pregnancy product. They may be interlaced with "advertorials" (aka advertisements created to look like articles)—articles that will tell you exactly how smart/beautiful/athletic your baby will be if you buy their product. I'm not saying that the story about the woman who birthed a mega-genius who could calculate figures using the quadratic equation by age two isn't true, but there's a slight chance that her baby's intelligence wasn't the result of the EDU700 Prenatal Education System. So take these magazines with a giant grain of salt.

Another good waiting room activity is napping. If you're going to be stuck there for a long period of time, there is nothing wrong with catching a little siesta. I kept my little airline neck pillow in my car and brought it with me whenever I went to the OB's office. Yes, it was slightly embarrassing being woken up by the nurse handing me a tissue to wipe the drool off of my chin, but who cares? It's not like you aren't already napping at work, at the gym and in line at the supermarket.

Señor Scale

It's easy to get excited when the nurse finally calls your name and invites you back into the doctor's lair. You've made it! You're going in! But your momentary excitement will certainly be short-lived, because just inside the door looms the bane of every pregnant mama's existence: Señor Scale.

Señor Scale is a daunting presence. Not only is he lean and lithe, but he's also pretty darn good at pointing out that you are neither lean nor lithe. And Señor Scale never lies. My scale at home is skewed a bit light—like it says I weigh 125 pounds when I really weigh more like 155. I like it that way. But Señor Scale at my OB's office says I weigh 155 and sometimes skews to 156 just for good measure. I hate him.

Needless to say, every time I entered the doctor's office door and spotted Señor Scale, the first thing I did was try to figure out how I could shed six pounds before I made it down the hall. I'd shrug off my coat (too hot), hand my purse to the nurse (too big) and step out of my sneakers (too sweaty) in hopes of maintaining some sense of dignity with Señor Scale. It never worked. Every week without fail, Señor Scale said I had gained at least a pound, usually more. Señor Scale is just plain mean, I'm telling you. One week, I actually started crying hysterically after Señor Scale told me that I weighed two pounds more than my husband. After I regained my composure, I blamed the tears on pregnancy hormones and quietly vowed to wear spiky shoes next time I got weighed. My secret revenge.

Anyway, I know that run-ins with Señor Scale can be disheartening. Ideally you should try to keep Señor Scale (and your doctor) happy, but you can't let Señor Scale dictate your mood.

The Telephone Nurse

After you're done with Señor Scale, you'll be led through a maze of hallways toward your room. But before you get to your room, you'll most likely pass a small desk where a busy woman is talking on the phone. You may not recognize this woman by sight, but you'll certainly recognize her voice. She is the telephone nurse. Yes, that's right, the woman who answered every single one of your pregnancy questions when you felt the need to call the doctor's office fourteen times last week.

In fact, before long, you're going to start thinking of this woman as your best friend. It'll start with a middle-of-the-night call "just to check and make sure it's okay to sleep on your back" and continue when you decide to call back "just to double-check." That'll progress to your asking for baby naming advice (no one else seems to give you unbiased suggestions) and your confiding in her that your deepest, darkest fear is accidentally pooing on the delivery room table.

Let me assure you, the feeling is *not* mutual. While you may think the telephone nurse's job is to give you on-the-spot attention for every medical concern you may have, she probably has at least thirty other needy pregnant women who also think they need on-the-spot attention. That means this woman is very, very busy. I'm not saying you shouldn't be calling your doctor's nurse whenever you have a question—you should—but simply that it's a good idea to be very, very nice to this person. After all, she is the one who is there for you when your mother-in-law is too tired to answer the phone.

I put my doctor's nurse Caroline on my speed dial. She was my lifeline whenever I had a medical pregnancy question. The woman knew *everything* and was so patient every time I called to whine about morning sickness, rant about weight gain or just accidentally pressed speed dial #3 instead of speed dial #2. And since Caroline was such a lifeline, I made it a point to be supernice to her whenever I saw her. I always stopped by the telephone nurse's desk to say hi, and sometimes I even brought her little treats.

So when you're being led past the nurse's area to your waiting room—even if you're still distraught over a little altercation with Señor Scale—try to put a smile on your face and say hi. Your nurse will appreciate knowing she's appreciated.

The Exam Room

You've made it! You're in the exam room and ready for the good stuff. But first, you wait. Again. Remember how I said that OBs tend to run late? Well, being in the exam room is no exception. Sure, you're one step closer to actually seeing your doctor, but that doesn't mean women aren't going into labor and babies aren't being born. So get comfortable—as comfortable as you can get wearing a backless gown.

You may get a little nervous when you're waiting in the exam room. It's not the stirrups looming on both sides of the table (although those have a way of making me nervous too)—but the fact that you only have a small window of time with your doctor and so many questions to ask. You might want to spend this time reviewing your already-prepared question list—or quickly scrawling every question you can think of on the back of a receipt you find in your purse. Either way, it's good to write down questions so you don't forget them when your doctor is actually standing in front of you.

While you're waiting, you'll also have plenty of time to become acquainted with the fun posters and pamphlets that will most likely be strewn about the exam room. This is your chance to fill your brain with all sorts of useless information about birth control failure rates and breast self-check procedures. Knowing random facts like this will make you very popular at dinner parties. You may even find a life-sized model of a human uterus in the exam room. Word to the wise: Tempting as it is, it's probably not a good idea to take apart the uterus model as they tend to be a bit difficult to put back together, and it may be a bit embarrassing when your doctor walks in and catches you building a Lego-like tower out of pelvic bones and fallopian tubes.

Eventually, your doctor will come in. First, you'll probably get the chance to update your doctor on your pregnancy happenings (I'm sure she's dying to know about the new crib bedding you found on Overstock.com) and ask your questions.

When I was pregnant, a lot of people told me that no question was too stupid for my doctor—and while that's a sweet thing to say—I'm going to go ahead and be blunt and tell you that there is such a thing as a stupid question. For example, you probably don't need to ask your doctor:

- How do I shave that increasingly more difficult-to-reach spot on my ankles? *(Let it grow, Jane of the Jungle.)*
- Where can I find those cute new maternity leggings? *(They're everywhere! Try Old Navy!)*

- How did I get pregnant in the first place? *(I think you know the answer to that.)*
- Can I have a pregnancy-long epidural? *(You can't as it doesn't exist. Nice try.)*
- Is it okay to eat ice cream for dinner and German chocolate cake for dessert? *(Of course it's okay. But remember Señor Scale. And don't forget the chocolate milk to wash it all down.)*
- Can I bring my dog into the delivery room? *(Probably not. For some reason, hospitals frown upon dog hair in sterile rooms.)*

But you can (and should) ask your doctor anything medically related that you want to know. Ask about the strange pain in your left hip that seems to hurt worse in the late afternoon or after you've walked down a flight of stairs. (It's called round ligament pain.) And ask about how to fall asleep without tossing and turning for hours. (Sleep on your left side and get a Snoogle Maternity Total Body Pillow.) And certainly ask about how you can get your horse pill prenatals down without instantly throwing up the second you swallow them. (I know of two people who were unable to take their prenatals until their midwives recommended Flintstones Gummies, a children's multivitamin. Apparently they are loaded with folic acid but are easier on your stomach.)

What to Expect at a Typical Medical Visit

Blood Pressure Check

Testing blood pressure is obviously totally noninvasive and non-painful. In the words of my four-year-old son, the machine will just give your arm a "great big bear hug." Your nurse will most likely want you to stop chitchatting for a few seconds so she can calculate your numbers.

Pregnancy tends to be a teensy bit stressful. It also tends to involve quite a bit of weight gain. As you probably realized last Thanksgiving when you went to stay at your grandma's house with seventy-four relatives, stress plus weight gain tends to lead to high blood pressure. Since high blood pressure can lead to bad things like preeclampsia, your doctor will probably get a read on your blood pressure at every appointment. If your blood pressure is high, don't panic! Your doctor will just keep a closer eye on you throughout your pregnancy to make sure you and your baby are both safe.

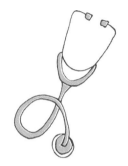

Fundal Height

Fundal height is a big, ominous sounding name that technically means "uterus height" but basically boils down to "belly size." At every appointment, your doctor is going to get out a tape measure and measure how many centimeters there are between your pelvic bone and your belly button to check how quickly your baby is growing. A good rule of thumb is that after you're eighteen weeks along, your fundal height should be about equal to your weeks of pregnancy. So if you're twenty-eight weeks along, your fundal height should be around twenty-eight centimeters. With that in mind, if your fundal height is forty-five or more, you might want to talk to your doctor about an induction.

Vaginal Checks and Cultures

I'm sure you know the drill from previous Pap smears—the stirrups, the swab, the cheery doctor trying to make you feel comfortable when you're clearly very, very uncomfortable. The reason for these tests is that they want to make extra sure there's nothing going on (or growing) down there that shouldn't be—like gonorrhea or chlamydia. If there *is* something going on, your doctor will want to take care of it before it has a chance of hurting your baby. Awkward, but necessary.

While she's down there, your doctor also might take a peek at your cervix to make sure it's closed tightly. Your cervix is the little passageway between your uterus and your vagina. It serves the very important purpose of keeping your baby inside of your uterus until it's time for delivery. If you need a visual, feel free to check it out on that uterus model in your OB's office.

Once your doctor has done one set of vaginal cultures and a cervix check, you're off the hook for a while. Most doctors won't do any additional cervical checks until the very end of your pregnancy. Once you've had your initial check, your doctor will probably leave well enough alone and let the cervix do its job until you're late in your third trimester.

Lastly, since you're probably going to have to take quite a few uncomfortable and icky tests throughout your pregnancy, you may want to consider implementing a "carrot cake rule" like my sister did. After the first vaginal culture of her pregnancy, she made a rule that anytime she had to have an invasive or irritating test at the OB's office, her husband had to stop and buy her a slice of carrot cake on the way home. Icky tests seem a lot more manageable when you can distract yourself with the thought of cream cheese frosting.

Doppler

At every exam, your doctor will bust out a Doppler transducer (about the size of a bar of soap), wave it over your belly and instantly you'll start hearing the sweet sound of your baby's heart rate. How cool is that? I could've sat on that exam table for hours listening to that delightful sound. Of course, my doctor had more important things to do—like delivering babies—so he usually only left the Doppler on long enough to make sure the baby's heart rate was strong and everything was going well.

You may be tempted to drop three hundred bucks on your own Doppler wand so you can listen to your baby's heart rate at home, but before you get out your MasterCard, let me warn you about two things: (1) Your doctor is probably much more skilled with the Doppler than you are; she may be able to find your baby's heart rate in 2.4 seconds, but you are more likely to spend an hour listening to your own abdominal grumblings; and (2) After you spend two hours listening to your intestines, you'll probably start stressing out about your inability to find your baby's heart rate and drive to your doctor's office so they can double-check. This is a lot of unnecessary anxiety for a pregnant mama (see "blood pressure") so you might want to avoid buying fancy at-home medical equipment if you're not a professional.

Ultrasounds

Without a doubt, ultrasounds were the highlight of my pregnancies —it was like I had a momentary window into my womb—and that tiny, blobby and nearly unidentifiable picture was so beautiful that I couldn't stop bawling. And to make it even sweeter, my ultrasound tech printed out these gorgeous, blurry black and white photos of my babies so that I could take them home and post them on my blog to show to the entire world. Trust me, people just love looking at blurry images of babies that they can't recognize. Really. What, you doubt me?

At the very least, your insurance should pay for one big mid-pregnancy ultrasound to check to make sure your baby is okay. More than that will depend entirely on your doctor and your insurance carrier. I have a friend who had really amazing insurance that paid for an ultrasound at each visit. (Can you imagine?) My insurance paid for one ultrasound at eight weeks to confirm the pregnancy, one ultrasound at twenty weeks for a "complete physiological exam" and one final ultrasound at thirty-six weeks to determine that the baby still had enough room to swim around in there.

I already mentioned this in the first trimester chapter, but since people tend to conveniently omit icky information when they're talking about ultrasounds, I'm going to have to be the bearer of bad news: Early pregnancy ultrasounds—ones performed before twelve weeks or so—are trans-vaginal ultrasounds. Because the baby is so small—and your stomach skin (or in my case, fat) is so thick—they won't be able to see the baby through a regular ultrasound. So, instead, they have to look through another, *er,* window.

The trans-vaginal ultrasound thing isn't as bad as it sounds. Basically, the ultrasound tech will dump a bunch of blue goop (that I'm assuming is some sort of lubricant) on a wand that's about the size of a supersized tampon. Very slowly, they'll insert the wand into, well, you know where. It is a bit awkward and uncomfortable at first, but as soon as you see that indistinct image on the screen, you'll be so transfixed that you won't care where the ultrasound wand is. The technician will probably spend some time counting the baby's heart beats per minute and measuring the baby's leg length and spine to determine your baby's exact due date and growth rates.

My advice: Don't even try to follow along. No matter how hard you try, you aren't going to be able to tell an arm from a heart or an eye from a foot this early in your pregnancy, so there's no use frustrating yourself. Instead, spend the time looking at that oh-so-adorable baby and dreaming about how she's going to look in that oh-so-adorable pair of corduroy overalls your mom just bought.

Once you reach your second trimester, your ultrasounds will

be exactly like you see on TV—complete with warm, blue goo on your big tummy and a somewhat recognizable image of your baby. These are the ultrasounds that you can (and should) invite your mom, your dad, your next-door neighbor and the woman you met in the waiting room to come see. At my twenty-week ultrasound with my daughter, I invited everyone I knew because I was so excited. When the tech announced that I was going to have a girl, the entire room erupted into screams and whoops. It was a regular old party in the OB's office.

Ultrasounds Continued: Finding Out the Sex of Your Baby

The best part about your twenty-week ultrasound is that you get to find out the sex of your baby. Do you like how quickly I've decided for you that you're *going* to find out the sex of your baby? I suppose it's *your* baby so you should have the right to decide if you want to be surprised by hearing "It's a boy!" or "It's a girl!" in the delivery room, but that doesn't mean I have to like it. I'm nosy. And I don't like waiting. And I like being forced to buy totally impractical pink or blue baby clothes when I go to baby showers.

My friend Rebecca is a waiter. She has somehow managed to make it through two twenty-week ultrasounds without peeking and she swears that the moment of surprise was worth the months of waiting. She also adds that she got tons of practical baby gear like diapers and wipes and changing pads at her baby showers, which, boring as it sounds, was a financial blessing. The not knowing still drives me nuts—but I guess if you're dead set on waiting to find out, I can be patient too.

I (obviously) did not wait to find out the sex of my babies. I found out as soon as humanly possible with both of them and I'm glad I did. I loved knowing. I was able to research names, paint my nursery, buy appropriately colored gear and pick out going home outfits that were supergirly or boyey. I'm a planner, so I loved that.

Plus—embarrassing confession time—with my first pregnancy, I'm glad I found out early because it took me some time to adjust to the idea that I was having a boy. For some reason, I had this idea that I would have all girl babies. I went into that first ultrasound absolutely certain that I was having a girl, and when the tech told me that I was having a boy, I was stunned. This is terrible to even admit—I was devastated. I'm the ultimate girly girl and had no idea what to even do with a boy. It took me the last few months of my pregnancy to get used to the idea of snips and snails, but I did eventually come around. And the instant I held my son, I fell in love and forgot all about my longing for a girl. My son is fabulous. I thank God every day that He gave me my wonderful firstborn son instead of the firstborn daughter that I thought I wanted. Proof that God knows what I need even when I don't.

Lab Work

The last stop on our little OB office tour is the lab. It may look like a friendly place with all those fun needles filling the cabinets and all those cups of pee lined up on the counter but don't be deceived: The lab is *not* as fun as it looks. The lab is where icky things happen— like blood tests and pee tests and glucose tests. All of these tests are superimportant, but they also tend to be invasive and annoying—not as invasive and annoying as Señor Scale, per se, but your time in the lab certainly won't rival your time with Mr. Chocolate Milkshake in the car on your way home. Here's what to expect.

Blood Draws

The techs in the lab seem to love leeching gallons and gallons of your blood through four-inch-wide needles. Okay, so I'm exaggerating a little, but I swear they take a good milk carton full of blood during that first appointment. The lab tech will roll up your sleeve and tie a band around your arm and then tell you that it might "pinch a little." At this point it's totally appropriate to turn your head and clasp your husband's hand until it turns blue. It'll give him good practice for when you're in labor. But unlike labor, the needle sting probably won't hurt nearly as badly as you expect it to. Trust me, I'm a drama queen and if it hurt, I'd still be whining and moaning about the pain right now.

While you're recovering from the needle trauma, you might want to ask the lab tech exactly why they need to draw what seems like your entire bloodstream. Or you can just trust me that each and every vial serves a very important purpose—namely, to make sure you and your baby are safe and healthy! I'm not going to get into all of the medical details (in case you've forgotten, I'm not a doctor), but they're looking for things like anemia, hepatitis B, HIV and rubella. If detected, most of the things they're looking for can be safely dealt with, so just remind yourself as they're putting on the Band-Aid that everything you just went through was for the good of your baby.

Glucose Tolerance Test

Another oh-so-fun test that your doctor will perform is the glucose tolerance test. Basically, your doctor wants to find out how your body is handling all of the Ding Dongs that you've been shoveling into your mouth 24-7 for the last three months. Sometimes pregnant mamas have a hard time producing and utilizing enough insulin to process sugar properly. This causes a distressing (but temporary) condition called gestational diabetes. And since gestational diabetes can be treated when you know about it early, your OB is going to check you for it—even if your pregnancy diet consists solely of steamed kale and quinoa.

The glucose tolerance test involves your drinking a smallish bottle of orangey liquid that tastes a lot like the Tang you made as a kid when you added double the powder and half the water. Sounds delicious, right? It is—if you like that sort of thing—but before you get all excited, let me warn you that drinking this bottle of Tang is a bit more difficult than you would think. In fact, I know several people who managed to mess it up.

Before my first glucose tolerance test, I had the brilliant idea to try to work the system a little. I figured that if I avoided sugar altogether for a few days before the test, my blood sugar would naturally be lower and I'd have a better chance of getting good, low numbers on the test. However, in trying to avoid sugar and only eating things like broccoli and asparagus, I ended up eating much less than I normally would've (just to be safe). Good idea in theory, bad idea in reality. I was already queasy when I woke up, and skipping breakfast (which they usually require you to do on the morning of the test) made me even more queasy. I drank my Tang and instantly threw up. I drank another bottle and threw up again. Four bottles later, they finally had to send me home to come back and take another test on another day. Note to self: Fast the morning of—not the week before—your glucose tolerance test.

My friend Rachel also managed to mess up her glucose tolerance test. Apparently she drank things like organic, pure-fruit apple juice as a kid and had never developed a taste for the finer things in life—because she took one sip of the Tang and gagged. She literally couldn't get the stuff down. So she sat there in the doctor's office for a half hour nursing the bottle. Eventually, the nurse told her that too much time had elapsed and she'd have to come back and take it again on a different day. Needless to say, she closed her eyes and chugged the thing on day two.

If you do manage to get—and keep—the Tang down, you'll be asked to wait in the waiting room for an hour while your blood sugar spikes nice and high and subsequently crashes to very low. With this in mind, this is not a good day to bring anybody with you to the OB's office. Sugar rushes and sugar drops tend to make people very, very cranky, so it's best to leave impatient, whiney toddlers and impatient, demanding husbands at home. This is a day to sequester yourself in a quiet corner of the waiting room with a novel or magazine and keep to yourself.

Once an hour has passed, the lab tech or nurse will draw your blood. If your blood sugar has returned to normal (or close to normal) within the hour, you're good to go. You can head to IHOP for some pancakes and syrup and try to re-create your earlier sugar high. If your blood sugar stays elevated, your doctor will probably ask you to come back to take a different (and equally fun) three-hour glucose tolerance test. I know lots of people (including myself!) who failed the first glucose tolerance test and did just fine on the three-hour one, so if your initial results are bad, try not to worry.

After your three-hour test, you may get the call that you do, in fact, have gestational diabetes. This is a bummer—but it's not nearly as menacing as it sounds. It's actually pretty common in pregnancy. As long as you work with your doctor (and possibly a registered dietitian) to manage it, you and your baby should be just fine. You'll have to make some dietary changes that I am certainly not qualified to explain, and you may have to take some prescribed medication, which is no fun, but is certainly worth it to keep your baby—and yourself—healthy.

Genetic Testing and Amniocentesis

Just when you think you don't have an ounce of blood left in your body for them to pilfer, your doctor might suggest a series of prenatal tests that are designed to determine if your baby is at risk for certain birth defects. Some of these tests, like the alpha-fetoprotein test, are mandated by law in most states. Others, like amniocentesis, are optional, but recommended if the mother is older than thirty-five or if she carries a genetic risk factor for things like Tay-Sachs or sickle-cell anemia.

All of these tests serve the purpose of determining the potential for a genetic defect in your unborn child. Sounds scary, doesn't it? Before I go any further, I want to point out that most of these tests do *not* confirm 100 percent that your baby is ill or has a birth defect. Instead, they tell you if your baby has an increased *likelihood* of having a certain illness or birth defect.

I know a woman who went in for her prenatal testing and was told that her unborn daughter had a severely deformed and under-developed brain. In fact, the doctor said that the little girl had absolutely no chance of surviving until delivery, and that even if she did survive, she would be born so severely disabled that she wouldn't survive more than a few hours outside of the womb. How's that for devastating?

The doctors suggested an abortion. My friend refused (thank God!) and decided to let the pregnancy run its course. In the meantime, thousands of people banded together to pray for this precious baby girl. A few weeks later, my friend had a second ultrasound—and her hopes were dashed again when the same diagnoses showed up on the scan. Severely deformed brain. No chance of survival. My friend started to question her resolve, but then she remembered that the God she serves is a lot bigger than an ultrasound diagnosis.

Here's where the story gets good. That baby *did* survive to delivery. Not only did she survive, but God healed her! She is now a *healthy* nine-year-old girl who loves to sing and dance. There is no sign of the devastating diagnosis that was once delivered to her poor mother.

I'm not telling you this story to make you all weepy and emotional (although, I did shed a few tears while writing it), but because I want to encourage you to really think and pray about how you're going to handle prenatal testing in your pregnancy. To me, it was kind of a no-brainer. First and foremost, there was no way I was going to abort a baby. Even if the doctors said there was no chance of survival (or a 100 percent chance of birth defect), I knew I wouldn't consider an abortion—especially in light of the miraculous story that I just told you. Second, I didn't want the emotional stress that would surely come if I found out that there *might* be something wrong with my baby.

I was very fortunate to have a Christian doctor who understood my feelings. We had a conversation about it and he allowed me to opt out of the optional prenatal testing. For the state-required ones, I made a deal with my doctor that he would only tell me the results if there was something that could be done about a possible defect. So if my baby had a disease that early detection could somehow help fix, I wanted to know. But if something showed up in the tests that simply meant watching and waiting, I didn't want to know. I'd rather find out at delivery when I could actually do something to help my baby.

The flip side of all this is some mamas want to be able to prepare themselves and their families for a potential birth defect or problem before the baby is born. This also allows them time to research their options for medical interventions and to line up the best possible care for their baby if something does show up. Several of my friends chose to take prenatal tests for this reason, and I certainly understand their rationale. Spend some time praying for clarity—because no matter how healthy or sick your baby is, God will be with you and knows what is right for you and your family.

Obviously, my friend's story is dramatic, and many people who receive negative results do have babies born with sicknesses or defects. Discuss the results of any tests you have with your doctor.

A Quick Tour of a Birthing Center

Before I finish talking about all of this medical stuff, I want to give you a quick rundown on birthing centers and midwives. Birthing centers and midwives are becoming a very popular option for pregnant mamas. They aren't for everyone (read: if you desperately want an epidural) but are a great option for mamas who are interested in a natural birth in a homey setting. I had my babies in a hospital (with an epidural, *thankyouverymuch*), so I can't really tell you much about birthing centers, but my friend Kristin—who has two kids, both born in birthing centers—has agreed to give me the scoop.*

All birthing centers are different—some won't accept women with high-risk pregnancies, some won't accept mothers over thirty-five and some are connected to hospitals and function very similarly. Make sure you go on a tour and do your research before making your choice.

What You Might Want to Know about Birthing Centers and Midwives

- Birthing centers look nothing like doctor's offices or hospitals. No utilitarian exam tables. No cold concrete floors. No fluorescent lights. You can expect comfy chairs, bright lighting, flowery blankets on beds and soothing music—all things that will make you feel much more comfortable throughout your pregnancy and especially during labor and delivery.
- You still get most of the perks you would at a doctor's office in a birthing center. I had always assumed that birthing centers didn't have modern medical equipment or participate in routine prenatal care. Not true. Most midwives perform ultrasounds and Doppler checks. Plus, you should get the same prenatal screens that you would in a hospital—from blood pressure checks to the glucose tolerance test.

- Midwives are highly trained medical professionals. Women don't just become midwives overnight. Instead, they go through years of schooling and training. Your midwife should know exactly how to detect potential problems in your pregnancy, make sure your baby is developing properly and might even know some cool tricks to help cure your morning sickness or how to flip a breach baby.
- Midwives know when to say no. Most midwives recognize that there are certain conditions that are above their level of expertise. One of my friends ended up having a very complicated pregnancy and about halfway through, her midwife referred her to an OB who was able to help.
- Birthing centers use lots of pain relief options. It's true that most birthing centers don't use epidurals, but that doesn't mean you'll be left to fend for yourself when it comes to pain in childbirth. The staff at a birthing center is usually well versed in the art of natural pain relief and will certainly give you lots of things to try—from breathing techniques to massage to acupressure—when you're in labor.
- You might get to sleep in a queen-sized bed—with your husband—after you have your baby. Unlike hospital beds—you know, tiny twin beds with metal rails and nurse call buttons—many birthing centers furnish their rooms with comfy queen-sized beds and the amenities you'd find at home. It makes the hours after you have your baby feel like a fun vacation. The downside to this fun vacation is that birthing centers generally don't have the plethora of advanced medical equipment that you'll find in hospitals. That means you may not have access to all of the monitors and pain relief options that you would at a hospital and you may have to be transferred to a hospital if complications arise.
- Your postchildbirth stay in a birthing center will be much shorter than a typical hospital stay. Most women stay two to three days in a hospital. Often birthing centers allow you to check out as

soon as a few hours after your baby is born. This can be a good thing (you'll probably be much more comfortable at home) and a bad thing (you'll have to call your midwife if you experience any problems or have questions).

- You can't change your mind about pain relief. If you're absolutely set on having a natural childbirth, a birthing center is a great place to have your baby because there is no one there who will try to convince you to get an epidural when you're in the throes of contractions. Of course, that means the flip side is true too. If you change your mind and decide that you do, after all, want an epidural, there won't be one available.

- Your insurance will probably cover part (or even most) of your stay. Birthing centers used to be considered "alternative medicine" and often weren't covered by major medical insurance plans. Not anymore! These days, most insurance plans pay for women to give birth in a birthing center. Call your insurance company (or the birthing center) to find out what's covered (and what's not).

- If there is a point during your delivery that your midwife feels that you or your baby is in danger, an ambulance should be called. A few months ago, my friend Melissa was giving birth in a birthing center when the midwife realized that the baby was stuck. She immediately transferred her to a hospital, and Melissa delivered a healthy baby boy via C-section. This obviously wasn't Melissa's first choice, but she was grateful that the midwife was so quick to transfer her when she realized there was a problem.

The Appointment Desk

You did it! You survived the needles, the stirrups, the sneering Señor Scale and even (gulp!) the waiting room bathroom—and you have a nice Band-Aid-covered cotton ball on your arm to show for it. Congrats. But you're not done yet, girlfriend. Before they'll let you out of the door, they're going to make you schedule a time to come back and do it all *again*. That's right, you're going to have to go *back*. Many, many times. And unlike your normal yearly visits to the OB, this time you won't even have to send yourself a postcard. That's because your next appointment is no more than a month away. But for now, you are free. So grab your bum cushion, head to Whole Foods and savor every bite of that carrot cake. You've earned it.

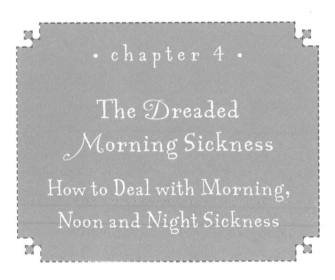

J don't know about you, but morning sickness kind of took me by surprise. I'd heard about it and I expected to feel a little queasy during my first trimester, but I never (ever) imagined morning sickness to feel like it did. I was expecting a little queasiness that could be cured by eating saltines; the constant morning, noon and night gut-wrenching nausea that I had went way, way beyond that.

For those first few blissful days after I found out about my pregnancy, everything was wonderful. I shopped for supersoft yellow-and-green onesies and strolled through bookstores hand in hand with my husband looking for parenting books and read about pregnancy. My husband took me out to romantic dinners where I ordered appetizers, dinner and dessert—and ate it all guiltlessly because I was eating for two.

It was as if I walked to the beat of a tiny voice singsonging "I'm pregnant! I'm pregnant!" Looking back on those days, I realize that I was naïvely sitting smack-dab in the middle of the calm before the storm. I was seven weeks along, and for some reason that equated to nearly an entire trimester in my brain. I figured I was well through the hard part and that I had stealthily slid under the morning sickness radar. I thought, *If it's going to hit me, wouldn't I be feeling something by now?*

I decided that I just had good genes. My mom told me that she had been a bit queasy during her first trimester but nothing that couldn't be fixed with a snack and a few minutes' rest. I thought I had lucked out and bypassed the morning sickness thing completely. I was loving life. I wasn't tired. I wasn't bloated. I was just hungry. Really, really hungry.

I'm not going to get into what I ate during those blissful early pregnancy days because I know that you'll probably puke on this book, which means you won't be able to finish reading it and get to the really good part when my morning sickness actually kicked in. But let's just say that I did my part and ate for two (or three). I decided pregnancy was a wonderful thing and that all those gals who complained were simply unlucky. I, on the other hand, was one of the fortunate ones.

Right.

Reality Hits

I thought I had the stomach flu. It was Mother's Day and I was eight weeks along. I remember going to brunch with my mom and ordering nothing but herbal tea. My mom looked at me with all of her motherly concern, so I explained that I must have "a touch of something" and that my stomach was feeling "a bit queasy." She told me to be careful. I was growing her grandbaby after all.

That afternoon, I threw up. I was still naïve enough to think it was the flu, and my husband brought me some Sprite and tucked me into bed. I woke up vomiting and continued throughout the night and the rest of the next day. I remember thinking that this was the worst flu I'd ever had and being glad that most stomach bugs last no more than two or three days.

Now you're going to think I'm really stupid. Go ahead and laugh at my expense; you need something to laugh about right now. That Monday afternoon, I called my OB and told them that I must have the stomach flu and wondered if there was anything they could give me because it was really putting a damper on my eating for two. The nurse probably had to put her hand over the phone so I couldn't hear her hysterical laughter.

The Ultimate Optimist

I had obviously been in denial. After the nurse set me straight, I hung up the phone and decided I could handle it. It was nothing that a million bazillion other moms before me hadn't suffered already. A little nausea here, a little vomiting there, over by ten weeks and then I would be in my glorious second trimester with a cute belly and the fabled increased sex drive to boot. Still an optimist.

Despite my earlier obliviousness, it didn't take me long to figure out that morning sickness isn't just a little nausea here, a little vomiting there. It's debilitating. It's depressing. It's enough to make a thrilled mother-to-be question ever wanting to be pregnant. You might already know that. And while I can't promise a cure, I can at least relate, so you know that you are definitely not alone. Misery loves company, and morning sickness definitely is miserable.

How to Cope

Technically speaking, something the size of a pea shouldn't be able to wreak much havoc in your life, but you'll learn fairly quickly as a parent that when there is trouble to be caused, size doesn't matter. That concept will become clear to you in about two years when you forget to put your Sharpie marker away after labeling your kid's sippy cup.

With that in mind, you probably have a million questions as to why your little pea is wreaking all this morning sickness havoc in your life. What's causing this ever-present nausea that doesn't even go away while you sleep? When will it go away? And, most importantly, what can you do to make yourself feel better?

The bad news is that even doctors with fancy degrees don't know exactly what causes morning sickness. Even worse, while they might have a few tricks up their sleeves, there is no tried and true cure. Seriously, someone needs to invent a magic morning sickness pill. I'm sure you'll get right on that just as soon as you're able to get off the couch and think clearly.

So while there is no cure-all pill for morning sickness, there are some tricks and tips that might help. My extensive medical research (aka my months spent wallowing on the couch while whining to my other pregnant friends about the woes of morning sickness) has taught me a few things. I don't know everything, but hopefully there will be a few gems in here that'll quell the queasiness for a bit. At the very least you'll be armed with tons of ammo for your next morning sickness whine session.

The Three Sub-Causes of Morning Sickness

In my not-so-expert opinion, there are three basic sub-causes of morning sickness. There's nausea caused by hunger (which my girlfriend Katie not-so-affectionately calls *ravenausea* for ravenously nauseous), there's nausea caused by scents, and there's nausea caused by movement or exercise. These aren't official terms (or diagnoses), so it's probably best not to try to explain to your OB that you have a bad case of *ravenausea* unless you want him to think you're a nut job. Still, self-diagnosing your personal morning sickness style can help you to seek the remedies that may work for you.

Hunger-Induced Nausea

Are you ravenously hungry about six minutes after dinner when you downed six hamburgers, two boxes of fries and a chocolate shake in four minutes flat? Have you had to upgrade from a regular purse to a giant satchel just so that you have room to carry your snacks? Have you caught yourself eating your dinner straight out of the pan as it cooks because you're just too hungry to wait? Then you have a case of *ravenausea*, or nausea caused whenever you get ravenously hungry, which is all the time.

A mama with hunger-induced nausea must constantly (and I mean constantly) feed the beast or she'll get sick. It's one of those catch-22 situations. If you don't eat, you get hungry, and if you get hungry, you get nauseous, which in turn, makes you not want to eat, which in turn makes you hungry, which (you guessed it) makes you nauseous.

My sister Alisa had hunger-induced nausea. During her first trimester, she kept a box of Cheerios by her bedside table and literally woke up every thirty minutes to eat a handful. She couldn't go more than twenty minutes without a snack and constantly had a box of crackers or a jar of peanuts within arm's reach. She said she felt pretty normal—as long as she was eating.

Unfortunately for girls who have hunger-induced nausea, it's nearly impossible to eat all the time. Constantly having your mouth full just isn't exactly flattering (or feasible). The good news is that eating 24-7 is easier to pull off than, say, avoiding moving or smelly things. (Just feel sorry for the exercise-induced-nausea gals who get sick every time they move—at least you can get off the couch!)

Tips for Gals with Hunger-Induced Nausea

- Keep snacks with you. At work. At home. In the middle of the night. While you're at the gym.
- Buy food in small portions. Sure, that industrial-sized box of granola bars looks appetizing now, but after you've eaten one or two, the thought of eating another one will probably make you gag.
- If you're hungry, eat. Right that instant. Waiting five minutes (even if you're in the middle of a superimportant meeting with your boss) isn't advisable.
- Eat several smaller meals throughout the day. I know that a triple cheeseburger and fries sounds delish, but eating a single cheeseburger now and a single cheeseburger in two hours will keep you feeling full (and therefore not sick) for longer.
- Add a little protein to your starches. You're probably craving sugary, carb-laden foods (when I was pregnant, I'd start drooling just thinking about things like white bread and oyster crackers), but you'll stay full longer (and therefore not nauseous) if you add a little protein to your snack. So spread a little peanut butter on your white bread or add a slice of cheese to your white saltine crackers.
- If you're craving it, eat it. There's really no use trying to substitute a low-fat frozen yogurt for a triple-decker chocolate-fudge cone when the cone is the only thing that'll hit the spot. You're pregnant. Live a little.
- If you're nauseous, eat something. Even if you don't want to. There will be times when you'd rather dance the Macarena in front of your co-workers while standing on a desk than eat a cracker. Force-feed yourself. You'll feel better. I promise.

Scent-Induced Nausea

Do you wake up gagging in the middle of the night because you can smell the leftover chicken in the refrigerator? Can you tell what your neighbors are making for dinner just by sniffing the air? Does a whiff of your friend's perfume send you running to the bathroom? If any of this sounds familiar, your nausea is caused by scent.

Scent-induced nausea gals have noses that decide to go into hyperdrive. The slightest change in scent—we're talking a whiff of pad thai that someone is eating twelve tables away—can make a scent-induced nausea gal heave instantly. My sister-in-law Annie gagged every time she drove by a Burger King—even if it was set three hundred feet off the road and she was whizzing by on the freeway.

A scent-nausea gal gets sick if she smells food, deodorant, BO, toothpaste, gum, bad breath, a restaurant, garbage, an open refrigerator, shampoo, mouthwash, laundry detergent, sweaty scalps, dirty hands and stinky T-shirts. I'm sure you can add to the list.

Oh, and there's also the smell of plain old water. Don't think it has a smell? Just ask a pregnant scent-nausea gal. Taking a sip of tap water straight from the sink is akin to catching a whiff of the lady in your office who pours on an entire bottle of perfume every single day. It can literally send a scent-induced nausea woman sprinting to the bathroom.

As you can imagine, scent-induced nausea women are a blast to be around. My friend (I won't mention names) put her husband under strict orders not to wear deodorant or use shampoo, *and* to make sure that he never smelled like BO, sweat or dirt. No problem, right? He also wasn't allowed to open the refrigerator, eat any smelly food, or drive by fast-food restaurants. He was thrilled. Now my husband says if we want to get pregnant again, I have to promise not to complain about his deodorant for the entire nine months. Oh, I wasn't going to mention names, was I?

Tips for Scent-Induced Nausea Gals

- Buy nose plugs. I know it's embarrassing to walk around with a clamp on your nose, but I can promise you that it's more embarrassing to throw up in a public place because you couldn't make it to the bathroom.
- Purchase some aromatherapy nausea-reducing spray and spritz it on yourself, your clothes and your pillow at night. (earthmamaangelbaby.com makes a great one called Happy Mama Spray that costs around ten dollars.)
- Avoid wearing scented lotions, perfumes or hair products.
- The scents of lemon and lavender tend to calm nausea. Buy some lemon or lavender oil at a supermarket and dab some on your wrist or just under your nose.
- Carry a cupful of lemon wedges with you. Sounds weird, but the smell of fresh lemon can overpower even the strongest smells.
- Leave the room before anyone opens the fridge.
- Put a couple of drops of orange juice into your water. It will overpower the smell and make it drinkable.
- Don't cook. Ever. Let your man cook for you—while you're out of the house (or at least out of the room).

Movement- or Exercise-Induced Nausea

Do you feel fine as long as you're sitting on the couch? Does moving (even a little bit) send you racing to the bathroom (which, in turn, makes you throw up more)? Does the mere thought of a treadmill make you reel? Does the sight of a woman running make you want to haul off and smack her? Then, you got it—you have a bad case of exercise-induced nausea.

Don't let the name fool you. I know that no one in her right mind actually exercises while suffering from morning sickness. Morning sickness is the perfect excuse to stay far, far away from the gym. But gals with exercise-induced nausea get nauseous from any movement. At all. Walking to the kitchen? Sick. Turning your head to see what's on TV? Sick. Getting up to go to the bathroom? Sick—but at least you're already in the bathroom.

If you have exercise-induced nausea, you feel sick any time you exert yourself physically, which basically means all the time. The thing about exercise-induced nausea is that it gets worse when you're tired or stressed. So really, the only way to control it is to lounge out in a comfy position as much as possible. I don't have to tell you twice, do I?

Tips for Exercise-Induced Nausea Gals

- Sleep a lot. If you're in bed by seven after taking a three-hour afternoon siesta, you're on the right track.
- Take it easy. If you do end up having to do something crazy like walk up a flight of stairs or, worse, go shopping, build in little breaks for yourself. Take a seat on a bench for a few minutes or stop and get a decaf latte halfway through shopping.
- Buy some sea (motion sickness) bands from the drugstore. They press on the pressure point on your wrist that calms nausea. If sea bands help, I suggest investing in a pair of Psi Bands (pronounced "sigh") (psibands.com), which work the same way but come in cute colors like turquoise and red and will definitely complement your outfit better than the gray drugstore bands.
- If you start to feel nauseous, sit down. Even if it means sitting down in the middle of the aisle at the grocery store.

- Create a "mission control center" near your favorite spot. Make sure that all of the stuff you need—water, the remote control, your laptop, your cell phone charger, snacks, your pre- natal vitamins, your sea bands, etc.—are within arm's reach of wherever you like to sit (on the couch, in the armchair). Once you're sitting down, you don't want to have to get up.
- Get a pregnancy massage. Or even better, get your husband to give you a pregnancy massage. Massage relieves stress, which can relieve nausea.
- Research acupressure points for nausea. Putting firm, consis- tent pressure on certain acupressure points can reduce nausea. The one caveat is that there are also acupressure points that can induce contractions, so it's probably best to call a licensed acupressurist if you are interested in this.
- Consider trying Vitamin B6. Vitamin B6 has been prescribed for pregnancy-induced nausea for years—my mom actually took it when she was pregnant with me. My friends Holly and Sam swear by it. Holly says Vitamin B6 was the best morning sickness remedy she found. (Note: Not to be a nag, but just to be supersure, ask your doctor before you try any drugs, vita- mins or herbal remedies.)

The Ultimate Trio

Some unlucky women get the ultimate trio of hunger-induced, scent-induced and exercise-induced nausea all at once. These wom- en only feel good when they are sprawled out on the couch in a scentless room as they munch on carbs while their husbands stand by ready to dote on their every whim. If you're one of those types, you might have to get creative with your morning sickness remedies.

If hunger, smells and movement nauseate you, try combining

tips from the lists above. For example, you might feel better if you dab a bit of lemon oil on your sea bands while eating Cheerios. Or eating a bag of crackers in bed in the morning before moving might work for you. It will take some trial and error, but you have nothing to lose, right?

A Working Mama's Guide to Working and Puking

During my first pregnancy, I was working as a high school Spanish teacher. We didn't have truckloads of money sitting around (but wouldn't that be nice?), so my husband and I decided that I would work through my pregnancy and save as many sick days as possible for my maternity leave. Sure, I was a bit tired and nauseous, but nothing I couldn't handle. So after a few days of self-pitying rest on the couch, I decided to head back to work.

I set my alarm for six in the morning and after tossing and turning and moaning for thirty minutes, I finally dragged myself out of bed. I gagged twice as I was brushing my teeth and then hoisted myself onto the floor of the shower and sat there for another thirty minutes while heaving and moaning. My husband begged me to get up, to get out, to do *something,* but I simply couldn't move.

I did (finally) make it to work that morning. I literally saw my students gasp at my still-wet hair and pale, pasty face as I walked into my first-period class. I made it through the warm-up activity before I started to feel queasy. I tried to sip some ginger ale in a coffee cup and immediately threw it up. I didn't even make it to the trash can. Instead, I threw up into my hands while standing in front of thirty-five high school freshmen. Needless to say I went home early that day.

I did eventually figure out how to be pregnant and work at the same time. It was hard. Harder than anything I had ever done, but I was able to drag myself to work most days. I confess that I wasn't the teacher that I was prepregnancy, but I tried my best and made it through most classes without crawling under my desk and taking a nap. Still, if you do need to work (and most gals do), I recommend following these rules for working while pregnant.

Eight "Working Mama" Rules for Early Pregnancy

- **Don't be heroic.** Sure, you'd like to save your sick days for maternity leave, but there is literally nothing that is worth the embarrassment of throwing up in front of a large group of people. Especially your co-workers (or even worse, high school students). If you're too sick to stand, you're probably too sick to go to work.
- **Have a support structure.** Even if you don't want to announce your pregnancy to every person you work with, find one trusted co-worker to be your confidant. Tell them about it, and you'll have a friend who can vouch for you when you're running late to a meeting or bring you a candy bar from the vending machine when you need a snack.
- **Don't forget your snacks.** Keep a snack at arm's reach at all times; stock up on healthy treats like trail mix, peanut butter crackers and dried fruit (or if you're like me, stock up on chocolate chip cookies and tell everyone that choco- late is the only thing you can keep down).
- **Don't be afraid to play the pregnancy card if you need to.** If your co-worker asks you to stay late to help crunch

numbers, the I'm-so-exhausted-from-this-pregnancy-that-I-can't-stay-up-past-seven-o'clock card works wonderfully at most jobs (and the best part is, it's true)!

- **Always know the way to the closest bathroom and the closest garbage can.** You never know when the nausea is going to hit you and you're going to have fewer than two seconds to find a toilet.
- **Bring a change of clothes to work.** Yes, every day. Maybe just leave them permanently in your car or desk.
- **Dress codes do not apply to pregnant women.** Use your discretion here, but generally if your feet won't fit in anything but flip-flops, that's fine. If the only pants you can button are your favorite jeans, that's fine. Oh, and if you show up to work with your hair wet every day from now until D-day, that's fine too.

Morning Sickness: Extreme Edition

If you're going through the morning sickness tips in this chapter, trying them all and finding that *none* of them work and you're still really, really sick, your morning sickness might be beyond normal run-of-the-mill morning sickness. About 3 percent of women get a rare pregnancy complication called hyperemesis gravidarum (HG)—a big fancy term that basically means really, really bad, horrible, debilitating (did I mention really bad?) morning sickness.

Morning sickness is no fun—for anyone. But if you are literally unable to eat and function, call your doctor (right *now*) about the possibility of HG. It can be dangerous for you or your baby, so if you think you might have this, seek medical help right away.

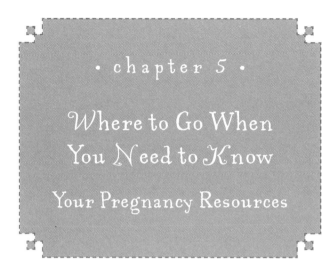

· chapter 5 ·

Where to Go When
You Need to Know

Your Pregnancy Resources

*P*anic time. It was six o'clock on a Sunday morning when I was about twenty-five weeks along and something *(ahem)* down *there* wasn't right. I had woken up early that morning with a burning, throbbing pain shooting from my bum down my legs, and I wasn't sure if this was (a) some weird sign of premature labor, (b) a sign that I had done too many squats the day before at the gym (highly unlikely), or (c) a figment of my imagination. I was ready to hop in the car and race to the nearest ER and pay a bazillion dollars in hospital fees when my (rational) husband grabbed me by the arm.

Enter Mr. Google. Turns out I had sciatica, a fun little pregnancy symptom caused by the uterus deciding to camp out on the sciatic nerve. Apparently, it's one of the most common symptoms of pregnancy. Aside from being extremely irritating and painful, it's completely harmless to both mama *and* baby. I'm not making this up. Google it if you don't believe me. You'll get 657,000 results.

Turns out Mr. Google is quite a guy. He saved me countless trips to the ER and thousands of dollars during my pregnancy. Sometimes I wonder how pregnant gals survived back in the old days (you know, like fifteen years ago) when they had no spur-of-the-moment, round-the-clock access to pregnancy information. They probably had to, like, call their doctors or their mothers or something.

But we live in the Google era! If you want to, you can get up at three in the morning to pee and spend the next two hours shopping for baby bedding (not that I ever did that). Or you can figure out exactly what is going on *down there* without suffering through an embarrassing conversation with the on-call doctor or (*eek!*) your mother-in-law.

Here's the thing about pregnant mamas: We're needy. We have loads of questions (When will my boobs stop growing?), tons of concerns (Will my baby ever, ever come *out?*) and will cry at the drop of a hat (read: whenever anyone so much as mentions sushi). It's okay to be needy! You're going through a lot right now! And you're going to need some support.

So I'm dedicating this chapter to getting a needy pregnant gal the resources and support that she needs. I'm not just talking about your typical resources like books and the Internet (although I will get to that), but also to other sources of support like the Bible, church, your husband, your mom, your girlfriends and yes, even your mother-in-law. One caveat: To be safe, you should always double-check any information that Mr. Google (or your mother-in-law) gives you about pregnancy with your doctor or midwife.

The Bible: Your Ultimate Pregnancy Resource

The Bible can and *should* be your ultimate pregnancy resource. God created pregnancy (and your baby) so it makes sense that His word is the ultimate pregnancy guide. In 2 Peter 1:3, we are told that "His divine power has given us everything we need for life and godliness." That doesn't mean that the Bible is the *only* resource we need in life, but simply gives us a proper perspective through which we can sort all other information.

I found the Bible to be a great source of peace during my pregnancies. Yes, its coverage of labor and delivery is a bit sparse (unless you count the rather disturbing anecdote about Jacob coming out grasping Esau's heel), but it has a lot to say about how God calms storms in your life. The Bible may not have much to say about pregnancy heartburn, but it has a lot to say about persevering through trials. (And if you've ever had pregnancy heartburn, you know that it's a trial.)

Sometimes, we try to gather loads and loads of information in order to gain a sense of control. Instead, what we really need is to spend time with the One who really *is* in control. I found that by turning to God's Word before turning to Google, I was able to calm a lot of worry and gain a great sense of serenity in my pregnancy.

The key to using the Bible as a pregnancy resource is to *actually* use the Bible as a pregnancy resource. The information you need isn't going to simply jump into your head from a closed book, but will come from careful reading, prayerful consideration and attentive listening to God's voice in your life. It takes thinking power—something that's probably been in short supply in your life ever since mommy brain kicked in. But a focused effort to turn to the Bible for support is a great way to assure yourself a peaceful pregnancy—and you definitely want that, don't you?

How to Use the Bible as a Pregnancy Resource

- **Put God on your electronic calendar.** If you're finding yourself pressing the sleep button seven times each morning, morning probably isn't the best time to set aside for God time. Figure out what works for you and pencil (no wait, pen) God in.
- **Focus.** The combo of pregnancy fatigue and mommy brain can make you brain-dead, so make a concerted effort to focus on each text and reflect on how it applies to your life and your pregnancy.
- **Read, reread and read again.** God's word is the *living* Word,

which means we can gain new insights from verses that we've read a billion times. And let's face it, sometimes you have to read the text a billion times to understand it anyway. Blame mommy brain.

- **Pray.** Sounds obvious (and easy) enough, but sometimes we all forget that God moves through prayer. So if you're really struggling with a certain aspect of your pregnant life, pray that God will reveal insight through His word.

- **Read the Cliffs Notes.** You know those cool study notes at the bottom of your study Bibles? They're actually chock-full of really interesting information and can help you to understand the text (and its application) better.

- **Get a pregnancy journal.** Pick up a pregnancy journal at your local Christian bookstore. It's a great place to jot down prayers and thoughts and can often inspire deeper Scripture reading and understanding.

Your Church: An Unexpected Resource

When the words *church* and *pregnancy* are uttered in the same sentence, one word automatically comes to mind: *casseroles*. I'm telling you, there's a secret class at all churches (I think I missed that Sunday) that teaches women the art of *casseroling* (my affectionate term for casserole-making). And once a woman has taken that class, she takes her casseroling duties very, very seriously.

Just mention that you might be pregnant within two hundred yards of a church, and you will have a King Ranch chicken casserole waiting on your doorstep when you get home. Show up at church with a baby bump, and you'll be eating nothing but tuna noodle for a week. And that's minor compared to what will happen once you have your baby. Then the casserolers (women who hand out casseroles to all in need) will use casseroling as an excuse to come over and see your cute baby. Your freezer will be so full that you'll have to store casseroles in your next-door neighbor's freezer until you have time to go shopping for an extra Deepfreeze.

We laugh, but the idea of casseroling is both wonderful and endearing. The thing about church folk is that, imperfect as they are, most truly love God *and* truly love people. When you're at your neediest (yes, that's right now), these God-fearing and people-loving people know just how to step in and give you what you need. And let's face it, when you don't feel like cooking and you *do* feel like eating, a warm, delicious casserole really hits the spot.

When you're pregnant, your church can be a great resource. It's hard at times to allow people to serve you—especially if you love to serve others. I'm not saying you should ignore others and be selfish (you shouldn't), but that you can and should accept the help of others who want to serve you. Allow yourself to be blessed by the people in your church who love you enough to make you a casserole (or mow your lawn or take you to the doctor's office).

Also, after you have your baby, you might want to consider heading to the kitchen and honing a casserole recipe for yourself, because once you've been served by casserolers, chances are you're going to want to become a casseroler yourself. You'll need to be ready for the next woman who announces her pregnancy within two hundred yards of your church.

A Real Person on the Line: A Real Pregnancy Resource

Think back to the last time you called somewhere, just to get connected to an automated phone system.

"Hello, and thank you for calling Pregnancy Information Hotline! Please *press one* if you're pregnant. *Press two* if you're not pregnant but wish you were. *Press three* if you're only calling because a friend of a friend's cousin might be pregnant and you're trying to help her figure it out."

You press one and get the next menu. "Thank you for calling. We need more information to better assist you. *Press one* if you're hoping that you're pregnant but not feeling any symptoms at all. *Press two* if you have been throwing up nonstop for the last three months and have missed your last seven periods, but are in oblivious denial about your potential pregnancy. *Press three* if you just realized that you dialed the wrong number and were really trying to call Preg and Nan's Pizza Company."

You press one and get the next menu. "Thank you. In order to transfer you to the right department, we need a bit more information..."

Just reading that makes me want to scream *representative* at the top of my lungs and throw my cell phone at the wall. Automated phone systems are so annoying! The creepy, ever-so-patient automated voice that calmly tells you what you cannot do is infuriating, but even worse is the fact that the machine just never quite gives me the answers I need. Sometimes there is just no substitution for a real human who can actually *think*.

Same goes for real life. Sometimes we get trapped in an automated support system where everything is automatic and impersonal. We keep pressing buttons and screaming for help, but our voice is never heard. While there's a definite need for books and Web sites and magazines, there's an even deeper need for real, interpersonal connections. Especially when you're at your neediest—which (have I mentioned?) is right now.

We have more access to people than ever before in history (imagine what our great-grandparents would've thought of a Blackberry!), yet it's easy to lose ourselves behind a screen of technology and avoid deeply connecting with people.

The good news is that people *love* talking about babies. Put a pregnant woman in a room with fifty strangers and within minutes she'll be bombarded with forty-five birth stories, sixteen tales of morning sickness and 2,234 snippets of advice. So you'll have no problem finding people willing to talk to you about your pregnancy. Even better, pregnancy is a great opportunity to build deep, lasting relationships with people. When you connect over something as important and life-altering as a baby, your relationship naturally gets more intimate and deeper. And that's a good thing.

So use your pregnancy as an excuse to wear sweats every day *and* as an excuse to deepen your relationships. Make it a point to share the good, the bad and the ugly points of your pregnancy with your husband, family and friends, and make it a point to reach out to actual people *before* you reach out to Google. Mr. Google's one smart guy, but you might be surprised by how much your friends and family actually know.

Your Husband: Your MAR (Most Adorable Resource)

I'm guessing that as your tummy expands, so do your husband's attempts to help. And let's face it, that's pretty adorable. He's probably the only person (besides your mother) who's as excited as you are about the baby. Plus, he's probably already proven himself to be invaluable when it comes to holding your hair while you're puking and fetching whatever you're craving at a moment's notice (even if it means a 2:00 AM trip to Whataburger). However, unless your last name is Duggar and this is your nineteenth baby, your hubby probably isn't the most knowledgeable person when it comes to pregnancy. Sure, he can Google recipes for sauerkraut-and-chorizo-quesadillas if you have a sudden hankering for German-Mexican cuisine, but I have yet to meet a man who enjoys talking about the intricacies of breast pumps at six o'clock on a Saturday morning.

Your husband may not be a wealth of pregnancy information, but he is a wealth of *you* information. He probably knows you better than anyone else in this world (which means he understands your current neediness pretty well). He also probably loves you more than anyone else in this world. So while he may not be the person to turn to if you need to know how to soothe breast tenderness, he's the perfect person to turn to when you need a hand to hold.

The thing about most husbands is that they really, really (really) want to do the right thing. They just don't know what the right thing is. Take my husband for example. When I was sick with morning sickness, he was convinced that if he could just find something that I wanted to eat, I would chow down and instantly feel better. So he was on a quest to find my magical-cure-for-morning-sickness food. The problem was that *nothing* sounded good and *just smelling* things made me puke. So it was a hopeless quest.

One night he came home from work with a sack full of food. He had burgers from Jack in the Box, sandwiches from Subway, pizza

from Double Dave's and several cartons of Ben & Jerry's that I'm still convinced were really for him. He had literally gone through every drive-thru in a ten-mile radius of our house hoping that one of the things he bought would hit the spot and I'd feel better. The second I caught a whiff of his bag-o-delights, I ran to the bathroom and puked my guts out. My husband ended up eating chewy, microwaved fast food for the next week.

I sat him down and explained to him that unless I

specifically told him that I was craving a double cheese with fries (in which case he should sprint to the car and get a burger into my hands as quickly as possible), he should probably just keep all food out of smelling range and assume that nothing was going to help. Instead of agreeing that it was probably best to avoid any future drive-thru incidents, he got all sad and mopey on me.

Turns out, he had really wanted to help, and since his efforts at helping had been a dismal failure, he felt like a dismal failure in the husband department. He really wanted to do the right thing, but he didn't know how to help. So he kept guessing—and guessing wrong. And his guessing wrong was making him feel distant from me and my pregnancy.

Here's a doozy for you: Many guys feel a little (get this) *jealous* of their wives for getting to bear their children. Of course they'd rather not have to deal with morning sickness, but they recognize that the act of carrying a baby is a great privilege. They also realize that mamas have a huge advantage when it comes to bonding with the baby—carrying a baby inside of you for nine months while nourishing him or her from your own body has a way of helping you connect. Daddies of the world want to share in this privilege and most will do anything they can to connect with the baby and the pregnancy.

The best thing you can do for your hubby (because I know you love him!) is let him be part of your pregnancy. That means not only sharing what's going on (yes, even if he won't admit it, he probably *does* want to hear that his baby is now the size of a chocolate-covered peanut), but also telling him explicitly how he can help share the burden. He wants to help. Give him a hand and tell him *exactly* how to help. You'll probably find that he's not only a great source of support, but that your pregnancy can also be a romantic, intimate time in your marriage.

Ways to Get Your Man Involved in Your Pregnancy

- Forward him all of the weekly pregnancy newsletters that you get delivered to your inbox—or, even better, sign him up for a subscription of his own. (And no, you're not the only one who signed up for seventeen of them.)

- Celebrate your pregnancy milestones together. When you reach your second trimester, surprise him by cooking a big dinner to celebrate. When you reach your third trimester, pick up a small present like a parenting book to remind him that he's about to be a dad.

- Make copies of your ultrasound photos and give them to your husband so he can put them on his desk at work.

- Send him to the store to fetch whatever you're *grrrraving* (yes, you're helping *him* by doing that).

- Pray for the baby together.

- Make your marriage a priority. So you haven't been feeling super-lovey-dovey lately (who does when they're nauseous, bloated and tired)? Still, your marriage is überimportant, so be careful not to neglect it just because you're pregnant. Make it a point to go on regular dates and to spend time with your husband (a red, lacy maternity baby doll won't hurt either).

- Have him help with the baby prep. Of course he's going to help assemble the crib and the dresser, but get him involved in the other (more fun) aspects of baby prep like the hospital route planning and stroller research.

- Read the Bible together. The Bible has lots to say about parenting—especially to dads—so set aside time to research what the ultimate authority on parenting has to say.

- Choose a name together. It can actually be fun to research and choose a name for your baby together. Unless, of course, your husband's taste in names is similar to Jason Lee's. In that case, start developing a plan to sign the birth certificate when your husband is in the hospital cafeteria for a coffee break.

Your Mama (and Your Mother-in-law): Your Experienced Resources

The ladies in your church bring you casseroles and your husband flits around trying to figure out what to do—and your mother, well, she goes shopping. Before you reach your second trimester, your child will have more pairs of shoes than you had during your entire childhood. By the time your baby is born, he or she will have more luxe velvet outfits than one little baby can possibly spit up on in a lifetime. And your mom is just getting started. Just wait until your little schnookum's first birthday.

Aside from being a top-notch baby wardrobe consultant, moms (and mothers-in-law) can also serve as wonderful pregnancy confidantes. They know pregnancy. They know you. And they're so excited about the baby that they can hardly sleep at night—or keep their wallets in their purses.

Here's another little-known fact about moms and mothers-in-law: They're actually *afraid* of meddling. Wipe that shocked look off of your face. I didn't say that they don't meddle. I said they're *afraid* of meddling. Now that I'm a mom, I'm starting to understand the dynamics of meddling. We moms love our babies so much that we want everything to go perfectly for them. So we talk. And make suggestions. And throw out ideas. We're not doing it to meddle, we're doing it to help.

The problem is that these so-called suggestions come across as moms trying to insert their will into their children's lives—and that tends to be a teensy bit annoying. So as a mom, you'll learn early on to be *afraid* of meddling. Your mom and mother-in-law are probably feeling the same way right now. They want to help. And suggest. And throw out ideas. But they do *not* want you to think they're meddling.

So help your mama (and your hubby's mama)! They really don't want to annoy the tar out of you (really, they don't). My sugges-tion is to give them something to meddle in so they don't meddle in everything. Put them in charge of researching the best baby gear, the best hospitals or the best cures for morning sickness. They'll happily jump at the opportunity to help (and in the meantime, you can lie on the couch and eat bonbons while they figure things out for you). How's that for killing two birds with one stone? Bye-bye meddling, hello new crib!

Also—and I hope this doesn't sound cheesy—I want to *suggest* that you give your mom and your mother-in-law some grace. When I was pregnant, I found myself losing my temper a lot more frequently, especially when it came to the people I loved the most. My mom took the brunt of it—and now that I have kids, I realize that my mom was only being a mom and looking out for me. So show your mom some grace. After all, she was the one who went through morning sickness, bloating and weight gain for *you.*

Get with Your Girlfriends: Your Gabfest Resource

Ask your husband what's up with that funny black line that magically appeared on your belly, and he'll probably ask you why you've been playing with the Sharpies. But call up your girlfriend, and she'll not only know the technical term (linea nigra), but she'll also be able to tell you exactly when it should appear (early in the second trimester) and whether it will fade after your pregnancy (it should).

Fact: Girls love talking about pregnancy. Just mention the word *pregnant* to any woman and she'll spend the next twenty minutes regaling you with horror stories about how her best friend's cousin gained weight like a sumo wrestler and the twenty minutes after that raving about how cute her next-door neighbor's newborn is. Girlfriends love stuff like that. Even if you're calling to discuss the intricacies of maternity leggings at nine o'clock on a Friday night, I guarantee any girl you know will put the DVR on pause to discuss.

With that in mind, there are certain topics that are probably best left to the "experts" (aka moms who have been there, done that). So when a seemingly bizarre symptom comes your way, pick up the phone, call a girlfriend and ask away.

Questions That Are Okay to Ask Your Girlfriends (but Probably Not Anyone Else)

Why in the world do I pee every time I laugh or sneeze?
Answer: Technical term: pelvic floor dysfunction. What it means? Your growing baby is squishing your bladder and stretching your pelvic floor. This makes it difficult for the bladder muscle to stay closed during sudden increases in pressure, like laughing or sneezing. Not-so-technical explanation: Your bladder will probably never regain its original strength. Sorry Charlie!

Why haven't I pooped in two weeks?
Answer: Not to compare your baby to a parasite, but your baby is leeching a lot of water from your system, making your large intestine pretty parched. Drink lots of water, eat lots of prunes and call your doctor if it gets really bad.

Will I always look like Chewbacca?
Answer: Nope! Pregnancy makes your hair grow at warp speed, but a postdelivery hormone drop will make your hair fall out at warp speed, so buy a good razor and enjoy the Pantene hair while you have it.

Why is my husband suddenly so annoying?
Answer: Nothing reminds you of your hubby's annoying quirks like a bad case of pregnancy resentment, so if you're thinking, *I'm so sick of watching you eat off-limits turkey sandwiches in those skinny jeans while I'm stuck here looking like a beached whale,* try to remind yourself that it's not *his* fault that he's skinnier than you. (Actually it is *partially* his fault. I'm just sayin'…) He can make it up to you after the baby's born by having trouble losing his sympathy weight and by changing lots of diapers.

Why can't I remember to feed the dog?
Answer: It's called "Mommy Brain," and it's not your fault. There are so many good, interesting thoughts floating around in that brain of yours that it's virtually impossible for you to remember everything. Perfect excuse to "forget" to go to the Neighborhood Association's next four-hour meeting.

Is it normal to have a lot of, *um, er,* discharge down there?
Answer: Whew! Got that one out in the open. Yes. It's normal. It happens to almost everyone, and yes, it will go away after you have the baby.

Will my boobs always hurt this badly?
Answer: No. The first trimester is going to hurt. The second trimester can be a little painful. During the third trimester, your boobs will be in their glory days: huge, perky and nearly pain-free.

I swear I haven't exercised in weeks so why am I sweating like I just ran a marathon?

Answer: You got a bun in your oven and that's exactly what you feel like—an oven. Crank on the AC because pregnancy makes your body temperature skyrocket.

Why do my nipples show through my ski jacket?

Answer: The girls are getting ready to breast-feed so get used to it. You can cover 'em up with fancy schmancy nipple hiders (yes, they actually make those) or just use plain-old Band-Aids and a super-thick bra (yes, they actually sell those too).

Pregnancy and Parenting Sites: Internet Resources

Type *pregnancy* into good ole Google and you'll get more than 148 million results. That's a lot of people talking about pregnancy out there in cyberspace! With the amount of time you've been spending on the couch recently, you may actually have time to wade through all 148 million sites, but since you're probably ready for a nap, I'll save you the trouble. I did it for you. Okay, so I didn't really open 148 million links, but I have spent some time studying the most popular pregnancy and parenting Web sites out there, and I can give you some insight into what you'll find on each one.

My Favorite Pregnancy Web Sites

1. Baby Center (babycenter.com)

   The Scoop: Baby Center has thousands (and thousands) of pregnancy articles to keep you informed, entertained and in the know during your pregnancy.

The Cherry on Top: I love the fact that Baby Center's articles are written by experts and triple-checked by doctors, making the information feel a little more trustworthy than the random site I found on Google that swore jumping jacks cured pregnancy heartburn.

2. BabyZone (babyzone.com)

The Scoop: Disney Family's BabyZone is the place to go for awesome pregnancy calculators and tools.

The Cherry on Top: I downloaded some (okay, all) of Baby-Zone's awesome widgets to my dashboard and was able to track my due date, see my baby's growth and get daily recipes.

3. The Bump (thebump.com)

The Scoop: The Bump has a huge Q&A section where you'll find tons of helpful answers to all of your pregnancy questions.

The Cherry on Top: I always look at the Bump first when I have a baby shower gift to buy. They have a supercool consolidation of baby registries from tons of top stores, making it übereasy and convenient to register and find registries. (Yep, if this is sounding familiar, it's because The Knot from your wedding-planning days is owned by the same people!)

4. CafeMom (cafemom.com)

The Scoop: CafeMom is like pulling up a chair, grabbing a cup of coffee and sitting down to chat with *millions* of pregnant mamas all at once. It's the biggest community of moms on the Web, so if you want to make virtual mom friends, it's the place to go.

The Cherry on Top: If you ask a question on CafeMom's boards, you'll get twenty-five friendly (and different) answers before you can order yourself a latte from the virtual barista.

5. ParentsConnect (parentsconnect.com)

The Scoop: Nickelodeon's ParentsConnect is the place where baby-naming folks hang out (making it the place to go for baby-naming advice). Plus, their weekly pregnancy newsletters are absolutely hilarious.

The Cherry on Top: Check out PC's "World's Biggest Online Baby Shower," a quarterly online party where you play hysterical baby shower games and win real prizes like strollers and diaper bags.

Getting Answers: Your Resources in Action

Now that we've covered all the bases, let's check out your resources in action.

Question: How can I avoid the dreaded stretch marks?

- Jesus said in John 16:33, "In this world you will have trouble. But take heart! I have overcome the world." And there's not a stretch mark in the world that Jesus hasn't overcome. But really, all joking aside, Jesus is *the* number one supportive resource you can lean on during this emotionally and physically trying time.
- Your mother lifts her shirt and shows you her battle scars, explaining how she's proud of her stretch marks as they remind her of you (*aw!*).
- Your mother-in-law tells you how she used a cream made from olive oil and coconut extract to home-remedy her stretch marks away.
- The church ladies make you a casserole.
- Your husband immediately runs to the store and buys the top-of-the-line stretch mark cream and starts to rub it on your belly. While he's out, he picks up three packages of hot dogs, a jar of pickles and a carton of Ben & Jerry's (for himself).

- Your girlfriends rant about what a sham the top-of-the-line stretch mark creams are and suggest that you use plain old olive oil before your shower each day.
- Then your girlfriend calls you back and tells you to forget it. Olive oil is expensive and it won't do any good anyway.
- Mr. Google has 825,000 ways. You just have to page through them. You'd better get going. Those stretch marks aren't going to avoid themselves.

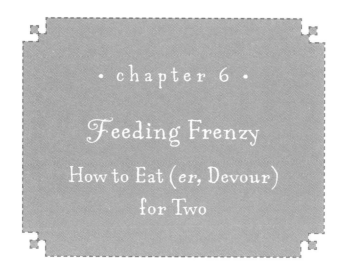

· chapter 6 ·

Feeding Frenzy

How to Eat (er, Devour) for Two

*B*efore we get started, let me just warn you that this chapter is bound to make you hungry. Of course, that's nothing new, given the fact that you go to bed hungry, wake up (at midnight) hungry, wake up (again) hungry and then spend most of your day (you guessed it) hungry. Nonetheless, I thought I'd warn you so you can go get yourself a snack before you start reading. The last thing you need right now is to be forced to think about food without actually having some in front of you to eat.

Since nagging hunger has likely become an integral part of your life, you've probably been eating a lot lately. And it's okay to eat a lot when you're pregnant! Even doctors and (get this) dietitians agree that pregnant women *need* to eat a lot. Not a lot *a lot*, like the entire sausage and pineapple pizza that you inhaled yesterday, but you definitely have the medical community's blessing to *eat*. And considering the fact that you will probably never again have your doctor's blessing to consume large amounts of fudge-ripple, take full advantage while you can.

I'm far from an expert on food. Of course, I love to eat, but I can't tell a calorie from a kilogram or a tablespoon of fat from a hunk of protein. My sister Alisa, however, is a bona fide registered dietitian, which means she has the burden of knowing *exactly* how many calories are in every bite of food she eats. That kind of knowledge is annoying when eating at an all-you-can-eat buffet, but it definitely comes in handy when you're pregnant and need to figure out how to navigate eating for two. With that in mind, I asked her to lend her expertise and help me with this chapter.

Before I go any further, I need to assure you that Alisa is a dietitian that you can *actually* trust. I have never seen her eat any tofu product that's made to resemble meat, and she has never *once* suggested that I replace my coffee habit with a wheatgrass-garlic tea habit. In fact, she's one of those dietitians that subscribes to the theory that everything—even chocolate—is okay in moderation. I don't even have to hide my Oreos when she comes over to visit.

So now that you can be certain that reading this chapter won't require you to eat tofurkey, let's talk (real) turkey: How much can you *really* eat while preggo? What exactly is going to happen to your body after you go on this extra-calorie binge? Is it really not okay to eat a turkey sandwich? And, most importantly, exactly how many calories are in that box of Cheez-Its that you devoured in the last five minutes?

How to Eat for Two

There are essentially two schools of thought on pregnancy eating. The first school—the one that I joined wholeheartedly—says that pregnancy is the one time in your life that you can gain weight without a social stigma, so you should relish every opportunity to eat anything and everything. The second school—the one adopted by hardhearted dietitians who have never been pregnant—says that your pregnancy diet and your nonpregnancy diet should essentially stay the same aside from a slight increase in calories in your second and third trimesters.

The truth probably lies somewhere in the middle. Eating for two isn't actually eating enough for two entire people, so loading up your plate with twice as much from the buffet line will only serve to make you feel (a) bloated and (b) fat. On the other hand, your baby is growing much quicker than say, your husband, so as much as he would like to convince you otherwise, it's probably best for you to have the last slice of pie.

According to Alisa—who has been pregnant and is very familiar with first trimester hot dog cravings—healthy pregnancy eating requires a careful balance between eating the right amount, figuring out what you can tolerate and getting the nutrients your baby needs to thrive. And since you probably don't have the get-up-and-go to figure out how to find that balance right now, here are Alisa's top tips on how to master the art of pregnancy eating.

How to Get into the Eating-for-Two Groove

- **Hop onto the minimeal bandwagon.** It's healthier (for everyone, not just pregnant mamas!) to eat five or six smaller meals instead of three gorge-yourself-silly meals each day. So if you eat breakfast at seven and then you're famished by say, eight o'clock, try eating several minimeals instead.
- **Carry snacks.** Pregnancy hunger has a way of making you do crazy things—like going through the drive-thru and ordering a ten-pack of tacos and then devouring them while sitting in the parking lot. Stave off hunger-induced craziness by stashing healthy snacks—like whole-grain granola bars or a bag of trail mix—in your purse, your car and your desk at work.

- **Give yourself some grace.** If you're craving tacos and the only thing that's going to hit the spot is tacos, go get yourself some tacos—perhaps two or three instead of ten—and pull into a parking spot and enjoy.
- **Try not to count calories.** Music to a hungry mama's ears, right? There's no point in worrying about exactly how many calories you should be eating. Yes, there are lots of guidelines on how much food you should be eating (more on that in a bit), but don't stress over it. If you're hungry, eat.
- **Don't forget to take your prenatals.** Unless you have a strange craving for spinach salad and are downing it by the pound, you're probably not getting enough folate in your diet. That means taking your prenatal vitamins is super-duper important. My trick for remembering? I stuck the entire bottle of pills in the cookie jar as the chances of me "forgetting" to eat a cookie every day was slim to none.
- **Drink a lot of water.** You and your baby both need water, so drink up, to the tune of eight (or more) glasses a day. (Pregnant mama trick: If water smells funny to you—and you're hardly the first pregnant mama to complain about the scent of fresh, pure water—try adding a squeeze of lemon or a splash of orange extract to mask the smell.)
- **Try to eat a balanced diet.** I'm not saying you have to kick your saltine cracker habit in one day, but try to slowly wean yourself off of the saltines and add something else—say, Kashi Original 7 Grain Snack Crackers—into the mix. This is good practice for when you have a toddler who refuses to eat anything other than macaroni and cheese for four weeks straight.
- **Keep real(ish) food on hand.** There are times when a string cheese or a handful of trail mix just isn't going to cut it. You need a *real* meal, and you certainly don't have thirty minutes to speed cook a gourmet dinner. I know that microwave dinners probably

don't measure up to your mama's pot roast, but you might want to stock up on some healthy, low-sodium frozen meals (yes, they make them—try Amy's Kitchen or Kashi) so you have something to eat when you don't have the energy to cook. You might want to keep a few meals on hand for your hubby as well, because according to my husband, after four nights, even PB and olive sandwiches get old.

Counting Calories

So with all this in mind, how many old-fashioned doughnuts can you *really* eat without feeling guilty? My exhaustive research (I Googled it) tells me that most doctors recommend that a pregnant woman should eat about three hundred extra calories a day, which is about one and a half doughnuts (just FYI). Of course, those three hundred extra calories don't have to be eaten in doughnuts. For example, you could also eat a half cup of Chunky Monkey or a small order of fries.

Just to make sure you have every morsel of information you need, I had Alisa share her research on the official recommendations for pregnancy eating. The American Dietetic Association (ADA) says that you don't really need any extra calories during your first trimester (boo!), 340 extra per day during your second trimester (better!) and 452 extra per day during your third trimester (that's more like it!). And if you must know, they also recommend limiting sweets *and* fats while pregnant, which means the ADA would probably frown upon my doughnut-and-ice-cream eating habits, but we'll just keep that between us.

These extra calories can be a good opportunity to gorge yourself on fast food, but most (smart) pregnant mamas use the extra calories to get more nutrition in their diets. If you want to make sure that your baby grows nice and big—and you *don't* grow nice and big—try to be strategic about your 340–452 calories. I'm not saying you can't occasionally indulge in something really ooey-gooey delicious, but on most days, try to pack some nutritional punch into your pregnancy snacks.

If you're anything like me, you're more of a wing-it gal than a count-every-calorie-that-passes-your-lips gal. And since you probably don't spend your days with a calculator and food log in hand, you might be wondering exactly what 340–452 calories looks like. Fortunately, Alisa *is* the kind of gal who carries a calculator and food log in her purse (sorry to out you like that, Alisa), so I asked her to give us a list of easy-to-whip-up snacks that are packed with nutrition and tasty to boot. Here's what she came up with.

Ten Delicious and Easy Snacks That Are Between 340 and 452 Calories

1. A big ole PB & J (or PB & banana) sandwich.
2. Eight smallish slices of cheddar cheese piled on crackers.
3. Two cups of popcorn with a glass of chocolate milk (butter allowed!).
4. A sliced apple dipped in peanut butter with a glass of milk.
5. A pita pocket stuffed with chicken salad.
6. A bagel with cream cheese.
7. A cheese quesadilla.
8. A bowl of tortilla chips with salsa or—even better—bean dip.
9. A cup of granola with milk or plain yogurt.
10. Two handfuls of trail mix and a glass of juice.

Getting on a Health Food Kick

All this talk of tofurkey and spinach salad probably has you craving something nice and healthy. (Go ahead, run to the fridge and grab yourself a low-salt, nitrate-free hot dog.) The reality is that even the worst eaters—I'm talking to you, O Queen of the Soft Serve—suddenly get supermotivated to eat superhealthily when they realize that everything that enters *their* body, enters their *baby's* body too. I'm not saying that to freak you out—well, not to freak you out too much—but when you think of it that way, it's really important to be purposeful about what you eat when you're pregnant.

All joking aside—and I do love a good tofurkey nugget joke—choosing to eat a healthy and balanced diet is one of the best things you can do for your baby. And while I've certainly made it clear that I indulged in the occasional treat, I also worked really hard to eat healthily when I was pregnant. (No, really, I did.) One thing I struggled with was knowing exactly *what* to eat. I had all sorts of food aversions and cravings, and by the time I had figured out what was actually consumable, my brain had no energy left to sort out the nutritional impact of what I was eating.

So I asked Alisa to make it really simple for us. She outlined the major nutrients that a pregnant mama needs and shared exactly how to get those nutrients without doing a lot of complicated cooking or label reading. That way, you can sit back and enjoy your deliciously healthy chicken-and-black-bean burrito in peace.

Packing a Nutritional Punch with Your Food Choices

- **Whole Grains.** From one carb-loving mama to another, I know you want *white* bread. And *white* pasta. And *white* chocolate. Oh, wait, never mind. Chocolate isn't a grain, is it? There's something about macaroni and Wonder Bread that will get any pregnant mama drooling. But whole grains are superhealthy, so do your best to whole-wheatify your white-carb habit. If you just can't get the 100 percent whole wheat stuff down, go for the fancy "white whole grain" stuff which still has some whole grains. Or mix half white pasta with half whole grain pasta. Or toss a few handfuls of whole wheat flour into your pancake mix. (Since you're probably wondering: Drowning the pancakes in maple syrup doesn't negate the fact that you're eating whole grains.)

- **Protein.** The old wives' tales say that if you're craving protein, you're having a boy and if you're craving fruit, you're having a girl. Well, turns out the old wives are wrong because I was positively carnivorous during both of my pregnancies and I have a boy and a girl. Protein is superimportant for your baby's growth, especially during the second and third trimesters. So try to get at least one serving of high quality lean protein in every meal through foods like peanut butter, soy and tofu products, eggs, low-fat dairy, poultry, fish, and lean beef.

- **Fiber.** Sorry to be graphic when you're eating, but pregnancy can make you *so* constipated! You could go old school and add Metamucil to your water every morning. Or you could just add a bunch of high-fiber foods to your diet. Load your plate up with whole grains, beans, fruits and veggies. While you're getting all fiber-filled, make sure to drink lots and lots of water (or prune juice). If you don't, you'll get *more* stopped up. And if you're thinking that there's no way that things could get *worse,* Alisa says they can and they will. I'm just going to trust her on that one.

- **Iron.** Did you know that your body actually *makes* blood for your baby? I'm not really sure how it works, but even after your baby starts making his or her own blood, you'll still be cranking a bunch of extra blood to make sure your baby has every drop that he or she needs. How cool is that? All that extra liquid not only gives credence to your theory that all of your weight gain thus far has been water weight, but also means your body needs lots of extra iron. Your prenatal vitamin should have a lot of iron in it, but your doctor may suggest an additional iron supplement if you start to get anemic. You can also get iron by eating things like spinach, red meat and iron-fortified cereals. (Bonus information: Alisa says iron is more readily absorbed in your diet if you eat it with vitamin C. So if you squeeze a lemon on your spinach or drink a glass of OJ with your cereal, your body will absorb more of the iron it needs.)

- **Calcium.** Your baby's bones, heart, teeth, nerves and muscles all need calcium to develop correctly. But don't fret: If your diet is lacking in calcium, your baby will just leech the calcium you have stored up in your bones. *Hello* osteoporosis! Let me guess: You're suddenly feeling supermotivated to go eat a container of yogurt. Do it! Dairy products like cheese, ice cream, milk and yogurt are the best sources of calcium. But if you can't eat dairy for some reason, you can also get calcium through fortified orange juice, spinach, broccoli and blackstrap molasses. Ice cream or spinach. Spinach or ice cream. Tough decision.

- **Vitamin D.** Calcium—you know, that mineral that your baby needs to grow almost everything—needs vitamin D to work. Most milk is fortified with vitamin D, so you probably get plenty that way, but vitamin D can also be made by your body when sunlight is absorbed into your skin. (How did God think of *that?*) If you live somewhere warm like Texas or Florida and enjoy a daily latte outside, you're probably all set. If you live in rainy Portland, Oregon, and/or are lactose intolerant, you might want to ask your doctor about a vitamin D supplement.

- **Folate/Folic Acid.** Here's a little dietetics lesson for you: Folate is a B vitamin found naturally in food, and folic acid is the synthetic form of the vitamin found in supplements. And the reason I'm telling you this seemingly useless information is so you can have a really cool fact to spout off at playgroup when the moms start talking about prenatal vitamins. But since we're talking about folate, I also want to point out that it plays a major role in your baby's brain and spinal cord development. So even if you're being supervigilant about taking your prenatals, you still might want to try to work some folate into your diet. The best sources of folate include citrus fruit (just watch out for heartburn), green leafy veggies, beans, and fortified breads and cereals.

• **Omega-3 Fatty Acids.** Omega-3 fatty acids are another brain-boosting nutrient. If you're wanting your kid to be admitted into Mensa by age four, it can't hurt to give him an omega-3 fatty acid boost in utero. The best way to get omega-3 is from fatty fish (like salmon), but there's a small concern over mercury (we'll get to that), so you can also load up on omega-3 through plant-based sources like walnuts, pecans, canola oil and flaxseed.

What Not to Eat

When I was pregnant, it really bugged me that I couldn't eat sushi. Ironically, I rarely have sushi when I'm not pregnant—raw fish really isn't my thing—but when I was pregnant, I craved salmon rolls every other day. I think it was the concept more than my love for sushi. It was the fact that I already had to give up so many things. It felt unfair that I had to give up sushi as well.

Unfair as it feels, there are good reasons that certain foods are banned when you're pregnant. It's not that the doctors and dietitians have conspired to make your pregnant life miserable. As far as I know, they haven't. It's that these foods can cause really bad (albeit really rare) problems for your baby. And in my opinion, miffed as I was that I had to give up sushi, the risk to my baby was reason enough to stay far, far away from everything on this list.

Foods and Drinks You Should Avoid While Pregnant

- **Raw Anything.** I take that back. I guess things like raw cauliflower and raw celery are okay—but why would you crave *those*? Raw animal proteins are a big no-no. Food-borne illnesses are never fun, but the risk of dehydration and complications increase significantly when you're pregnant, so make sure your meat and seafood is fully cooked. Steaks and roasts should be cooked to medium or medium well and all chicken, seafood and pork should be fully cooked.
- **Sushi.** This goes back to the "raw anything" rule.
- **Raw Eggs.** Again with the raw food thing. And yes, this means no eating raw cookie dough until your baby is born. Unless, of course, you find a workaround. For example, you could wait to put the raw eggs in until the very end and swipe a few pre-egg bites. Just saying.
- **Unpasteurized Cheeses.** Soft cheeses have gotten a bad rap because in the past, most were unpasteurized and therefore, unsafe for pregnant mamas to eat. But these days, most Bries and Gorgonzolas are totally safe for pregnant moms. Just make sure you read the label and it says "made with pasteurized milk" before digging in.
- **Lunchmeat.** This is a big one. Lunchmeats can (rarely) carry *Listeria,* an icky bug that's pretty harmless to most people but can be superdangerous for a pregnant mama (ask your doctor). Just to make sure you don't put your baby at risk, it's best that you don't eat lunchmeat unless it has been heated to *steaming.* So that means your cold deli sandwich is out, but Quiznos is in. (*Mmm.* Toasty!)
- **Unpasteurized Juices.** You know those fancy fresh-pressed juices they make at the health food store? They also have an increased

chance of carrying icky food-borne illness—so go ahead and just buy yourself an Odwalla and save yourself the worry.

- **Artificial Sweeteners.** Before you start a petition to have me lynched for trying to tell you to give up your Diet Coke, let me just qualify this with the fact that I'm not saying "absolutely no" to artificial sweeteners. I'm just making sure you have all the facts. There is a lot of controversy surrounding the safety of artificial sweeteners—and what's more, they haven't been extensively studied in pregnancy, so we don't know exactly how they affect an unborn baby. With that in mind, if you must have it, it might be a good idea just to drink regular old Coke for a while.

- **Energy Drinks.** Energy drinks have a lot of caffeine, which has been linked to an increased chance of miscarriage and in high amounts can hinder your baby's development. So, nuh-uh.

- **Herbal Teas and Supplements.** Like energy drinks, herbal teas contain (you guessed it) herbs. I'm not going to go as far as to say you should avoid herbal tea altogether, because 99 percent of herbal teas are just fine. But certain tea ingredients, like raspberry leaf, can cause premature labor. It's best to run anything herbal by your doctor before you take it. I actually brought a box of my favorite tea to my first doctor's appointment (I was concerned, okay) so my doctor could look over the ingredients. He checked the ingredients and gave me the go-ahead to drink without worrying.

- **Advil or Motrin.** Okay, so I know this is a medicine and not a food, but since you ingest it, I figured I'd mention it here. Ibuprofen—fabulous as it is for curing headaches—can cause bleeding in pregnancy and should be avoided.

- **Liver and Kidney.** Just in case you love yourself a big steaming plate of liver 'n' onions (sorry, I'm gagging right now), it's probably best to avoid organ meats while pregnant. It has something to do with toxins and—honestly, I didn't read any further than that because I figured that the chances of a liver-loving pregnant mama reading this book are slim to none.

- **Alcohol.** There. I said it. And now I have to explain myself. I'm pretty opinionated about alcohol and pregnancy, so I'm dedicating the entire following section of this book to the subject. And, yes, in my opinion, alcohol should be avoided at all costs while pregnant. Read on to find out why.

The Big Alcohol Debate

Alcohol and pregnancy has become a touchy subject lately, which is kind of strange because for the last thirty years or so—think post-*Mad Men*—it's been pretty commonly accepted knowledge that pregnant women and alcohol don't mix.

Here's the deal with alcohol and pregnancy: Early exposure to alcohol in utero can cause central nervous system damage—meaning the baby's brain doesn't develop or function the way it should. This results in fetal alcohol syndrome, the name for a variety of lifelong impairments that are the product of this central nervous system damage. It's a big deal. Since we're talking about unborn babies here, most doctors (and pregnant mamas) started to follow a no-alcohol-while-pregnant rule. In fact, back in 1988, it became federal law that all alcoholic beverages had to be labeled with a warning about the risks of drinking while pregnant.

But things have changed. Recent research has shown that the riskiest time for fetal alcohol syndrome is early in the pregnancy. With this in mind, several major medical journals as well as the UK Department of Health have concluded that consuming small amounts of alcohol late in pregnancy doesn't significantly increase the risks and is probably okay.

I don't know about you, but *doesn't significantly increase* and *probably okay* are not phrases that make me feel superconfident—especially when we're talking about the health and well-being of my baby. I guess to me, no glass of wine is worth the risk of a lifelong disability for my child.

So as opinionated as I sound, I want to go on record as disagreeing with people who say it's okay to drink alcohol while pregnant. I'm a don't-drink-while-pregnant kind of gal, and I'll probably stay that way for the foreseeable future, regardless of what new research is saying. The good news is that a significant part of the medical establishment agrees with me: Both the CDC and the Mayo Clinic hold firm to their no-alcohol-while-pregnant recommendations.

Now that I've gone on this alcohol rant, I probably need to talk a few of you down from the ledge. If you had a glass of wine (or two) before you found out you were pregnant, don't freak out. One of my friends went out to dinner for her birthday at a Mexican restaurant and had a margarita. The next morning, she woke up and it dawned on her that her period was late. Sure enough, she was pregnant. She beat herself up over that margarita for weeks—until her doctor finally assured her that it was *not* a huge deal.

Her doctor explained to her that during the really early weeks of pregnancy, when that fertilized egg is floating down your fallopian tube waiting to implant, it's not getting nourished from your bloodstream, so the alcohol you may drink won't even touch your baby. Once the egg does implant, the hormones will flood your body and you will most likely know you are pregnant fairly quickly. So while this is definitely not an excuse to go on a prepregnancy-test margarita binge, it means that a drink or three before you know you're pregnant isn't something to stress about.

In summary, here is a list of Erin's Pregnancy and Alcohol Rules (feel free to print these out and tack them on the wall in the bathroom of your favorite restaurant):

- Alcohol and pregnancy just don't mix. Order a virgin piña colada—it'll still come with the fancy tiny umbrella.
- You have enough to freak out about—so don't freak out if you accidentally had a margarita before you found out you were pregnant.
- If you *are* freaking out, call your doctor just to be sure—but don't listen to your doctor if she says you can drink *another* margarita.
- Spread the word. Let's start another no-alcohol-while-pregnant revolution.

Just Sayin' No to the Joe

Confession time: I did *not* give up caffeine cold turkey when I got pregnant. I wanted to. The day after I found out that I was pregnant, I made a valiant attempt and made it all the way until ten o'clock before driving to Seattle's Best for a café au lait. I even tried to trick my body into thinking that decaf would suffice, but I'm a full-caf girl at heart. I had a really hard time giving up my morning cup of joe.

In the midst of my struggle to overcome my caffeine addiction (yes, I admit, I was addicted), I called my doctor to get the whole scoop. He told me that all the no-coffee-while-pregnant hype was based on a study that showed that taking in large doses of caffeine could increase the risk of miscarriage and low birth weight. My doctor suggested that I try to limit my coffee intake to one (or max, two) cups a day. That said, you should check with your doctor or midwife to find out what he or she recommends as far as caffeine intake.

With that in mind, I really tried to cut back on the coffee (and eventually did wean myself to a max of one cup a day). One thing I did was start brewing pots of half-caf early in my pregnancy and could hardly tell the difference. I thought that was an ingenious idea, but it turns out that everyone else had the same idea. I noticed bags of half-caf beans on sale at the supermarket the other day. Who knew?

Fish and Pregnancy

Fish is another maybe/maybe-not pregnancy thing. It's really, really good for your baby and really, really bad for your baby at the same time. Fish is good for your baby because it contains omega-3 fatty acids, which are brain-building supernutrients that give your baby's brain development a boost—and you want that. But fish is bad for your baby because our oceans have become really polluted with mercury. Since fish live in and breathe that ocean water, they have a bunch of mercury floating around inside of them, and you don't want your baby getting a bunch of that.

So the rule with fish and pregnancy is that you shouldn't eat more than two servings a week (that goes for when you're breast-feeding too), and you should avoid really big fish like shark, sword-fish, tilefish and king mackerel, which have been swimming around in the mercury-filled ocean for months on end. If you love tuna, go for the "chunk light" variety, as the albacore tend to have higher mercury content. If you love salmon, go for wild sockeye, not farmed or Atlantic.

Also, if you want your kid to get the omega-3 brain-development boost but aren't a big seafood lover, try drizzling some flaxseed oil on your toast in the morning or add a handful of walnuts to your trail mix. Both walnuts and flaxseed are good plant-food sources of omega-3s that don't carry the risk of mercury poisoning.

Pregnancy Weight Gain

Before I finish this chapter on eating, I need to tackle pregnancy weight gain. I know that's probably not your favorite subject (it's certainly not mine), but considering the fact that weight gain is a pretty definite part of pregnancy, it's a necessary evil in a chapter about eating.

I have yet to meet a real, live pregnant mama who looks like the women in the maternity store ads. I'm convinced that the women in those pictures aren't real. Okay, so they're probably real women, but I'm certain that they aren't really pregnant. Those perfectly round baby bumps sitting atop toned calves and size zero hips are way too good to be true.

Of course, when I got pregnant for the first time, I really, truly believed that's exactly how I would look. I had visions of cute maternity leggings paired with figure-showing maternity T's. I imagined charming strappy sandals paired with my favorite bootcut jeans (because naturally, I'd still be able to wear them as my hips would certainly stay my prepreggo size). I actually *wanted* to start gaining weight so I could start looking adorably pregnant. I didn't know better. No one told me the women in those darned ads aren't real! Anyway, if you want the dirty details on what actually *will* happen, I'll just start from the beginning.

The first place you're going to start gaining weight is in your breasts. Your husband will probably notice it first. His inability to wipe that telltale goofy grin off of his face will be your first sign. Unfortunately, along with rapid growth, your boobs will probably also be excruciatingly tender, so you might need to implement a look-but-don't-touch rule with said husband. (Note to any husbands who happen to have picked up this book: The tenderness typically goes away in the second trimester, so be patient! Your day will come!)

Here's the thing: While having cleavage like a Victoria's Secret model is great at home, it's probably something to avoid at places like church and work. Most of the shirts from your prepregnancy days will probably be too low cut and too tight to wear in public, so you might want to invest in some new (read: bigger) shirts, or even better, figure out ways to hide that bursting décolletage. I found that colorful silk scarves and long beaded necklaces were great (and cute!) ways to cover up.

Next in the weight-gain parade come your thighs and hips. Remember how I thought I would be able to wear my favorite boot-cut jeans throughout my pregnancy? Well, I was wrong. Dead wrong. In fact, I'm pretty sure my favorite jeans didn't make it through my first trimester. Instead, in one fell swoop, my thighs gained four pounds each, my butt gained one, and my hips decided to widen (you know, in early preparation for labor). Good-bye buttons, hello elastic waistbands!

Next comes your face. One day during my second pregnancy, my son was sitting on my lap. He proudly pointed to my chin and counted to four. "One...two...three...four! Four, Mama!" I asked him what he was counting and he shrugged and said "Your chins. You have four." Delightful child, isn't he? But the sad part is that he was right. I seemed to grow a new chin every other day.

As if the boob-butt-face trio isn't enough, next come the appendages. Strappy sandals? No way! Cute cuff bracelets? You wish. I used to think that weight gain in bony areas like fingers, toes and wrists was next to impossible, but I learned the hard way. I now know that rule number one of pregnant mama weight gain is that you can and *will* gain weight in every crack, crevice and appendage of your body. Nothing is exempt.

Just to help drive this point home a bit more, here's a chart of commonly eaten pregnancy foods and the amount of weight you'll probably gain from eating them. I'm not telling you to avoid these things, but simply what you can expect when you're eating.

Food	Weight You'll Gain
Carrot	1 pound
Entire jar of pickles	2 pounds
Cheeseburger	5 pounds (all to your hips)
French fries	2 pounds + 4 pounds water weight
Chocolate milkshake	3 pounds

Two boxes of saltines	4 pounds + 2 pounds water weight
Stick of sugar-free gum	1 pound + 6 pounds for the Ho-Hos that you eat 20 minutes later when you realize that the gum was no substitute for what you were craving

Weight Gain by the Numbers

I ended up gaining fifty-two pounds during my first pregnancy. I know, I know. That's *waaay* above the "recommended" range for weight gain, but range shmange. I was *hungry!* I've come to terms with the fact that pregnancy weight gain is inevitable. I went into pregnancy fully expecting to gain the recommended amount and not an ounce more and found myself ballooning past that number on the scale before I'd even started my third trimester.

At first I blamed it on the scale at the doctor's office. Those things get a lot of use and they're bound to break under the strain (*ha!*) eventually. When I realized that the scale seemed pretty sturdy, I started to blame my weight gain on water retention. That sounded like a good excuse. I was certain my little guy was just swimming in amniotic fluid and that the weight would melt away after I delivered. When that didn't happen, I realized that I had gained my pregnancy weight the old-fashioned way: by indulging in a few too many midnight bags of Ruffles.

The thing about pregnancy weight gain is that it's nothing like your typical I-gained-ten-pounds-over-the-holidays-and-now-have-to-eat-spinach-salad-until-March weight gain. Gaining weight when you're pregnant is essential for the health of your baby—so it's a good thing. But it's still weight gain. And since too much weight gain can affect your baby's future health, you need to be very careful to keep it in check (says the girl who gained fifty-two pounds). The key here is to do your best to eat healthily *and* eat well without going overboard (and devouring a triple hot fudge banana split every day). That won't do you or your baby any good at all.

So, You Hungry?

When I was about thirteen weeks pregnant, my family went on vacation to one of those all-inclusive resorts. There were about ten restaurant choices, so there were a billion different things for me to choose to eat at any given moment. I was in heaven. If I got queasy from the chow mein, I didn't have to worry about there being leftover chow mein in the fridge the next morning. If I totally dug the cheese fries, there would certainly be more waiting the next day. That's how a pregnant mama needs to eat.

Of course, my husband balked at my idea of staying at the all-inclusive resort for the remaining twenty-seven weeks of my pregnancy. I had to go back to the real world and learn to eat like a real person. And that's hard when you don't have a personal chef waiting at your beck and call.

I want to close this chapter by reminding you to allow yourself not to be perfect. I remember feeling like I was a bad mother and wife because I didn't have the time, energy or money to cook perfectly balanced pregnancy meals every day. I did the best I could, but there were plenty of days that we had fast food for dinner. There were also plenty of days when I left my husband to fend for himself.

So, yes, ideally, you'd eat a perfectly balanced diet of whole grains, lean proteins and vegetables. Ideally, you'll gain exactly the right amount of weight and not a pound more, and you'll look like one of those women in the maternity clothes ads. But while we're wishing, it would also be ideal if pregnancy didn't last nine months, and they made maternity jeans that actually stayed on. Since none of those things are going to happen, I'm giving you permission to give yourself a break.

Do the best you can. Trust God. Pray for your baby. And go eat a cheeseburger. Or a tofeeseburger. Your choice.

· c h a p t e r 7 ·

Work It, Mama!

Exercise and Pregnancy

We've already established that pregnant mamas tend to be a bit crazy, and I'll be the first to admit that pregnant mamas who exercise are the craziest of the bunch (no offense!). I used pregnancy as an excuse to stay far, far away from the gym and ignore the fact that I was gaining weight by the minute—which might have something to do with the fact that I gained fifty-two pounds. So if your tennis shoes have been languishing in the back of your closet for months (and you'd like to keep them there), feel free to head to the kitchen and get yourself a Ding Dong and then thumb ahead to the next chapter. I give you permission.

Since I'm of the do-as-I-say-and-not-as-I-do mentality, I figured I'd be remiss if I didn't give you some information about exercise and pregnancy. Since I'm certainly not the one to tell you about it, I consulted my friend Nicole Cruz, who not only owns a really cool boot camp for stroller-mommies but is also pregnant, which means she is one of the few people I know who actually exercises while pregnant.

Before you write her off as crazy, let me point out that she's a certified personal trainer who knows a thing or seven about exercise. Plus, she has this really, really cute baby bump from the front, and you can't even tell she's pregnant from behind because her buns are so tight and her thighs are superslim (sorry, Nicole, I wasn't really checking you out from behind). If that's not motivation to figure out a way to get your tennis shoes on over your swollen ankles, I don't know what is!

In reality, there are lots of benefits to exercising while pregnant. (Yes, I said it.) I might even go as far as to say that I would *consider* exercising during my next pregnancy, but we'll go ahead and cross that bridge when we get there. In the meantime, here are the essentials if you do decide you want to don your spandex and hop on the elliptical machine.

Top 9 Reasons to Exercise While Pregnant

1. **Your baby will be healthier.** The increased blood flow and oxygen flow that comes when you exercise means the service at your baby's 24-7 diner just got a whole lot faster.

2. **Your husband will be less annoying.** Or maybe you'll just be in a better mood. The endorphins that kick in while you exercise can help combat pregnancy-related moodiness (not that you've ever struggled with *that*).

3. **You'll gain less weight when pregnant.** This is of course very subjective—as "less" weight can still mean gaining seventy-eight pounds—but if dragging yourself out on a twenty-minute walk saves you some anxiety at weigh-in time, it's probably worth it.

4. **You'll decrease your risk of icky pregnancy illnesses.** Women who exercise are up to 20 percent less likely to get gestational diabetes. If there's anything worse than exercising while pregnant, it's being unable to eat pancakes and syrup while pregnant.

5. **You'll sleep better.** I'm guessing that people who run marathons go straight to snoozeville the night after the big race. Same goes for pregnant women. Walk a mile, fall asleep faster. Attempt to run a marathon, fall asleep about one mile into the race.

6. **Your labor will be short and sweet.** Okay, no guarantees on this one. In fact, I had pretty easy labors, and I didn't exercise a lick during my pregnancies—Scout's honor! But most medical professionals and exercise fanatics will agree that being in good shape can't hurt when you go into labor.

7. **You'll develop good habits.** If you're in the habit of going to the gym—even if it's just to hang out at the smoothie bar— you'll probably stay in the habit after your baby is born. Also, just as an added bonus, studies have shown that the kids of active parents tend to be more active themselves. It may *sound* like a bad thing to have an active toddler, but as long as your kid isn't near your cat or an electrical outlet, it's a good thing. Active kids tend to be healthier *and* happier.

8. **You'll make mommy friends.** Remember how I said Nicole runs a stroller boot camp? Well, there are mamas all over the country offering similar prenatal and postnatal classes that are really fun (no, really). Exercising with other pregnant mamas is a great way to make lifelong mommy friends.

9. **You'll lose your baby weight faster.** Don't delude yourself here: It's nine months up, nine months (give or take a few) down, no matter *what* you do. You will not be leaving the hospital in your skinny jeans, but exercising while pregnant may make it so you leave the hospital in your skinniest maternity jeans, which is a good start.

Where Do I Even Start?

Let's say I've somehow convinced you to put down that Ding Dong and go dig around in your closet for some tennies. You've even gone as far as to slip into some spandex running tights (the ones your husband bought you for Christmas three years ago that still had the tags on) and an old T-shirt. You have even pulled your hair into a ponytail. You're looking sporty, but how do you actually start *being* sporty?

I think the thing that kept me from exercising—aside from the fact that I was really, really tired and really, really wanted to stay on the couch—was that I didn't even know where to start. I had no idea where to begin, and the last thing I wanted was to be *that* lady who speed-walked around the neighborhood wearing hand and ankle weights.

I also didn't have a bazillion dollars to join a fancy schmancy fitness gym and hire a personal trainer. That would've been great, but I had baby clothes to buy! If you have a bazillion extra dollars, then I highly recommend that you hire a personal trainer to help you sculpt your body into a lean, mean pregnancy machine. Otherwise, you can just glean some of Nicole's personal trainer expertise here for free. (Caveat: Always check with your doctor or midwife before starting any exercise program—just to be extra safe.)

Erin's Easy (and Cheap!) Ways to Exercise When You're Pregnant

- **Go on a walk.** Walking is fun (well, fun for people who consider exercise fun), easy and low-impact, which makes it perfect for pregnant mamas. Plus, if you drag your husband along, you can plan out your baby's future as you walk.
- **Do (pregnancy) jazzercise.** I love exercise videos. I am the least coordinated person in the world, but that has never stopped me from donning my leg warmers and blasting eighties music while dancing around my living room. The good news is that there are lots of great pregnancy exercise DVDs available (check them

out from the library!) that will get you safely moving and grooving in your living room. Nicole's favorite is a DVD set called *Preggi Bellies,* which sounds supercutesy, but actually has lots of fun(ish) belly-and-body-sculpting exercises.

- **Lift weights.** When I was pregnant, one of my friends told me about an exercise video that encouraged pregnant mamas to use soup cans to do resistance training. Kind of makes you wonder what would happen to your exercise routine if you got hungry and accidentally ate one of your "dumbbells." Anyway, if you don't want to use soup, you can pick up a couple of two- to five-pound weights at a sporting goods store (they cost a few dollars each) and do things like arm curls and leg lifts during the commercial breaks when you watch TV.

- **Head to the pool.** There are definite pros and cons to swimming while pregnant. The big pro is that being submerged in cold water guarantees that you won't overheat like you would if you say, went running in November when it was snowing. Also, swimming is low impact—meaning your achin' back won't hurt worse than it already does when you're done. The con to swimming is that most pools require you to wear "appropriate attire," which means you'll probably have to squeeze your body into a maternity swimsuit (and if you've ever seen a maternity swimsuit, you know why that is *not* a good thing!).

- **Take a class.** Exercising with a bunch of other pregnant women who are just as fat and tired as you are is probably very appealing. Plus, sweating together with other pregnant mamas can help you to create a bond of sisterhood that's tighter than your prepregnancy sports bra.

- **Modify your current workout.** If you're one of those girls who exercised *before* you were pregnant, you can modify your typical workout to match your pregnancy workout needs. With a few exceptions (which I'll get into later in this chapter), most exercise programs are just fine for pregnant women.

- **Stretch.** Let me be explicit here: There will come a time that you will have both of your legs in stirrups while the rest of your body is attached to monitors, IV bags and your husband's purpling hand. This is when having some flexibility will come in handy.
- **Go online.** Technically, Web surfing doesn't count as exercise, but head to Fit Pregnancy (fitpregnancy.com) and Baby Fit (babyfit.com) where you'll find pregnancy exercise ideas, as well as advice from certified trainers on exactly how to do things like strength training or cardio.

Exercising Your Pelvic Floor

The one exception I had to my no-exercise-during-pregnancy rule was pelvic floor exercises. Seeing as how you probably had no idea what your pelvic floor was until you got pregnant, you've probably never even considered exercising it. But word on the street is that keeping your pelvic floor strong can not only make your labor easier, but it can also make it so you don't pee your pants every time you sneeze for the rest of your life. Since you'd probably rather not start wearing Poise Pads when you're thirty, you might want to consider starting a little pelvic floor exercise routine.

Another detail about your pelvic floor that warrants mention is that its strength and flexibility have a direct correlation to your sexual enjoyment after pregnancy. Pregnancy (and delivery) put a lot of strain on the muscles down there, and stretched out and flabby muscles aren't exactly sexy (this goes for all muscles, not just pelvic floor muscles, by the way). It's in your best interest to keep your pelvic floor as healthy and strong as possible.

Now that I've adequately frightened (*er,* motivated) you into starting a pelvic floor exercise program, I probably need to explain how to do it. The best way to exercise your pelvic floor is to do Kegel exercises. I'm sure you've heard of them, but just in case you haven't, let me give you a quick demo.

Head to the bathroom. If you don't have to pee, go drink a thirty-two-ounce glass of lemonade and then go to the bathroom. As soon as you start to pee, squeeze the muscles down there until the urine stops. Start peeing again. Stop. Pee. Stop. See how that works? Once you've practiced in the bathroom for a while, you can probably graduate to doing Kegels anywhere and everywhere (just don't actually pee while you're doing them unless you're on the toilet). Try doing them while you wait at the OB's office. Or when you're in your car on the way to work. Or when you're watching TV. The thing about Kegels is that you can't do too many of them, so get in the habit of doing them whenever you can.

What You Can't Do

I want to start this section out with a big, giant disclaimer: Before you do *any* exercise while pregnant, you need to talk to your doctor or midwife. Because now that I've told you all of the sporty things that you can (and probably should) do while pregnant, I would be negligent if I didn't get into the things that you can't (and definitely shouldn't) do while pregnant. There is a whole list of pregnancy-related medical conditions that make exercise a big no-no while pregnant. I have had very little medical training and I am certainly not qualified to advise you on these matters, so I'm going to defer to the medical professionals. So call your doctor. Right now.

Once your doctor has cleared you to exercise, there are still a few don'ts (and some "try-not-tos") when it comes to pregnancy exercise.

The Six Big Don'ts of Pregnancy Exercise

- **Don't push it.** Too high of a heart rate can be dangerous for both you and your baby. Your heart rate naturally increases when you're pregnant, so you're already starting out at a deficit. A good rule of thumb is to make sure that you can always carry on a conversation while exercising. If you can't talk in complete, coherent sentences, you're pushing it too hard.

- **Don't get too hot.** I know, I know. You're *already* too hot. But don't let yourself get hotter. Technically, you shouldn't let your core temperature get higher than a hundred and two degrees, so try to exercise during the coolest part of the day if you're going outside. If it's a really hot day, it's probably best to just stay inside in the air conditioning. Also, as much as I love spandex, your aqua spandex catsuit (*ha!*) should probably be saved for times when you're not exercising. Tight clothes don't allow your body to breathe and make you hotter.
- **Don't get dehydrated.** Drink plenty of water (or lemon-lime Slurpees if that's what you're craving) before, during and after your workout.
- **Don't lie on your back.** When you lie on your back, your uterus tends to squish a big artery that brings blood both to your brain and to the baby. Early in your pregnancy, it's fine, but once you hit about sixteen weeks, you should avoid any exercises that involve lying on your back on the floor. Feel free to use a balance ball if you're really gung ho. I'm sure you're superbummed that you can't do sit-ups for the remainder of your pregnancy, but it's a sacrifice that you'll have to make for the health of your baby.
- **Don't try to be graceful.** I know you feel all svelte and lithe right now, but pregnancy has a way of messing with your sense of balance. That means if you try to do an exercise that requires balance (say, running on a treadmill or riding a bike), you might end up falling on your face.
- **Don't forget your warm-up and cool-down.** I know it seems like adding a ten-minute warm-up and cool-down to your exercise routine just feels like adding more *exercise* to your exercise routine,

but you probably need to suck it up and do it anyway. Skipping your stretching can cause your muscles to get more sore, and skipping your cool-down can result in dizziness—two things that you don't want to be worrying about when you're carrying around (at least) thirty extra pounds.

Extreme Sports

I showed up for my first OB visit with a bathing suit on. It was early summer and my husband and I were looking forward to a long summer at the lake. Our friends had just purchased a brand-new ski boat, so we were going to ski, wakeboard and tube the summer away. I put on my sunscreen in the waiting room.

After my OB did the usual poking and prodding, he asked if I had any questions. I smiled and offhandedly asked, "I can water ski, right?" It was almost a rhetorical question. I had never even considered the idea that he would say no. But guess what? He said no! I was momentarily devastated (was I going to have to drive the boat *all* summer?) but then I realized that he was probably saying it for my baby's good.

High-speed and high-impact sports like waterskiing, skiing, snowboarding, horseback riding and bobsledding carry with them a high risk for falls, which means there's a risk to you *and* your baby. You probably don't care about yourself (what's a broken arm here or there?), but you certainly want to make sure your baby is as protected as possible. So it's probably best to stay off the slopes and out of the lake when you're pregnant.

Same goes for any sport that carries a risk of your getting hit hard in the stomach with a ball or flying object. That means you'll probably have to give up your weekly game of dodgeball. Bummer! But don't worry, you'll get lots more dodgeball practice when your baby is in grammar school and you have to go into the gym for a parent-teacher conference.

That Wasn't So Bad, Was It? Was It?!

I'm going to end this chapter with an inspirational story about the merits of pregnancy exercise. Cue *Chariots of Fire* music. Sit back, relax, have a laugh at my expense and see why pregnancy exercise might not be such a bad idea.

One of my family's traditions is to run—and please take the term *run* very loosely—the Turkey Trot Fun Run every Thanksgiving. We sign up for the city-hosted race and head downtown early on Thanksgiving morning to make a preemptive strike against the heaps of turkey we'll certainly eat later that day. My son was born in December, so I was eight-months pregnant when the Turkey Trot rolled around in 2005. Not one to buck tradition, I signed up for it anyway.

Please note that I was *not* in any sort of shape to be running at that point. Exercise had become a distant (and very fuzzy) memory to me—something that I was sure I'd think about again some-day, but I certainly wasn't going to consider anytime soon. So I was a little delusional to think that I could actually haul my super-pregnant and superbloated body over a three-mile course. But for some reason, I signed up anyway. My mom said she'd stay with me.

When the gun went off, I was way in the back of a crowd of ten thousand runners, so I started well behind the starting line. It was one of those courses that starts and finishes on the same big hill, so as soon as the race started, the organizers race to take down the big "start" banner and put up the big "finish" banner. I had made it about halfway down the hill when the finish banner went up. I had made it about three quarters of the way down the hill when they announced that the first runners were making their way to the fin-ish line. That's right. People were *finishing* before I'd even crossed the *starting* line. Here's the clincher: Right as I made my way under the big start banner, another pregnant mama raced past me and through the finish line. She had just run three whole miles in the time it took me to walk three hundred yards. She turned to me and smiled and said "Oh! When are you due? I'm due on December twenty-fifth." That was my due date. I was mortified. And if you *must* know, I did *not* finish the race.

I confess: This whole incident inspired me not to be a *complete* pregnancy sloth in future pregnancies. I mean, there's no possible way I'm going to be running three-mile races for time when eight months pregnant, but it might be a good thing to be able to reach the *starting* line while eight months pregnant.

Feeling inspired? I'm glad we had this little chat. The best thing you can do right now is grab a pencil and write *exercise* on your calendar. Probably not for today, though. Tomorrow will work.

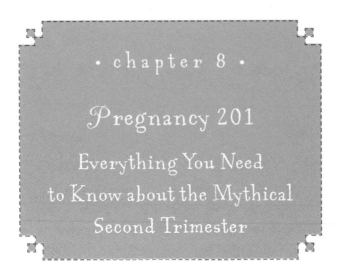

chapter 8

Pregnancy 201

Everything You Need to Know about the Mythical Second Trimester

$\mathcal{I}$f I had been granted three wishes when I was nine weeks along, I would've wished for a good night's sleep, a Bugaboo stroller (a gal's gotta dream) and a free pass into my second trimester. Forget about all that first trimester hobbelty-hoo and skip straight to the good stuff—that magical time when I would have an adorable belly sticking out over my still-buttoned jeans *and* I'd be allowed to eat three hundred extra calories a day.

Your second trimester is time to par-*tay!* It's the honeymoon period of your pregnancy—time to kick up your heels, crack open a jar of pickles and celebrate all that you've accomplished. Just don't celebrate too hard. Even if you're in your second trimester, you're still pregnant, which means too much exertion can lead to regression into first trimester symptoms. And you do *not* want that.

Just so I can score some sympathy points, I don't think I ever really experienced a second trimester. My pregnancies started out in the first trimester like everyone else's with nausea, vomiting, bloating and fatigue in full force. The problem is that my first trimesters didn't end at fourteen weeks like the baby books said they would.

Instead, my morning sickness and fatigue hung on for longer, finally making their exit somewhere around twenty-four weeks when they had more than outstayed their welcome. And since the second trimester technically ends at twenty-eight weeks, I don't count my second trimester as a trimester. It was more like a nice little "minimester" between my first and third trimesters.

The good news is that most women *do* have second trimesters. You'll probably start feeling better between ten and fourteen weeks and by the time you're sixteen weeks along, you'll have enough energy to shop for baby clothes online, take a shower *and* make dinner—all in the same day. At this point, you'll probably want to run through the streets, screaming with joy and dancing in victory. But don't. You'll just embarrass yourself.

Instead, your second trimester is the time to do all the things that you daydreamed about while camped out on your couch in your sweats. Like decorating your nursery. And eating ice cream. And surviving an entire day without running to the bathroom to puke.

But remember, it's easy to overdo it in your second trimester. You're coming off of a two-month stint on the couch and the second trimester energy burst can make you feel a bit invincible. You may suddenly feel the urge to volunteer to plan the church musical or make dinner for one hundred and forty-three of your closest friends. Don't. You may think you have the energy now, but wait until you've written an e-mail to all of the cast members or peeled fifteen carrots. You'll be tired enough to go right back to your now perma-indented spot on the couch.

Aside from eating every morsel in your refrigerator and obsessing over baby names, your top priority in trimester number two should be to rest. That means no heptathlons, no late-night TV marathons (sorry Letterman!) and *no* vacuuming (involves too much lifting and moving). That will just have to wait until you've had your baby and the only thing that will lull your little cutie-pie to sleep is the nonstop white noise of the vacuum. You'll know *exactly* what I'm talking about six months from now, so try not to worry about your dirty carpets until then.

So now that my grandmotherish lecture on not overdoing it is over (no, really, I promise, no more lecturing for at least six... *er,* make that three...pages), it's time to start talking about all the fab things you *can* do during your second trimester. In the next few months, you're going to experience all sorts of exciting things. Like getting an entire new (maternity) wardrobe and finding out the sex of the baby. And speaking of scx, during your second trimester, you might want to start, *ahem,* having it again. But we'll get to that later. For now, let's just do our best to put all that first trimester fatigue and nausea behind us and focus on our second trimester bliss.

Mommy Madness

Before we go any further, I need to address a giant pink or blue elephant in the room: mommy madness. Up until now, you may have believed that the pregnancy hormones surging through your body are only affecting you physically. Take a deep breath because the next few sentences might hurt a little. Those hormones also bring about some pretty palpable emotional changes—changes that may make you seem a bit nutty. So if you've been wondering why everyone is looking at you like you're psychotic, let me break it to you gently: It's because you're acting crazy.

Not that I know anything about hormone-induced psychosis, but if I *did* I would probably tell you about the button-down shirt incident. I had borrowed my husband's favorite white button-down shirt and my husband had the gall to ask me where it was. (It was in my car, okay?) I snarled at him and told him to leave me alone. Five minutes later, I had forgotten I wanted him to leave me alone and I was in his lap weeping uncontrollably because my friend had sent me an e-card with baby pandas on it. Since I was weeping in his lap, my husband took that as a sign that I was ready to tell him where his shirt was. I wasn't. I snarled again.

Of course, I was being entirely rational and sane, but in retrospect, I realize that there's a slight chance that pregnancy hormones played a teeny-tiny role in my actions. With that in mind, it's probably a good idea to think of pregnancy as a forty-weeks long, severe bout of PMS. You may not even realize it's happening, but those pesky pregnancy hormones flooding your body might just make you do and say a few crazy things. It's not your fault. It's your husband's! Just kidding.

Reality check time. (You knew that was coming, didn't you?) Even if you have a really, really good excuse to be acting crazy (and pregnancy is a really, really good excuse), it's still not okay to be grumpy, mean, nasty or moody. God wants us to be patient and kind and love others as He first loved us. So even if your husband is really, *really* grating on you by asking you about his button-down shirt, you should probably just patiently and kindly tell him where it is. Just saying.

In our maddest mommy moments, we tend to turn on the people who love us most. Instead, turn to Him. Jesus tells us, "My grace is sufficient for you, for my power is made perfect in weakness" (2 Corinthians 12:9). How powerful is that? When we are weak (read: acting crazy), God's power is even *more* perfect. And God's perfect power is all you need to get through even the ugliest hormonal messes.

Ask God to quiet the emotional voices screaming in your head and to fill you with the fruit of the Spirit. If you need it drilled into your head (like I did most days), read and reread Galatians 5:22 and ask God to give you more of His Spirit, which results in more love, joy, peace, patience, kindness, goodness and faithfulness (and gentleness and self-control) in your life. Ask Him to keep you from saying anything you shouldn't say. And while you're at it, ask Him to help your husband to be less annoying.

Last (but certainly not least), if you find yourself sticking your swollen foot into your mouth, don't be afraid to ask for forgiveness. It's easy to feel like you can't dig your way out once you've gotten in deep (hence the fact that my husband's white button-down lived in my car for a week after the aforementioned incident). But people tend to be forgiving—especially of pregnant women. So say you're sorry and remember that as soon as you have your baby, you'll be well-rested and entirely sane and *never* struggle with keeping a handle on all of your emotions again (*ha!*).

Getting Some Sleep

I know I promised no more lectures for a while, but this is important: You need to rest! Remember what I said about taking care of you? Well, now more than ever, it's superimportant. Your little bundle is packing on the pounds right now. You have officially become your baby's growth-fueling, 24-7 buffet restaurant, which takes a lot of energy!

It's ironic that right when you need lots of energy, you lose your ability to sleep. Pregnancy insomnia starts about seven minutes after you take your pregnancy test, but it really kicks in during your second trimester. It's superfrustrating. And, yes, it's entirely appropriate to wake your husband up to tell him you can't sleep. If you're not sleeping, there's absolutely no reason that your husband should be snoring away like a baby over there. At least that's how I felt when I had pregnancy hormones surging through my body.

Anyway, I'm normally the kind of girl who can fall asleep on the couch with all the lights on and *American Idol* blaring. But when I was pregnant, I tossed and turned for hours trying to get comfortable—only to wake up four minutes later because I had to pee. And then I'd spend another hour tossing and turning trying to get comfy again. It was an awful cycle that not only contributed to my inability to leave the couch, but also contributed to my pregnancy-induced psychosis. Not good.

After spending a few nights sulking on the couch while watching middle-of-the-night infomercials, I realized that drastic times call for drastic measures. I hopped on Facebook and changed my status message to: "Someone help me! If I'm not asleep in ten minutes, I'm going to name this baby Snooze!" Sure enough, my girlfriends came to my rescue.

The best get-to-sleep trick I learned is to whine and moan and grumble in your bed until your husband gets fed up and buys you a one-hundred-dollar pregnancy pillow. I know you'd rather blow a hundred bucks on teensy tiny baby booties, but from a once-pregnant-mama to a pregnant-mama, it's worth every penny. In case you haven't seen one, they're these long, squiggly pillows that wrap behind your back, between your legs, around your waist and over your chest until you're all snuggled into this comfy nest with all of your floppy pregnancy parts supported. And when everything is supported and snuggled, you finally are comfortable enough to drift off into dreamland.

Another great trick is a prebed footbath and a foot massage if your hubby so desires (and he probably will if it means you'll actually go to sleep). Unfortunately for you bath lovers, there's a rule about keeping your core temperature low (ask your doctor), so you have to keep the water nice and tepid. But there is no rule about keeping your feet cool, so forgo the whole-body chill session and give those tootsies a long, steaming hot and bubbly soak every night before bed. The added bonus is that a foot soak can help eliminate middle-of-the-night leg cramps, something that may become a frequent occurrence late in your pregnancy.

One of my friends suggested light exercise before bed as it had helped her to sleep better while she was pregnant. Seeing as how I avoided exercise at all cost during my pregnancy (see Chapter 7), I didn't even try that one. But if you're really brave (okay, desperate), feel free to go on a quick jaunt around your neighborhood right before bedtime.

The last trick I learned is to eat before bedtime (I don't have to tell you that twice, do I?). When you're hungry, you can't sleep, so a prebed snack (coupled with a midnight snack if you wake up) can definitely help you catch some zzz's. The trick is to eat something that has protein in it so you stay full longer. Try a piece of toast with some melted cheese on it or crackers with peanut butter. Or if you're really serious about getting some sleep, I suggest a glass of warm milk paired with a few—or seven or eight—chocolate chip cookies.

Before I get off my lecture kick (for good this time, I think), I just want to reiterate that you need your sleep so you should do *whatever* it takes to get it. Don't be a sleep martyr here and go sleep on the couch because you're worried that your tossing and turning is keeping your husband awake. Worrying about your getting enough sleep is keeping your husband up. That, paired with your moaning and complaining, of course. So stop the insanity and start snoozing.

Being a Working Mama

We aren't living in the fifties, girls. That means—more likely than not—that you probably have a job that goes beyond doing your husband's ironing and making pot roast. You may have even gone to school to get a degree—and not just a Mrs. degree. With that in mind, you're probably going to have to make some decisions in the next few months as to whether you're going to be a working mama, a stay-at-home mama or some combo of the two.

The idea of being a stay-at-home mom is, well, let's just say *popular* in Christian circles. From the moment I got pregnant, everyone I knew started talking to me about how important it was for me to stay home with my kids. It was best for them, best for me, best for everyone. I knew that there was some merit in what they said, but to be completely honest, I had a really hard time with the idea. At the time, I was working as a high school Spanish teacher, and I loved my job. I had worked hard to get there. And I just wasn't sure I was ready to give it up.

There's also this thing called money and we weren't rolling in it. I knew that if we wanted to keep paying the mortgage and eating, I'd have to work some. I asked my boss about going back to work part-time and she was adamantly against it. (Apparently students need full-time supervision. Who knew?) I looked at the childcare costs of going back to work full-time and realized that I'd barely net anything on a teacher's salary. Nothing seemed to be the right fit.

I freaked out. I cried. I worried. And my husband? He was completely chill about the whole thing. He knew God would provide—and if that meant my staying home full time or going back to work when the baby was six weeks old, it would all work out. So after a lot of worrying and freaking out on my part and a lot of praying on my husband's part, we decided to take a wait-and-see approach. I told my boss I was taking a semester off and that I'd let her know by May if I was going to start the new school year.

Then, my mind was made up on the day my son Joey was born. The instant I saw him, I realized that I wasn't going to be able to leave him every day to work full time. I could hardly stand to leave him alone to go pee! I forgot all about my teaching career—I was going to be a stay-at-home mom.

But then—there's always a *but,* isn't there?—we got an electric bill that we couldn't pay on the heels of an emotionally trying week when I felt completely cooped up and lonely in the house. And suddenly, staying at home didn't seem feasible. Or even like something I wanted to do. I didn't know what to do. I felt like any choice I made would be the wrong one.

In the end, I got a part-time job as a writer and editor where I could work from home. It worked out well for us. I earned a little money. I felt like I was doing something for me that went beyond laundry and peek-a-boo. And my job didn't take a ton of time so I worked while my son napped and was able to be there for him when he woke up.

With this in mind, during your second trimester, you might want to spend some time thinking and praying with your husband about what you're going to do work-wise after your baby is born. I also want to assure you that this is a very individual and personal decision that has many factors—financial, emotional, spiritual, physical. Your friends may be diehard stay-at-homers, but if you decide that having a career is what's best for you and your family, then go for it. There is not one right answer.

Finally, a lot of moms get creative with their work. Many moms I know work from home, and this is a great solution if you can swing it. Here are a few of the things my friends do at home...just to get your creative juices flowing.

Work-from-Home Career Ideas

- My sister-in-law Mollie asked her boss if she could try doing her current job from home. To her surprise, he agreed to let her try. She's found that she's much more productive at home without the distractions of the office. And best of all, she gets to see her son a whole lot more.
- My friend Amy started a Silpada jewelry business from home and it's been super successful. I have friends who sell Silpada, lia sophia, Scentsy and even baby clothes from home.

- Look online. You'd be surprised at how many part-time jobs allow telecommuting. That's how I got my job as a writer for a Web site five years ago.
- See if your doctor needs a medical transcriptionist. Or if your friend who owns a business needs help writing e-mails or doing invoicing. A lot of small businesses hire part-time workers to do administrative work after hours.
- Get crafty. If you're a crafter, see if you can sell your goods online at Etsy.
- Consult. My sister Alisa is a registered dietitian, so she does nutritional consults from home when her daughter is sleeping. My friend Mel is a counselor, so she does on-the-phone assessments while her kids are in preschool.
- Freelance. My friend Melissa is a copy editor. She freelance copy-edits for several big firms while her three kids sleep. Companies also hire freelance writers, bookkeepers, transcriptionists, techies, Web designers and phone tutors.

Maternity Clothes

If you're a first-timer, you probably won't need to buy maternity clothes until you're about twenty weeks along. Your ab muscles are still tight and strong (enjoy 'em while you got 'em), so your belly will stay nice and flat and seemingly unpregnant for the first few months of your pregnancy.

If you're a second-timer, third-timer or twelfth-timer, the aforementioned ab muscles haven't been tight or strong since early in your first pregnancy, so you probably won't be able to button your pants starting at week three. By the time you're six and a half weeks along, you'll need to wear maternity pants. Kidding! I'm sure you'll make it to at least seven weeks before you have to bust out the full-paneled khakis.

Don't get too excited—the fact that your belly hasn't popped does not mean you'll still be able to fit into your regular clothes. Your ab muscles may be holding your belly in, but there are no muscles holding in your ready-for-birthing hips, your arm flab or your newly acquired neck folds. Those will show up when you're about ten weeks along and won't go away until your baby enters kindergarten.

Most gals start their second trimester in the looking-fat-but-not-looking-pregnant stage. But a few weeks in, you'll probably start the transition into the still-looking-fat-but-also-looking-slightly-pregnant stage. A month or two later, you'll finally get to the looking-really-fat-and-really-pregnant stage. And that's when you'll know that you have officially graduated into maternity clothes!

Although you may have already picked up a maternity shirt here or a pants-holding-up elastic belly band there, you probably will need to make one ginormous shopping trip to pick out your maternity clothes. One of my friends went online and printed out a maternity-clothes shopping checklist that told her to buy X number of shirts and X pairs of jeans, which is a good idea in theory but entirely useless in my opinion. I mean, mommy brain and all, you can probably figure out that you'll need to wear a bottom and a top every *single* day. So if you do laundry a lot, you won't need much. If you're me, you'll need sixteen outfits.

With that in mind, you might want to assess your individual clothing needs and write your *own* shopping list. Look in your closet and see what clothes you normally wear and plan your new wardrobe to be a scaled-down version of that. It'll help to have a list of things you actually need so you don't end up with seventeen super-cute shirts and not a single pair of pants to wear with them.

If you still need more guidance, I'm happy to help (I like shopping almost as much as I hate laundry). Here are my personal ten commandments of maternity clothes shopping.

10 Commandments of Maternity Clothes Shopping

1. **Buy big.** You may think you're huge right now, but you ain't seen nothin' yet! Try it on, and if it fits now, buy two sizes up.

2. **Don't use the fake belly pillow.** In case you've never been to the maternity store, they have these cute little fake belly pillows in the dressing room so that you can try on clothes and see what you'll look like with a baby bump. Cute, but *do not* use them! They're entirely misleading. The baby bump pillow fails to account for extra poundage that you're sure to put on in your hips, thighs, butt and arms. So unless they invent a thigh-flab and an arm-hump pillow, you probably should just assume that any clothes you buy will *not* look like that when you put them on two months from now.

3. **Think loose.** This is kind of a double-edged sword. Tight shirts do a great job of showing off your baby bump (a plus), but they also show off your back fat and your saggy arms (a minus). So unless you're super-duper sure you can pull it off (ask one of your girlfriends), it's probably best to stick with clothes that have more cotton than spandex.

4. **Think airy.** You're already cooking like an Easy-Bake Oven, so find clothes that are made from light fabrics that let a little breeze in. It doesn't matter how cute the maternity dress is, if it clings to you or gets dark, soggy pit stains before lunchtime, you're not going to wear it.

5. **Consider where you're going to wear the outfit.** You probably have a real life and a real job, so that thin-as-air silky sundress with spaghetti straps might be great for a walk in the park, but it's probably not the best get-up for your church Bible study. And unless you do a lot of park walking, you might want to

save your money for something more practical—like a bra that actually fits. Same goes for work wear. Unless your boss is super-cool, you probably aren't going to be wearing a belly-baring T-shirt to your next meeting that says "knocked up."

6. **Check out your cleavage in the mirror before you buy.** Remember, your boobs have grown sixteen sizes in the last two months (as if you could forget). That means the V-neck number that used to be entirely appropriate to wear to lunch with your in-laws now makes you look like Pamela Anderson.

7. **Buy maternity drawers.** You may think you can save money and wear your regular old underpants throughout your pregnancy. Guess again. Maternity panties have more coverage so you won't spend your days searching for a private place to pick your panties out of your butt. By the way, if you're a thong girl, they have those in the maternity section too—not sure what's different from a regular thong, but they sure feel more comfortable!

8. **Buy a maternity bra.** It's certainly not news to you that your boobs get bigger while you're pregnant. What may come as a surprise is that they are going to keep growing. And growing. And growing some more. So while it may seem like a good idea to stock up on the buy-one-get-six-free maternity bra sale, it's probably best to buy one or two maternity bras now, knowing that you will have to upgrade in a few months.

9. **Don't spend a fortune.** You're only wearing these clothes for a few months, so it's hard to justify slapping down a hundred bucks on a pair of maternity jeans. Buy the things you really need (i.e., the superadorable but entirely impractical hot pink maternity salsa dress) and skip the things you don't need (i.e., a boring pair of tan polyester pants with a full-paneled waist). Wait. Maybe I got that backward.

10. **Buy enough.** I just told you not to spend a fortune on maternity

clothes (which is good advice) but you also do *not* want to risk late-pregnancy wardrobe fatigue. You're going to be wearing maternity clothes nonstop for the next few months, so you're going to get a little (okay, a lot) tired of them. I remember being so sick of my maternity shirts that I decided it would be a good idea to "borrow" one of my husband's giant baseball T-shirts and pair it with one of my knit skirts. Apparently I looked a bit ridiculous (who would've thought?) because one of my friends cornered me at church and offered to let me borrow some of her maternity clothes.

Now, Let's Really Talk about Sex, Baby

The last few months, you've probably gotten out of the ole lovemaking routine. But now that you've turned a corner and your first trimester woes have all but disappeared, suddenly sex isn't sounding like such a terrible thing. Buh-bye flannel pj's. Hello low-cut (and figure-flaw-hiding) maternity baby doll.

Of course, sex doesn't quite work the way it used to (you know, when you were lithe enough to slither into just about any position you wanted to). Now you have to deal with things like gushing hormones, mood-swinging libido and the giant preggo belly that just happens to get in the way of, well, everything. Here's how to deal.

Sex 201 for Second Trimester Mamas

- **Get creative with your, um, positions.** For obvious reasons, the missionary position probably isn't going to work anymore. I'm sure your husband will be happy to oblige if you ask him to try out some alternatives to see what works for you.
- **Do it. A lot.** Those gushing hormones that I've been ranting

about do have their benefits—namely, a giant second trimester libido burst. That means you're actually going to want to have sex. A lot. Take advantage while you're still thin enough to leave the lights on and awake enough not to fall asleep while you're doing it.

- **Get some lingerie.** If you're feeling insecure about your blossoming belly (or blossoming breasts, butt, hips and arms), pick up some pregnancy lingerie. Yes, they actually make pregnancy lingerie (try cakelingerie.com) and yes, it does a great job of covering up all the places that you're feeling insecure about.
- **Bare it all.** I know I just told you to cover up, but my husband swears that I look my best while pregnant (even though it's a proven fact that I gain an inch-thick layer of fat around my entire body). Most likely, your hubby thinks your pregnant belly is hot, too, so don't be afraid to flaunt it while you got it.
- **Get some K-Y Jelly.** The same hormones that are responsible for your second-trimester libido burst (a good thing) also tend to make you a little dry down there (a bad thing). So pick up a jumbo-sized tube of lubricant and use it liberally.
- **Get all *Song of Solomon* on him.** God designed sex to be an intimate form of communication between husband and wife. And since God designed it, He probably knows a thing or two about it. Reading the *Song of Solomon* together is a good place to start.

A Babymoon

Speaking of sex, you might want to think about going on a "babymoon" during your second trimester. The theory goes that pregnant couples should go on a big hurrah of a vacation before their baby comes because they'll never be able to go on vacation again without (a) hiring a babysitter, (b) making sixty-five teary-eyed phone calls per day to said babysitter, and (c) sobbing hysterically the entire drive to the airport. Since the chances are slim that you'll even be able to pry the little schnookums off of your breast for the next year or so, it's probably a good idea to just go now.

I have a friend who went on a lavish weeklong vacation to Hawaii for her babymoon. She and her husband checked themselves into a spa and they spent the week getting massages, eating delicious food and lying on the beach. That sounds wonderful, right? So if you have the money, put this book down right now and go book yourself a spa vacation.

Unfortunately, I did *not* have the money for a vacation like that—or any vacation for that matter. My husband and I were saving every penny we had for the baby (and in hopes that I wouldn't have to go back to work right away), so springing for a sixty-dollar room at Motel 8 was a stretch. We did end up splurging and driving to San Antonio and enjoying a nice dinner out and a night away. It was great, but my favorite babymoon story comes from a friend of mine who didn't have any money at all. She planned a staycation babymoon with her husband. They spent an entire week doing adorable romantic things together like going on picnics, cooking dinner, going on walks in the park and lying in bed picking out baby names. All together now: *awwww*.

Having Fun Yet?

The other day, I took my kids to Jumpy Gym (you'll become well acquainted with these giant inflatable contraptions in the next few years). My son was running around, jumping in the inflatable castles and laughing hysterically. I asked him if he was having fun yet and he said: "I know I'm having too much fun when I can't stop laughing!"

How's that for clever insight from the mind of a four-year-old? When we're in the midst of our pregnancies, it's easy to get caught up in the waiting and the planning and not allow ourselves to get caught up in the *joy* of pregnancy. Pregnancy can be a time of utmost joy and laughter for you, where you can't stop delighting in the incredible gift God has given you.

While you probably stop laughing from time to time (say, when you're getting weighed at the OB's office), I want to encourage you to allow your pregnancy to be a time of laughter. Allow yourself to get caught up in God's grace and the tiny life that's growing inside of you. Allow yourself to enjoy your pregnancy and to enjoy the changes taking place. Allow yourself time to laugh. *You'll know you're having too much fun when you can't stop laughing.*

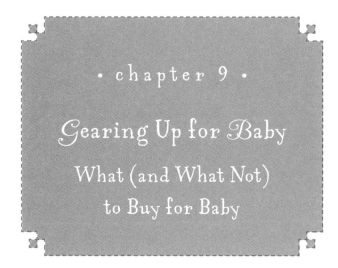

· chapter 9 ·

Gearing Up for Baby

What (and What Not) to Buy for Baby

There are a lot of rumors swirling around when it comes to baby gear. You may hear that you can wrap your baby in old T-shirts and put him or her to sleep in a laundry basket instead of a bassinet. You may hear that you can use wet paper towels as wipes and baking soda to cure diaper rash. You may even hear that you can get by with four measly cloth diapers—by washing three as your baby wears one. These rumors—while intriguing—are all lies spread around by people whose main goal is making your life much, much more difficult.

The truth is that babies need a *lot* of gear. Not four strollers, seventy-nine baby blankets, fifty-four bottles and a wipe warmer like the baby superstore would like you to believe, but you'll definitely be spending some money at the baby store in the next few months. Baby stores tend to have the exact opposite philosophy as your four-cloth-diaper-maximum friend—they would have you believe that every item that has ever been invented for a baby is an absolute necessity. I'm not saying the two battery-powered in-car bottle warmers wouldn't be handy, but the truth is that you'll probably never use either of them.

Since you'd prefer not to walk around the baby store with the word *sucker* written on a Post-it note on your forehead, you need to be armed with some information *before* you go shopping. Once you step inside the sliding doors at the baby superstore, it's all over; you'll want everything! So before you go shopping, let's spend some time sorting the good from the bad, the necessary from the unnecessary and the borrowable from the un-borrowable—so you can get everything your bouncing little money-sucker (*er,* bundle of joy) needs without bouncing your checking account.

What Baby *Really* Needs

The best way to shop for baby gear is to bring along a trusted friend to help you sort through the must-haves and the don't-needs. Or, if you don't have a trusted friend, bring along your hubby, who won't be as easily swayed by the adorable ducky bedding. Or, if not him, bring your mother, whose favorite pastime is shopping for baby gear. As a last resort, bring along your annoying coworker who is always bragging about how much money she saved when shopping for baby gear. Whatever you do, do *not* go alone. It's just not safe to send a hormonal pregnant mama shopping without adequate reinforcement.

Another thing to remember is that you don't have to buy every item that your baby might possibly need for the first eighteen years of his or her life right now. Most stores will actually let you bring your baby in with you—so if a moment comes along after your baby is born when you realize you actually do need a battery-powered in-car bottle warmer, you can head to the store *with* your baby and buy one.

With that in mind, I want to point out that there are certain things that you can probably wait to buy until after your baby is born. Case in point: a high chair. You will eventually need a high chair, but most babies don't start eating solids until they are five or six months old. So if you buy a high chair now, it's just going to collect dust in your kitchen for the next six months. Better idea: Spend your time worrying about things you'll need when your baby is a newborn and wait until the baby dust has settled before you pick up things like high chairs, booster seats and SAT prep guides.

So what do you *really* need to go buy right now? When I was pregnant, I would've been thrilled to get a big ole kit with everything-baby-needs-and-a-bottle-warmer-to-boot stork-delivered to my doorstep. But nobody makes those—I checked. So you're going to have to figure out your baby gear needs on your own. Here are my recommendations:

Erin's Essential Gear List

My absolute necessities list is pretty short. It includes:
1. Somewhere for baby to sleep
2. Diapers and wipers
3. Something for baby to wear
4. A properly installed car seat

Somewhere for Baby to Sleep (and, No, the Car Seat Doesn't Count)

Just in case you don't believe me when I tell you the gear lists at the superstores go a bit overboard—I just checked out the gear list at a baby superstore in our area and they suggested that new babies need five (yes, *five*) different types of cribs. They recommend a regular crib, a cosleeper, a bassinet, a Pack 'n' Play and a Moses basket. Unless you have a cosleeping, bassinet-using, breast-feeding, bottle-using, constantly-traveling and colicky baby, you do *not* need all of these—but you will definitely need at least one, maybe two.

Here's the scoop to help you decide:

Crib. Naturally, your bed will probably be your baby's favorite place to sleep, but having a crib will give you a place to put your baby when you need a little *(ahem)* alone time in your bed. Plus, your baby's crib will serve to keep your baby safe, confined and comfortable for the first two or three years of his or her life.

Cosleeper. A cosleeper is a minicrib that either attaches to the side of your bed or sits on top of your mattress next to you. Cosleepers are superconvenient if you're breast-feeding and don't want to drag yourself out of bed every two hours to nurse. You can literally just roll over, pop your boob in your baby's mouth and fall back asleep (not that I've ever done *that*).

Bassinet. A bassinet is a smallish crib that you can put right next to your bed so your baby can sleep really close to you without actually being in your bed. These are handy if your nursery is across the house from your bedroom or if you're a really heavy sleeper and want to make sure you hear every whimper or sigh your baby makes. These also come in handy if your baby requires rocking to fall asleep—because a bassinet is much easier to rock from the comfort of your bed than, say, a full-sized crib.

Pack 'n' Play. This is a portable crib that you can set up quickly and easily anywhere you go—which means you'll be schlepping the thing back and forth to Grandma's house on a weekly (or daily) basis.

Moses Basket. A Moses basket is exactly what you would imagine it to be: a cute, wicker basket with padding so your baby can sleep comfortably on the move. Moses baskets are a great place for your baby to take a little snooze while you make dinner or visit with friends. One caveat: If you do get a Moses Basket, it will only work when your baby is teeny tiny and unable to sit or crawl. Once your baby is big enough to move, a tiny wicker wall will do nothing to stop an escape attempt.

Diapers and Wipes—and Lots of 'Em.

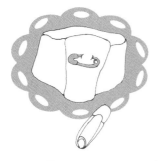

I don't think anyone is going to tell you that you don't need diapers—but nearly everyone you know will have an opinion on what kind of diapers you should buy. Since everyone else will be opinionated, I'd be remiss if I didn't join the gang and spout off my opinions as well. For the first few weeks, I highly recommend Pampers Swaddlers disposable diapers. I know they're expensive—and your baby will go through them at a rate of two per minute—but there is no alternative for newborns as far as I'm concerned. Swaddlers are dummy-proof, which means that when your husband puts one on your baby backward and upside down, it'll still keep your baby clean and dry. As you can imagine, they're essential.

Later, once your husband has had some diapering practice, you can wean yourself off of the Pampers Swaddlers and try out other types of diapers. The key here is to realize that certain diapers will fit *your* baby better than others, so you probably shouldn't spend an enormous amount on diapers before your baby is born. Case in point: My son wore Huggies and they fit him perfectly. When I was pregnant with my daughter, I stocked up on Huggies, only to find out they didn't fit her as well. By didn't fit her as well, I mean they gapped at the legs and urine poured out of the leg holes onto my lap every time she peed.

Another thing to consider when buying diapers is cloth versus disposable. I'm not going to get superopinionated about this because there are definite pros and cons to both disposable and cloth diapering. With my son, I used disposable diapers. The big, gigantic, undeniable pro with disposable diapers is that you have way less laundry. And considering the fact that your baby will drool, spit up and poop on about fourteen outfits a day, less laundry is certainly a desirable goal. Disposable diapers are also really handy. You can just throw away the dirty diaper, slap a clean one on and you're off. But the convenience comes at a price—both to your pocketbook and to the environment. Disposables cost about twice as much as cloth and, even more alarming, they can sit in landfills for up to five hundred years without biodegrading.

Because of this (and because Huggies really weren't working for her), I decided to try cloth diapering with my daughter. Cloth diapers are generally better for the environment—although using cloth diapers usually means using more water, so you might want to take that into consideration if you live in a drought-prone area. Cloth diapers are also much less expensive than disposables. But I confess: I didn't last very long on the cloth diapering front. I loved the idea of cloth diapers, but I just couldn't keep up with the laundry.

My fallback option with my daughter was gDiapers. (Get 'em at gdiapers.com.) gDiapers are a cloth and disposable hybrid. They have a cloth outer shell with a disposable, biodegradable (and flushable!) insert. They're pretty cool; you get all of the benefits of both cloth and disposable diapers. Plus, they're absolutely adorable. What could be cuter than an almost-naked baby in a cute, colored (and did I mention ruffled) diaper? The drawbacks? They're *expensive,* and since I'm being completely honest here, the flushing process for the liners is a bit more extensive than I had imagined. Let's just say it involves a three-minute wait and a swish stick. Still, if you want an eco-friendly choice with convenience, gDiapers are it.

Wherever you need diapers, you also need wipes. I recommend the plain old grocery store baby wipes that come in the jumbo-sized packs. If you want to get really fancy, you can go with the natural kind or the aloe-infused kind or even the smells-like-baby-powder-and-soothing-lavender kind. But whatever you do, do *not* get any ideas about making your own wipes. A woman at my sister's child-birthing class decided that making her own wipes out of supersoft flannel cloth and pure spring water would be a way to save money and would be healthier for her baby's skin. My sister came home thinking that the whole make-your-own-wipes idea was something she might want to try—and I, being the experienced mom, had to set her straight. The whole idea was obviously contrived by someone who has never had to change a screaming, poopy newborn at two in the morning while running back and forth to the bathroom to dampen supersoft cloths with bottles of spring water. Once you think of it that way, the idea doesn't sound so great anymore, does it?

The only real requirements that I have for wipes is that they are wet, easy to find and that you're able to get them out of the package with one hand. If you want to be thrifty, buy one plastic tub of wipes and then a bunch of refill packs and restock the plastic tub as you run out. I'm pretty certain I'm still using the same blue plastic tub that I got at one of my son's baby showers five years ago.

Something for Baby to Wear

Your baby needs clothes, but that's probably not going to be an issue, what with your mother-in-law's knitting habit and your mom's shopping habit. After all, every grandma I know seems to think that it's their mission in life to adequately clothe their grandchild from day one. And by adequately clothe, I mean make sure that the baby has at least one of everything on sale at Gymboree at any given time.

The trick here is sizing. On average, babies weigh about seven-and-a-half pounds when born, so they'll fit nicely in newborn-sized clothing. But the thing about averages is that there are always babies who break the odds. I have a friend who birthed a twelve-pound baby (naturally!) and he was able to fit into size three–six-month clothes right away. My daughter was tiny—like six-pounds tiny—so she swam in the newborn stuff. I didn't want her to be naked for the first few weeks of her life—and I certainly didn't trust my husband to pick out clothes for her by himself—so I had my husband swing by the mall when we were on our way home from the hospital. I left him in the car with the baby and ran in and picked up a few preemie outfits.

My suggestion is to buy (and wash) a few newborn-sized outfits. Wait to buy the rest until your baby arrives and you know exactly how big (or small) he or she is so you can purchase the appropriate size. That way you won't end up with a bunch of extra newborn-sized clothes that your baby will only wear once. You can always send your mom to the store later or use baby clothes shopping as an excuse to leave the baby with your husband and get out of the house for an hour.

Another thing I'm including in this "something to wear" section is receiving blankets. Your baby will end up wearing blankets in the form of a swaddle for at least the first few weeks of his or her life. Swaddling blankets—or if you want to get really fancy, a Velcro swaddler—are key if you want to get any sleep at all when your baby is a newborn. So my best old-timer mom advice is to stock up—your baby will need at least five—and keep them clean so you have one available any time you need one.

A Properly Installed Car Seat

They actually won't let you leave the hospital with the baby—even if you're Britney Spears—unless your baby is fastened into a properly installed car seat. With this in mind, you probably want to (a) buy a car seat and (b) figure out how to properly install it before you start having contractions. This is necessary because frantic, last-minute car seat installation doesn't always lend itself to *proper* car seat installation. I know this because my poor, sweet (and have I mentioned procrastinating?) husband didn't quite get around to properly installing the car seat when I asked him to do it three weeks *before* my due date. When it came time for me to go to the hospital two days *after* my due date, it still wasn't installed. Let's just say that contracting pregnant mamas who just want to get to the hospital and get an epidural are not necessarily forgiving of such omissions.

If you're wondering what kind of car seat to buy, I suggest an infant seat. Eventually, your baby will need a convertible car seat (infant seats only hold babies up to twenty-two pounds), but for the first several months of your baby's life, an infant seat will prove invaluable. Infant seats are two-piece car seats with a seat part that clicks into a base in your car so you can easily take your baby in and out of the car. This is a lifesaver for a tired new mama because it's almost a guarantee that your baby will fall asleep in the car about six minutes before you arrive at your destination. If you have an infant seat, it's a simple pull, click and lift. If you don't, you'll spend twenty minutes trying to unstrap your baby without waking him or her up and another twenty minutes chastising yourself for not driving around the block for twenty minutes so your baby could nap longer.

Other Things Baby May Need

As you probably suspected, the four things on my baby essentials list aren't the only things I'm going to recommend that you buy. Those are just the only universal things that I think every single baby in the world will need. There are also a bunch of things that you may or may not need depending on where you live, your life-style, whether you plan on working or not and (most importantly) whether you're able to show any sort of restraint when tempted by adorable baby shoes. Here's my maybe/maybe not list:

Stroller. I didn't put a stroller on the required list because there's a possibility that you'll never use one. Really. I know someone whose stroller is still in its box in her garage because she rarely leaves the house with her baby, and when she does, it's usually to go to the grocery store or Grandma's house. If that's the case, your money is probably better spent on comfy pajamas and magazines. But if you do plan on ever going to the mall or the park or anywhere else with your baby, you might want a stroller. My personal recommenda-tion is to get one of those snap-n-go stroller frames for your infant seat and then a lightweight, easy-to-carry umbrella stroller for when your baby outgrows the infant seat.

Breast Pump. If you plan on going back to work, or on leaving your baby with Grandma for a few hours to go out on a date with your husband, you'll want to get a breast pump. If you don't think you'll use it much, you can probably get by with a small, inexpen-sive hand pump. If you plan on going back to work or donating gallons of milk to a milk bank, you may want to invest in a fancy electric pump. Some cost four hundred dollars—an insane amount of money—but it'll be worth every penny when you're able to quickly (and painlessly) pump a bottle of milk while crouched in the bathroom stall during your lunch break at work.

Diaper Pail. My brother hates the smell of stinky diapers so much that he actually makes his wife dispose of dirty diapers in the gar-bage can outside every single time she changes one—even if it's in the middle of the night and snowing. But since there's no way I'd go out in the cold in my jammies to throw away a dirty diaper, I needed a diaper pail. I've tried several—and if you want my opinion, your best bet is probably a plain old kitchen garbage pail, the kind that you can step on a little pedal to make the lid open and then close without touching. If you really want a pail that's made especially for diapers (you know, so your baby's diaper pail can match his or her crib bedding), try a Diaper Champ. It's a little trickier to use than a plain-old garbage can, but it gets the job done.

Sling. I confess: My purchasing a baby sling was more about me than it was about my babies. It's not that they didn't benefit—they did get to cruise around all snuggled into my body with a clear view of the world— but the real beneficiary here was me. My sling was not only adorable, but it covered up my still-not-gone baby tummy and looked supercute with most of my outfits. New mamas look gorgeous carrying around babies in slings. When you're four weeks post-partum and feeling haggard, having a fashion accessory that makes you feel cute is a very, very good thing.

Baby Carrier. Fashionistas, you can go ahead and skip this in favor of the sling. But for those of you who consider the functionality of your baby carriers more important than their stylishness, you might want to think about getting a nonsling-type baby carrier. I loved my sling, but there were times that my Baby Björn worked best. Plus, chances are you're never going to be able to convince your hubby to carry your baby around in a pink flowered sling. But he will probably be happy to snuggle your baby into a manly Björn.

Bottles. Yes, you'll probably need some bottles. But you won't need a ton right away. If you plan on breast-feeding, your nurses or lactation consultants will probably suggest you wait a few weeks before trying a bottle. If you don't breast-feed, you'll probably get a ton of bottle samples in the hospital and will be able to try them all out before you go stock up.

Baby Swaddler. Swaddling will soon become one of your most cherished skills as it is often the only way to get a newborn to sleep. That said, if you're like me and happen to be...let's call it *manually challenged* when it comes to burrito-wrapping tiny infants, you might want to invest in a Velcro-closure swaddling blanket, which takes all the work out of swaddling so you can get your baby to sleep *fast*. Worth every penny, if you ask me.

Diaper Bag. You will never be able to leave your house again with just your purse and your cell phone. Once you have your baby, at the very least you'll need diapers, wipes, bottles, toys, snacks, outfits and a partridge in a pear tree. And while you could try to carry all of this stuff in a plastic shopping bag, a diaper bag may be a better option. I recommend something made from sturdy canvas—because it will get dirty—and something that's manly enough for your husband to carry, so you don't have to be the one lugging the thing around everywhere you go. Husbands tend to frown upon carrying anything that's pink, flowery or argyle.

Infant Nail Clippers. Let's be honest here. Baby nail clippers may sound like something you think you're going to need, but the reality is that your baby will squirm, cry and wiggle every time you try to hold his or her hand still for more than three seconds. I know many mothers who have resorted to biting their children's nails, using a nail file or simply letting them grow until they break off naturally. But if you want to give the whole sharp-metal-object-next-to-your baby's-soft-tender-skin thing a try, go for it.

Boppy (or Other Brand) Nursing Pillow. I got a Boppy at my baby shower. I had no idea what it was—or that it would soon be one of my favorite material things in the world right up there with the rockin' prepregnancy jeans my husband got me on our honeymoon. In fact, when I went on vacation a few years back, I checked my Boppy as my second piece of luggage because I just couldn't bear the thought of going a week without it. Here's how it works: You lay the Boppy (a horseshoe-shaped pillow) on your lap and your baby on the Boppy while you're breast-feeding, and you suddenly have two free arms to do fun things like read magazines, crochet baby sweaters and surf the Web for baby advice. Indispensable, really.

Nursing Cover-up. Nursing cover-ups are great. If you're a first-time mom—especially if your baby is younger than two months old—the time and effort it will take to get your baby latched on and breast-feeding will probably not lend itself to spur-of-the-moment public breast-feeding sessions. But that's not to say you can't try. And eventually, you'll get really, really good at it, and at that point, feel free to slip the cover-up on and breast-feed your baby while eating lunch with your girlfriends, watching a soccer game or grocery shopping at Costco.

Infant Bath and Hooded Towel. Yes, you can bathe your baby in the big old bathtub or the kitchen sink, but your baby will look so cute with those pudgy little legs splashing in that itty-bitty tub. And a hooded bath towel—especially one with ears or a face—is pretty much a necessity. No grandmother will let you get by with giving your baby his or her first bath and not sending hooded towel pictures.

Baby Monitor. Technically, a baby monitor isn't a necessity at all. There's really no doubt that you'll hear your baby's louder-than-

Audio-Adrenaline cries—even if your baby is sleeping in a crib all the way across the house. But most new mamas have a distinct fear that they'll somehow sleep through their baby's 3:00 AM cries and that their baby will do something terrible like settle down and fall back asleep all on his or her own. Since not having a monitor will probably stress you out, it might be a good idea to just get one. If you want to get really fancy, pick up a video monitor. My sister has one and I admit that it is awfully fun crowding around the screen to watch her adorable daughter snooze.

Shoes. Your baby needs cute little crib shoes about as much as you need six-inch-high red stilettos. And we all know how much a pregnant mama needs hot red stilettos. So buy as many pairs of tiny brown cowboy boots and pink Mary Janes as you can afford, but don't be disappointed when they won't stay on your baby's feet for more than six minutes.

Rocking Chair. I know that you've read every single sleep book in the world and you consider yourself a near-expert on baby sleep solutions—but guess what: Your baby will still probably keep you up all night long for the first six months of his or her life. With that in mind, you might as well have a comfy place to sit while you're up all night. A soft, comfy rocker with arms that's wide-enough-to-hold-you-and-the-baby is the perfect solution.

Changing Table with a Changing Pad. This isn't required. You can change your baby on the cold, hard floor or on your nice clean bed if you want. But a changing table with a washable changing pad really comes in handy when your baby decides to make a really, *really* dirty diaper in the middle of the night.

Your Newborn's First Week's Medical Needs

You have two choices here. You can either (a) stock up on a few medical necessities now so you're all prepared when you come home with your baby, or (b) send your husband to the store for the medical necessities right after you get home. Which, I'd like to remind you, would mean you'd be at home *alone* with the baby—and while that may not sound scary now, wait until you're two days postpartum and on the edge of utter exhaustion. At that point, you'll be glad you stocked up before you had the baby.

- **Alcohol Wipes.** You'll need these to clean your baby's umbilical cord until it falls off—about three to six weeks after he or she is born.
- **Petroleum Jelly.** If you have a boy and choose to circumcise, you'll need to dab petroleum jelly (aka Vaseline) on the wound for a few days to keep it from getting infected.
- **No-scratch Mittens.** Babies are born with razor-sharp fingernails—and no sense of control. You baby will scratch, claw and draw blood from any skin surface he or she touches—including his own face. Get some soft mittens to protect that cute little mug and yours as well.
- **Thermometer.** God willing, you won't use this until your baby is in kindergarten, but it's probably a good idea to have a rectal thermometer on hand in case your baby starts to spike a fever. I don't want to freak you out, but my daughter got sick when she was nine days old and ended up spending a week in the children's hospital. As it turned out, she was fine, but the only sign that she was sick was that she had a fever. We were glad we'd had a thermometer on hand.

- **Baby Hats.** No, I'm not talking about the cute little flowered bonnet your mom bought for your baby. These are tiny, cotton stocking hats that you can buy in bulk in the baby section. The reason they sell these in bulk is that newborns can't regulate their temperature, so even if your baby is born in August, he or she will probably still need to wear a hat for a few weeks.

Baby Showers and Registering

A lot to take in, isn't it? Before you have a panic attack trying to figure out how you're going to pay for all of this, I'll let you in on a little secret: You're *not* going to pay for all of it. Your friends and family members are going to help. Lucky for you, most people know that having a baby is expensive—and those same people love picking out cute baby gear—which means your friends and family members will probably throw you a baby shower.

Baby showers are a ton of fun—I mean, really, who doesn't love looking at melted candy bars in diapers? But even cooler, your friends and family will probably use your shower as an opportunity to show their love and excitement about your baby by showering you with all sorts of baby gear. What a wonderful gift! I was so grateful when my friends threw me a shower—and even more grateful that I didn't have to go into debt to buy a crib!

Before you have your shower, you may want to register. I know, I know, some people balk at the idea of asking for gifts on a registry, and that's their prerogative. But since the idea of storing fifteen non-returnable baby bathtubs in my garage doesn't necessarily appeal to me, I think registering is a great idea. It's a way to show your friends and relatives what you like, what you need and what you already have. Here are my baby registry tips:

- **Do not (I repeat, do *not*) bring your husband.** He does not care about baby booties the way you do and will probably do anything it takes to get you out of the store as quickly as possible. Bring along a friend or your mother.

- **Try to register for inexpensive items as well as expensive ones.** Some of my best girlfriends all banded together to buy me a much appreciated and very expensive baby swing off my registry. But most of the people who come to your shower will probably be looking for a gift in the twenty-to-fifty-dollar range. It's frustrating to look at a registry and only see items that you just can't afford to buy.

- **Register for things you really need—like baby thermometers and receiving blankets.** Things like pink flowered baby dresses and argyle sweater vests tend to buy themselves, so you probably don't need to register for them.

- **Register online first and save yourself a marathon session at the baby store—and the swollen ankles that are sure to come after.** Once you've added the basics online, you can head to the store to double-check your selections and check out the things you need to see in person before including them.

- **Register at more than one store.** That way your friends have a variety of places and things to choose from—and don't have to drive across town to get to the tiny boutique where you registered if they have a Target next door.

Buying Used

It'd be nice to have all brand-spanking-new gear for your baby, and you *will* get a lot of brand-spanking-new baby gear at your shower. But you'll also probably end up buying a lot of stuff yourself. Since it'd probably be nice to have some money left over to eat once your baby is born, you might want to consider looking into ways to be frugal when it comes to baby gear. When I was pregnant with my son, I literally spent every penny we had (and some that we didn't) on baby gear. I didn't have any friends or siblings to borrow gear from and I had this idea in my head that it was dangerous to buy used baby gear. (It's not.) So I spent a fortune on a shiny new crib and changing table—only to have my baby spit up all over them. Not worth it.

I learned my lesson with my second baby. She got a few new things (I couldn't resist the cute girl gear), but I was also more than willing to buy used items. The good news is that it's totally safe to buy most baby gear—from strollers to cribs—used. So go crazy. Okay, go crazy with a lot of caution and research behind your craziness.

Rules for Buying Used Baby Gear

- **Research recalls.** Sometimes baby paraphernalia gets recalled—and while stores usually pull recalled gear off of shelves, Craigslist doesn't have the same policy. Before you buy a used baby item, ask the owner to give you the brand and model number and check with the Consumer Product Safety Commission (cpsc. gov) to see if it's ever been recalled.
- **Check the date.** This is especially important for cribs and car seats. Cribs made before 1992 have slats that are wider than two-and-three-eighths inches, which can pose a strangulation risk. Older cribs can also have splintered wood and lead-based paint. Even more serious—car seats are considered "expired" six years after their manufacture date because the plastic starts to break down and they don't hold up as well in crashes. Most car seats and cribs should have a manufacturer's sticker on the side, so check the date before you buy.
- **Look for damage.** Check the bottom legs of a crib to see if it's been chewed on by a dog or a cat, and check the rails to see if they've been chewed on by a baby (yes, babies chew on cribs—

good to know, right?). If the crib has biting damage, make sure it's not splintered or your baby could get a sliver. Likewise, check car seats for cracks or strange angles that could signal that it's been in an accident.

- **Make sure it's clean.** Sorry, this is just a personal preference, but I'm not a big fan of grimy spit-up dried on my baby gear. Spit-up can be cleaned off with a strong disinfectant wipe. I probably don't have to say this, but if the seller hasn't done you the favor and cleaned it for you, make sure you clean it carefully before putting your baby in it.

Gear You Should Consider Buying New

- **Car Seat.** Car seats are considered safe if (a) they're less than six years old and (b) they've never been involved in an accident and (c) they haven't been recalled. So unless you know the complete history of your car seat, you should probably buy new.
- **Crib Mattress.** You'll soon find out that even the biggest, thickest diaper can and will leak. And while crib mattresses are plastic-lined, they aren't totally waterproof, so I just felt icky having my sweet (and clean) baby sleep on a mattress that had been peed on. If you're okay with that, then feel free; just clean it really well. But since you asked for my opinion, I'll give it to you: Forego your daily latte for a month (you're not supposed to be having much caffeine anyway!) and use the money to get your baby a squeaky clean mattress.
- **Breast Pump (or at the Very Least, Breast Pump Parts).** Before I can even explain this, I'm going to need to give you a little structural analysis of breast pumps. Electric pumps have three parts: the pump part, the connecting tubes and the breast-sucking parts. The breast-sucking parts actually suck the milk out of your breasts and into the bottles, and (for obvious reasons) you don't

want to use someone else's breast-sucking parts. *Eww.* But I'm going to go out on a limb here—in my totally nonprofessional opinion, I don't see a problem with buying or borrowing a used breast pump. I've spent a lot of time getting acquainted with the intricacies of breast pumps, and the actual pump and the tubes never actually touch the breast or the milk. So if you have a chance to save some big bucks and get a used breast pump, go for it. You have my permission. And in case you're wondering, you can buy replacement breast-sucking parts in the baby section at Target or Walmart. Bet you never knew they sold *those* there!

- **Changing Pad.** This goes along the same lines as the used mattress thing. While I'm sure that a used changing pad is just fine—and your baby is probably just going to poop and pee on the thing in a matter of days anyway—it still makes me feel squeamish imagining that someone else's baby has already pooped and peed on it. If you have to buy a used one, make sure to clean it really well and buy one of those supersoft fuzzy covers.

Decorating Your Baby's Nursery

I had my son's nursery all planned out. It was going to be a retro-sports themed nursery, complete with old school black-and-white framed photos of baseball players, a hand-stitched quilt from a boutique downtown and a cute little baseball mobile with mini real-wood bats and leather mitts. But before I could pick (low-VOC) paint colors, my husband stopped me in my tracks. He had this strange aversion to spending $380 on a hand-stitched baby quilt considering that *we'd* always slept on a $39.99 bed-in-a-bag. And he thought $90 antique touched-up photos might not be appreciated by a two-month-old. As cute as it all was, he was right.

It does seem a bit extreme to spend a bazillion dollars on baby quilts and decorations when your baby is probably going to spend more time pooping on them than enjoying their beauty. Plus, after the pooping-on-everything stage comes the having-big-opinions-about-everything stage, so you'll probably be ponying up for Superman bedding or Pink Princess sheets in a few years anyway. You have a billion things to spend money on right now—pedicure, anyone?—so saving a few bucks on your baby's nursery isn't going to hurt anyone.

After my husband put the kibosh on my retro-sports nursery, I went on a mission to zazz up my son's nursery on the cheap. Now, I admit that I tend to go a bit overboard on the zazz (yes, I'm *that* mom who pulled an all-nighter to hand-paint flowers on my daughter's nursery wall two days before she was born), but I like things when they are cute and fun and decorated. So I busted out some decorating magazines, honed my crafting skills and got busy.

My son still ended up with a sports nursery, but instead of ninety-dollar photos, he had funky baseball canvases painted by yours truly. Instead of the hand-stitched quilt, he had a much cheaper baseball comforter, and instead of the spendy all-leather mobile, I made one with a kit from the craft store. Yes, it took some time—but when you're eight months pregnant and up all night timing Braxton Hicks contractions, time is one thing you have. So with that said, here are my best (and cheapest) nursery zazzing ideas.

Ways to *Zazz* Your Nursery on the Cheap

- **Paint the walls.** Solid colors are great, but if you really want to add *zazz,* go Picasso on the room and paint your own mural. If that sounds a bit too artistic for you, try using stencils. Or paint simple geometric shapes. Or write the words to your favorite Bible verse, nursery rhyme or song. Still sound too daunting? Put a tarp down and splatter paint.
- **Go antiquing.** Head to the flea market and find cool antiques that

will work in your baby's nursery (just make sure to keep things out of baby's reach!). Swap out the light with a cool chandelier, restore old side tables or bookshelves to store toys or paint an old trunk and fill it with baby blankets.

• **Paint letters.** Pick up some wooden letters at the craft store (they cost less than a buck each!) and paint them yourself using waterproof, acrylic paint. My kids both have their names spelled out on their walls.

• **Hang up your baby's bedding.** Current SIDS-prevention rules—which you should follow to a tee—say that babies under the age of one year shouldn't have anything in their cribs except for a sheet and a light blanket. But that doesn't mean that the gorgeous hand-stitched quilt your mom made needs to languish in the closet. Hang up a towel bar and drape the quilt over it for an instant wall decoration.

• **Get some sticky wall decals.** Pick up a couple of rolls of decals (they cost less than ten dollars at Target and Walmart) and instantly transform your baby's room into a jungle, a flower garden, a racetrack or whatever.

• **Make some DIY art.** I get that you're not Monet (neither am I) and that the closest thing to a masterpiece you've made is your self-portrait from the seventh grade, but that doesn't have to stop you from making some supercool DIY art for your baby's nursery. Try framing a few coordinating sheets of twelve-by-twelve scrapbooking paper. Or make a collage out of pictures. Or get some paints and a blank canvas and see where it takes you. Hey, if that Russian painter Malevich can make millions off of a single black square on a canvas, imagine what you can do.

• **Make a shadowbox.** A shadowbox is like a three-dimensional picture frame that you can fill with colorful, fun and interesting objects. Pick one up at the craft store and fill it with something colorful. Try dried flowers, buttons, baby shoes, matchbox cars, tiny bouncy balls or ribbons.

- **Hang things from the ceiling.** If you're making an airplane room, get a few plastic airplanes and hang them from the ceiling using fishing line. If you're making a garden-themed room, pick up some big fabric butterflies from the craft store and make them fly.
- **Use mirrors.** Babies love to look at faces—especially their own. So pick up a variety of colorfully framed mirrors and hang them all over the walls.
- **Hang some wallpaper.** Wallpaper has gotten a bad rap recently—and rightfully so considering the awful blue seashell stuff that has graced every cheap hotel room for the last half century. But wallpaper isn't all bad. One of my friends used a tropical floral print wallpaper in her daughter's nursery. Not only did it look really funky and cool, but it also gave her daughter something interesting to look at as she fell asleep. Win-win.

Disclaimer: Remember, anytime you use paint while pregnant—whether it's painting letters or refinishing antiques—you should always use low-VOC paint and keep the room well ventilated.

My Last Words before Setting You Free at the Baby Superstore

You, my friend, are about to be turned loose into the jungle of the baby superstore. You will be armed only with a registry gun and some animal crackers. Your mission: to survive the day without registering for sixteen pairs of baby shoes and spilling the entire bag of animal crackers in the stroller section. Ready, set, shop!

Kidding! You will not get this all done in a day! There's a reason that pregnancy is nine months long—so that you have time to get all of your baby gear shopping done in short one- or two-hour bursts to avoid pregnancy exhaustion. Your real mission: Take it slow, take it easy and make it fun.

chapter 10

Name Games

How to Choose the Perfect Name for Your Baby

For every Jacob, Emily and Sarah in the world, there's also a poor little Supernova Spice who has to explain "it's Supernova Spice, two words" every single time someone asks her name. Poor little Supernova Spice's parents were either trying to be original or cruel—no one is quite sure—but it's quite certain that they've set their daughter up for years of teasing and even more years of identity crisis as she tries to figure out why her parents felt the need to name her after a galactic event and a cooking ingredient.

For obvious reasons, choosing your baby's name is probably the most important decision you'll make during your pregnancy. It's not something to be taken lightly (like, say, your decision to have chocolate chip ice cream instead of cherry tonight), or even somewhat seriously (like deciding which crib bedding to buy)—but something to be taken very, very seriously. After all, this is something that will stick with your baby *forever*.

Now that I've sufficiently freaked you out, I want to assure you that it's pretty hard to mess up on a baby name. It *is* possible (see *Supernova Spice*), but as long as you prayerfully consider your choices and do your research, you'll probably pick something that both you and your baby will love. So don't stress. Otherwise you might get baby naming block—a very serious condition cured only by complete abstinence from baby name books. And you do *not* want to give up your baby name books.

Interestingly, some parents are taking the baby naming responsibility so seriously that they actually hire professional name consultants (yes, that's a real job title) to do the suggesting for them. I read an article about a family that hired a name consultant for four hundred smackaroos to tell them the perfect name for their son. Of course, the name consultant did lots of hemming and hawing and eventually came up with the exact name that the parents had already been considering. Seems like a waste of four hundred bucks if you ask me. You don't need a fancy baby naming consultant or even a degree in advance naming linguistics (with a minor in telepathy), to name your baby. Really. I'm going to go out on a limb and say that you are 100 percent capable of figuring out the perfect name all by yourself—with some help from me, forty of your closest friends, all the members of a baby naming Web site and your mother-in-law. Let's get started.

How I Named My Son

When I was pregnant with my son, I felt pretty overwhelmed with the naming decision. For years, I had liked the name Jack, and I had assumed that I would name my firstborn son Jack. Unfortunately, I got a bit antsy and when my husband got me a golden retriever puppy about four years before we had kids, I named the puppy Jack. When I found out I was having a boy, I had the brilliant idea to start calling the dog Buddy so we could still name our son Jack. Pretty smart, right?

Wrong. Turns out Jack the dog had gotten pretty attached to

his name. So when I walked into the kitchen and caught him with his front paws on the counter scavenging for food, he simply looked at me like I was crazy when I shouted "No, Buddy! Get down!" Eventually, we gave up on the idea of changing our dog's name and decided to find a different name for our yet-to-be-born and yet-to-be-attached-to-his-name son.

After that, my husband and I had quite a few—let's call them heated—discussions about our son's name. The problem was that my husband gravitated toward hipster names like Rowan and Evan. I, on the other hand, liked common names with biblical meaning. I was gunning for names like Joseph, Luke and Peter. We had a really hard time finding a name that met both of our requirements.

Of course, calling our son "baby boy" for months wasn't an option, so while we haggled over real names, my husband and I started calling our son Cheeto (you know, after the cheesy chips that I was craving). The name stuck and before long, everyone was calling our yet-to-be-born son Cheeto. There was a moment in time that I actually considered just forgetting about the baby naming pressure and calling the kid Cheeto. Mommy madness at its best. Fortunately, I got over that one and went back to the drawing board with my husband.

We still hadn't reached a consensus when my due date (finally) arrived. In fact, when we were driving to the hospital at four o'clock on the morning that I was set to be induced, I scribbled out three names on a scrap of paper: Rowan, Evan and Luke. I oh-so-nobly handed my husband the paper scrap and told him that after the baby was born, he could decide—hoping and praying that after he'd seen me go through labor and delivery, he'd give me what I wanted and call the baby Luke.

But it was not to be. Sometime after my induction and before the contractions really kicked in, one of us came up with the name Josiah. We looked it up on the hospital Wi-Fi and found out that it means "the Lord saves." My husband loved it because it was unique and hip. I loved it because it had Biblical significance and could be shortened to my favorite common nickname, Joey. We had found a winner—just in the nick of time: *Josiah Cameron*.

My Daughter's Name

It literally took us three minutes to decide on my daughter's name, which was a refreshing change compared to the months and months of agonizing we did with Josiah. I told my husband my favorite two girl's names. He said he loved both of them. We picked Kate, meaning "pure." I also told my husband that I wanted Kate's middle name to be after my mom, Ellen. He liked that too. And *voilà!: Kate Ellen*. It really was that simple.

Naming Resources

My brother-in-law Peter's aunts and uncles are named Aaron, Adele, Alan, Arva and Avis. The story goes that his Grandmother was too cheap to buy the entire baby names book, so she tore the first page out in the checkout line and stuffed it into her pocket. When the time came to name her babies, she only had *A* names to choose from, so she just went down the list and chose them—in alphabetical order.

Fortunately, these days you won't have to steal pages from a baby names book to get access to great baby naming information. In fact, you have access to everything—from the low-tech to the high-tech to the time-wasting—all at your fingertips. And whether you're looking for baby naming ideas or just wanting to get more information about the name you've already chosen, there are hundreds of places to go to learn everything you want to know about baby names. Here are my favorites:

Baby Names Made Easy: The Complete Reverse-Dictionary of Baby Names. I'm of the opinion that there's just no substitute for a good baby naming book, especially one that you can highlight, circle and mark up until you've narrowed it down to your very favorites. I personally like this book because it's organized by category instead of alphabetically, which would've been very helpful for my brother-in-law's grandmother. Just think, she could've ended up with all of her kids named after flowers or animals instead of the letter A.

Baby Name Wizard (babynamewizard.com). This was my all-time favorite naming tool (read: thing to do) when I was pregnant. You basically plug your favorite name into the name wizard and it shows you a graph of the name's popularity over the last one hundred and fifty years. So, for example, my daughter's name, Kate, spiked in the twenties and again in the past ten years. And really, what could be better than baby names, historical graphs and color-coded charts? It's even cooler than it sounds. Really.

Baby Names World (babynamesworld.com). Not only can you find hundreds of thousands of names, but you can put your favorites into a baby names list that people can vote on, which not only will help you to avoid a Supernova Spice incident, but also will give you honest and somewhat nonbiased feedback on your favorites.

Baby Names Optimizer (babynamesoptimizer.com). Baby Names Optimizer is the place to go if you are having trouble coming up with a baby name idea to start with. You start by answering a bunch of questions about your naming preferences (e.g., what letters are your favorites, meanings you like and the types of names you like) and then it generates a list of twenty names that fit your preferences.

Babble's Baby Names Tool (babble.com/baby-names). Just in case you're curious what your baby's future name will look like when he or she calls someone on their iPhone, there's an app for that. With Babble's baby names tool, you can load your favorite baby name and then see what it will look like on a high school diploma, a birthday cake or even on a star on the Hollywood Walk of Fame.

Hot Names

Your baby's name is your decision—and no one (not even me) should try to sway your opinion. But that doesn't mean I'm not going to try. Look, the search for a name can be agonizing and tedious, and with so many names to choose from, it's easy to get stuck. So at the very least, I can sort things out for you and give you some ideas of what's hot and what's *not*. Just helping you out here.

Popular Names

I personally love popular names. There's just something about a name that everyone's going to know how to pronounce and spell (maybe that's the ex-teacher in me talking). So I have never been averse to picking a popular baby name. But a lot of people shy away from popular names, thinking that it will result in their baby being one of ten "Ethans" in their first grade class. But that's not exactly true. Take the name Jacob, for example. It's been the most popular name on the Social Security Administration's top baby names for years—and yet last year, according to SSA statistics, roughly fifty-five hundred out of every million babies were named Jacob. That's less than 1 percent. So that means that even if you name your baby the most popular name in the country, chances are he will still be the only kid in his class with that name.

Unique Names

I'm not against unique baby names. In fact, some of my favorite names have been beautiful, original names that my friends have created. I am, however, against *ridiculous* baby names. There's no reason to name your child something preposterous just because you want them to be the only person with that name on the planet. But with some thought and consideration, it's fairly easy to avoid a naming faux pas—ahem, *Moxie Crimefighter*—and find something that fits your unique style without being comical.

My sister and her husband really wanted to find something distinctive yet beautiful for their daughter. My sister stumbled upon the name Hadassah in a Francine Rivers novel and fell in love with it. Hadassah is not only a biblical name, but it's also Hebrew for Esther, our late grandmother's name. My niece, Hadassah Rose, always gets compliments on her name because it's unique, but not so out there that it's ridiculous. That's the goal of a unique name.

Family Names

I love the idea of naming your baby in honor of a cherished relative. What a tribute to the person you're naming the baby after—and what a great way to carry on your family's naming traditions for future generations. One caveat: This only works if you actually like the names that have been used in your family.

Case in point: My great-grandfather's first name was Jibbo—no joke. My brother Troy had a moment of lunacy when he decided it might be a good idea to name his firstborn son Gibson (not bad) with the nickname Jibbo (horrible). My sister-in-law went along with it because she didn't have the heart to make fun of a family name. Much to my sister-in-law's relief, my sister and I caught wind of this and quickly set my brother straight that—family name or not—Jibbo is *not* a good baby naming decision. They ended up using another family name (Glen) and calling their son one of my all-time favorite names—Jude Glen.

Classic Names

Old-fashioned names have made a big comeback lately—in fact, if you look at the kids in my son's class, you might even feel like you're back in the 1920s. He has friends named Jack, Henry, Emma, Catherine and Abigail. I love that! One of my friends named her sons *Charles William* and *Edward James*—and her little boys definitely live up to their strong, traditional names.

Not Names

There are certain words that should never, ever be considered names. Yes, I'm talking to you, Ms. I-want-to-think-of-a-creative-name-that-no-one-else-will-think-of. I'm not saying you shouldn't go for a unique name, but simply that a line has to be drawn some-where. Okay, so I'm being too opinionated again. Your baby's name is your decision 100 percent, and I shouldn't be doing anything to try to sway you. But, really, if you're dead set on one of the follow-ing names, please, please put this book down and call four of your best friends and ask them for their serious opinion. If they all give you their blessing, then go ahead. If not, read this chapter again and please try to think of something else.

• **Food Names.** Foods just don't work as names. There are

exceptions—one of my favorite names *ever* is the name Olive. I also love Clementine, Rosemary and Reuben. But as a general rule, if you can eat it, you shouldn't name your child after it. Peaches, Plum and Honey: not my favorites. Hamburger, Pizza and Avocado: absolute no-nos.

- **Places.** This one is tricky. There are some place names that are great. I once knew a girl named Berlin and it was the cutest thing ever. I also like names like Dallas, Brooklyn, Memphis and even Paris. My issue comes when people name kids after the place where they were conceived. That just makes for an awkward future conversation with your kid when he or she asks you why you chose the name you did.

- **Superheroes.** Sorry, I'm just not going to endorse the idea of naming a child Batman or Spiderman or Wonder Woman. If you absolutely must find an outlet for your comic book obsession, go for Clark Kent or Peter Parker.

- **Color Names.** Again, there are exceptions. Violet is absolutely adorable. I'm not opposed to Azul or Blanca. Magenta or Chartreuse? Not so much.

- **Band Name.** If your favorite band is *Caedmon's Call,* then naming your baby Caedmon is fine. If you're *Audio-Adrenaline*'s number one fan, the names Audio or Adrenaline should not be considered. Period.

- **Anything Ending in Dot Com.** I once knew someone who thought it would be a good idea to name her son *matthew.com*. Her rationale was something confusing about it being an easy jump from name to domain, but regardless, we'll just chalk that one up to mommy madness and move on. Go with Matthew. Or Com. But no dot-coms in names. EVER.

- **Crazy Spellings.** I used to be a teacher. And when you name your kid Miaaannkkaser (pronounced Bianca), it just annoys people—including your kid. Go for Bianca. With a B-I-A-N-C-A.

- **Punny Names.** The kid named Ben Dover probably only exists in playground jokes—at least I hope so—but people inadvertently give their kids punny names all the time. If you have a last name that sounds like something else, you should think really hard about any possible puns that could come from your name choice. That means if your last name is Barr, avoid the first name Candy, and if your last name is Case, it's probably best to leave Justin off your list.

- **Bad Initials.** My dad's initials are G.A.S.—and his grandparents couldn't resist the urge to buy him sweaters with his initials embroidered on them. Enough said.

What's in a Name?

A name is a whole lot more than something you choose in a baby book. Names have meanings, and the meaning of your baby's name will definitely have an impact on your child. I'm not saying a name's meaning will change who your child is—because calling your daughter Faith will no more guarantee that she becomes a woman of faith any more than calling your son Rusty will guarantee your baby will have red hair. But the name you choose for your child will give him or her a glimpse of what matters to you. Choosing a name that means truth will communicate to your child that truthfulness is a character trait that is important to you. Similarly, giving your child a name that means hope can demonstrate your desire for your baby to also put their hope in Christ.

In the Bible, Mary was told by the angel Gabriel to name her son Jesus. Jesus means "the Lord saves" in Hebrew. By calling His son Jesus, God made it clear from day one that Jesus was *the* Messiah sent to save the entire world. In Luke 24:47, Jesus says that "and repentance and forgiveness of sins will be preached in His name to all nations." In this case, He's using the word *name* to mean His entire character—meaning that the entire character of God—and God's gift of salvation would be shared with every human through the name of His son Jesus Christ. Fascinating, right?

Similarly, you've probably noticed that in the Bible, many people had names that meant something. The name Peter means *rock*—and in Matthew 16:18, Jesus says, "Upon this rock, I will build my church, and the gates of Hades will not overcome it." Jesus called Peter to be the rock that served as the base for the entire Christian church. And Peter, armed with his holy task, stepped up and became the rock that Jesus knew he was. His name represented a character trait that His heavenly father valued, and Peter chose to live up to his name's calling.

My sister-in-law Stevi loves to study names and their meanings. My brother Troy swears she's read the book *100,000 Baby Names* from cover to cover at least four times, which is quite an accomplishment considering the book has no story line and no pictures. Anyway, they're pregnant right now and in the process of choosing a name for their baby—sex still to be discovered. They've already decided on the adorable Greta Mae for a girl (*aw!*) but they're still working on a boy's name.

One name they're considering is the name Paul. Not only is it a family name on *both* sides, but it's also supercute. I mean, really, imagine a little towheaded Paulie running around. But now I'm getting ahead of myself. Their one hang-up on the name is that Paul means small, and my sister-in-law is nervous that the baby will grow up thinking he's small in their eyes. Of course, he probably would never think anything like that, but just in case, I did some research on the meaning behind the name. It actually doesn't mean small as in "small in stature" or "small in importance," but instead, means humble—as in "small to yourself." That's a cool, noble character trait, right?

My point here is that there's no need to agonize over your favorite name's meaning—but simply to take a name's meaning into consideration. For me, the meanings of my kid's names just make them even more special. I probably would've chosen the names regardless, but knowing that my kids' names mean "the Lord saves" and "purity" makes me like them even more.

Fighting over a Name

Here's the catch with baby names: It takes two to make a baby—and with this in mind, your husband is probably going to want to help choose a baby name. I know what you're thinking: Didn't he already do *enough*?! But, really, as much as you'd like to name little Miss Madeline and Mister Deacon on your own, naming your baby should be a joint endeavor.

This is where it gets complicated. Your husband doesn't like Madeline because he once knew a girl named Madeline in the second grade, and she smelled like peas. Oh, and Deacon is okay, but he thinks he likes the name Ashton better because, well, in his opinion, Deacon is wimpy. Let the name games begin!

How to Pick a Name without Picking a Fight

- **Make cross-off lists.** Each of you gets to write down your ten favorite names and then each of you gets to cross the five names you like least off of your partner's list—no questions asked. That means you can eliminate the option of Bertha in one fell swoop, even if it's a family name that his mother is insisting upon. But remember, that means he can also cross off Zephaniah, regardless of whether it's currently your favorite.
- **Let someone mediate.** Let a close (and trusted) friend mediate your baby naming discussion. Give this person the right to eliminate any names that might be causing unseen tension and to suggest names that you might both like.
- **Have a name finding challenge.** Challenge your husband and

yourself to find at least four new names—names that are on neither of your favorite's list—that you *both* like. Use the new list as a starting point for future baby naming discussions.

- **Find alternate sources.** If the baby names book has proven to be a bust, try to find alternate sources. Go to the movies and sit through the credits to see if there are any names you like. Scour magazines and books for bylines and cool names. Head to the grocery store and see what other moms are calling their kids. (And no, "you-get-over-here-this-instant" is probably not the kid's real name.)
- **Wait until after the baby is born to decide.** Just wait... I know it's hard, but maybe you'll get inspiration for the perfect name after you've seen your baby's face.
- **Draw the name out of a hat.** If you have a bunch of choices that you can't narrow down, pick the name out of the hat. If you draw something you both like, it's settled. If both of you look at the name and scowl, you'll be able to delete it from your list.

Sharing Your Baby's Name

Before I go any further, I feel like I need to divulge some pertinent information: I kept my baby names hush-hush until I made the big announcement after they were born. I know that annoys the tar out of some of you. Trust me, I never heard the end of it from my sisters. But it was totally worth annoying all of our friends and relatives because it was *so much fun* having a little just-between-us secret and a big birth-day announcement.

I actually didn't mean to be a secret keeper. I've never been able to keep anything a secret for more than two seconds in my entire life. But when people asked us what our son's name was going to be, I couldn't tell them because I didn't *know*. We decided in the hospital, remember? But after a while, I started to enjoy the whole not telling thing. People would guess, people would make suggestions and best of all, people would squirm in frustration. And I kind of liked it when people squirmed in frustration. I was pregnant, okay? I needed some entertainment.

After all the fun we had not telling anyone our son's name, we decided to do the same thing with our daughter. We didn't tell a soul and had all sorts of fun keeping our little secret for the entire nine months of pregnancy. And when baby Kate was born, we invited our family into the room and announced her name. Everyone oohed and aahed and told us how much they loved the name Kate. They had no choice but to say that—the birth certificate was signed—so the last thing anyone was going to do was say "Have you considered the name Jenny?"

That's the big advantage to keeping your baby's name a secret: No one can be opinionated about your choice of names. If your great Aunt Tilda wants you to name the baby after her Uncle Gerolld with two *l*s, you can just say, "We're not telling the name, so you'll have to wait and see." And once little Gerold with one *l* is born, Aunt Tilda won't be able to say a thing about it because by that point, little Gerold will already be wearing a T-shirt with his name embroidered across the front. It takes a lot of pressure off.

Of course, there are disadvantages to keeping your baby's name a secret—namely the lack of ridiculously cute personalized baby gear. My son came home from the hospital to a nursery with no wooden letters spelling his name in his nursery, no personalized car seat cover, no onesies that had his initials embroidered across the front and—perhaps most distressing—no personalized nursing pillow. I'm not saying these things are necessary, but they're awfully nice if you ever get confused as to whose onesie it is in your baby's dresser drawer. And, really, who can resist a baby who has his or her name emblazoned across his little booty?

My Favorites

I just can't end this chapter without telling you my top name choices. Okay, so I probably can, but I don't want to. So here they are—my top ten boy's names and top ten girl's names. (By the way, I'd love to hear your favorites too!) E-mail me! (erin@christianmamasguide.com.)

My Top 10 Boys Names

10. William (Will)
9. Luke
8. Max
7. Elijah (Eli)
6. Asa
5. Andrew
4. Peter
3. Henry
2. Edward
1. Josiah

My Top 10 Girls Names

10. Violet
9. Isla
8. Grace
7. Eve
6. Sarah
5. Abigail (Abby)
4. Stella
3. Faith
2. Kate
1. I'm not telling…because it's my favorite name and I fully intend on using it if I ever have another baby girl. Sorry, Charlie. Oh, Charlie… I love that name. Maybe I should add it to my list.

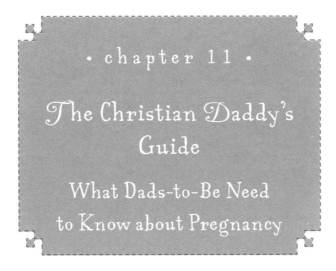

*Y*ou're probably starting to wonder about your husband's role in all of this. I mean, he did do the impregnating, but since then, he's had very little responsibility aside from running to the store to pick up a carton of fudge ripple. If we're being honest, he's had it pretty easy with this whole pregnancy thing.

The funny thing is that most guys *think* that pregnancy is pretty rough on them. The other day a friend asked us if we were thinking about having another baby and my husband had the gall to say, "I'm not sure if I'm ready to go through pregnancy again." Oh really. *He's* not sure *he's* ready? I mean, he did have to go through a lot—with all those times I made him hold my hair while I puked my guts out and all. Poor guy. Okay, okay. I'm sure I wasn't a picnic to be around while I was pregnant. Can you blame me?

Anyway, since pregnancy obviously affects the men in our lives—and since your husband is probably begging for a chance to get in on the pregnancy book reading action, I figured I'd dedicate a chapter to pregnant daddies. Unfortunately, since I've (a) never been a guy and (b) never dealt with a pregnant wife, I'm probably not the foremost expert on this subject. With that in mind, I've recruited a panel of been-there-done-that dads who are willing to share all of their pregnancy advice with other dads-to-be. So here it is: *The Christian Daddy's Guide to Having a Baby.*

Meet Our Panelists

Peter considers himself an expert on labor and delivery support—and is pretty certain that if his wife would agree to let him try out the tubes that you can attach to your shoulder to stimulate breast-feeding at the hospital, aka "supplemental breast-feeding system," he could also become an expert on breast-feeding.

Troy just managed to get his wife knocked up for the second time and proudly holds his wife's hair whenever she pukes, as long as there's not a Gonzaga game on TV. Troy considers himself an authority on middle-of-the-night grocery store trips and somehow managed to assemble his son's crib without making a single mistake.

Cameron (yep, that's my husband) secretly considers himself the King of Morning Sickness. He's spent so much time talking to pharmacists, doctors and Mr. Google about morning sickness cures that he fervently believes he can cure any woman's first trimester woes—except, of course, mine.

Michael is a first-time daddy who realized a little too late that dealing with pregnancy hormones takes as much finesse as dealing with a difficult business client—or worse, a difficult boss.

Here's what they think you—and your baby daddy—need to know:

Troy on Pregnancy Tests

Lesson #456
It doesn't matter how much a pregnancy test costs, you should let your wife take as many as she wants.

My wife is addicted to pregnancy tests. If there was such a thing as PTA (Pregnancy Testers Anonymous), I'd make her join. When we were trying to conceive, she was taking them at a rate of twelve per month. That's right. She'd take one two weeks before her period was due "just to make sure she hadn't miscalculated her cycle" and then take one again the next day "just in case she was one day off." This continued for a week or two before she upped her daily quota to two tests a day "just in case one was a dud." Her pregnancy test habit was costing us more than fifty bucks a month, and it would have been more had I not (lovingly) banned her from the expensive digital tests that sell for as much as ten dollars each!

I mean, seriously, what's wrong with finding out the old-fashioned way (i.e., waiting until you're three months along and you start to show)? I tried to explain this to her (after hiding the box of pregnancy tests in the back of my closet), but she wasn't buying it. In fact, she had the audacity to get all teary-eyed and explain to me about how comforted she would be by getting a positive result early. And take it from a guy who knows, when your maybe-pregnant wife gets teary-eyed on you, there's no going back. I caved and gave her what she wanted.

Lesson learned: Fifty dollars a month is a small price to pay to indulge your could-be-pregnant wife—even if her idea of indulgence involves peeing on a superexpensive stick.

Michael on Mommy Madness

Lesson #721
There is no arguing with a pregnant woman.

I learned early on that it's undoubtedly easier to support your wife's emotionally charged irrationality than to try to argue that she's being irrational. For example, if she's insisting that the nursery must be painted *tonight*—even though it's three o'clock and your baby isn't due for five months—it may be in your best interest to brew a pot of strong coffee and finish painting the nursery *tonight*.

There are ways, however, to convince your wife that *your* rational thoughts were *her* ideas. The challenge is finding ways to hide pills of logic in puddings of affirmation or agreeability. For example:

- Of course you're not keeping me up at night with your constant tossing and turning and snoring and snorting. Not at all. (*Pudding of affirmation.*) But if you want to, maybe we could make a really comfortable pregnancy nest for you in the guest room—complete with a table for water and chapstick and a minimum of fifteen pillows to support your belly. Come on. I'll help you. (*Pill of logic.*)
- I'm so glad that you're cleaning the "superdingy and obviously germ-ridden" baseboards with my toothbrush. I was getting concerned about them too. (*Pudding of affirmation.*) But I'm worried you're going to go into premature labor with all of that scrubbing. Why don't you come over here and I'll give you a foot rub? (*Pill of logic.*)
- You're not being irrational at all. (*Pudding of affirmation.*) But why don't you take the evening off and relax a little. You know, lock yourself in a cool, quiet room and read the Bible for a few hours while I watch this game on TV? I'll bring you a glass of water. (*Pill of logic.*)

• Of course the scale at the doctor's office is wrong, because there is no way that you could have gained 68 pounds already. (*Pudding of affirmation.*) But just to make you feel better, I'll eat this entire carton of Chubby Hubby, because I know that there's nothing like my gaining a few pounds of sympathy weight to make you feel better about yourself. (*Pill of logic.*)

Lesson learned: There's a fine line between advocate and accomplice; there's an even finer line between encourager and enabler. It is possible to be a supportive husband without allowing your wife's pregnancy hormones to overtake your life.

Cameron on Morning Sickness

Lesson #823
There is no known cure for morning sickness.

When my wife was in the throes of morning sickness, I would've gone to great lengths to cure her. She was miserable. And since she was miserable, I was miserable. And since living in a household with two miserable people is a pretty pitiful existence, I made it my mission to cure my wife's morning sickness. I tried everything.

One of my wife's pregnancy books suggested over-the-counter nausea medication, so I went to the pharmacy at ten o'clock one night to pick her up a bottle. She took one whiff of the cherry goo and ran to the bathroom and puked.

My sister-in-law suggested the potato chip and lemonade diet (apparently the salty-sweet combo can stun a stomach into relaxing). My wife ran to the bathroom and puked.

My mom suggested separating liquids and solids. My wife ran to the bathroom and puked.

My wife's friend suggested sea bands. Another middle-of-the-night trip to the drugstore. And when I got home, my wife ran to the bathroom and puked.

I read online that eating bland, flavorless foods helped. I brought my wife white rice. And guess what? She ran to the bathroom and puked.

All this running to the bathroom and puking taught me one thing: There is NO cure for morning sickness. But that doesn't mean you shouldn't try. When your wife is sick—and trust me, morning sickness is the absolute sickest I've ever seen my wife—you need to be her knight in shining armor. She needs you right now. And even if curing morning sickness seems futile, you still need to try to find a way.

Lesson learned: Even if you try fifty different cures and your wife runs to the bathroom puking fifty different times, you still need to pick yourself up, head to Mr. Google and try to find cure #51.

Troy on Pregnancy Eating

Lesson #945
Making a giant batch of carnitas so your wife
doesn't have to cook all week may seem like a sweet idea,
but it will only result in your eating carnitas for
breakfast, lunch and dinner for a week.

My wife hates cooking when she's pregnant, so I had the brilliant idea to whip up a giant batch of carnitas in the Crock-Pot so my wife wouldn't have to cook for a week. *Aw,* aren't I sweet?

Turns out that after smelling the carnitas simmering in the Crock-Pot all day, my wife gagged at the thought of eating it. She had cereal. I had carnitas every day for a week and still have Tupperwares of carnitas in the freezer waiting for the day that I can stomach the idea of eating more.

Lesson learned: Cooking for your pregnant wife is a good thing. But cooking in bulk for your pregnant wife will only result in your eating leftovers for a month. So use your Costco membership for things like diapers and wipes—not chicken potpies.

Cameron on Registering for Baby Gear

Lesson #1,232
You do not have to pretend to like being at Buy Buy Baby just to impress your wife...she's already impressed.

Remember when you registered for your wedding? That was fun, right? I mean, if you consider discussing the intricacies of china patterns and flatware fun. Admit it, you would've rather been at home watching football, or at the very least getting a snack in the food court, than standing in the china section trying to pretend like you were interested in how many settings of china you were going to need to carry you through your first dinner party.

The thing is, back before you were married, you had to pretend like you were interested because you hadn't married the girl yet. And to be honest, you kind of *were* interested because you loved the girl and wanted to show an interest in her. But you're married now—and with the responsibility of being a married man, you are afforded certain privileges. One of those is that you do not have to subject yourself to a marathon session at the baby store discussing the ins and outs of breast pumps. Especially since the sheer thought of that giant suction-cup thing being attached to your wife's breast probably makes you shudder.

The trick to getting out of going to the baby store to register is simple: Make your wife believe that you would be a useless dud of a helper at the store and that one of her friends or family members would be much more helpful. I sent my wife with her mother and sister. I even offered to buy them lunch so they could take a breather from the tedious registering. They were, of course, thrilled to spend the day shopping and lunching together, and in the meantime, I avoided a scary run-in with the breast pump aisle.

Lesson learned: Your wife will appreciate the opportunity to go shopping with her friends almost as much as you appreciate the opportunity to watch football all day in quiet. So let her.

Michael on the OB's Office

Lesson #1,543
The OB's office is much, much scarier than it sounds—
but you should go anyway.

The first time I walked into the OB's office, I realized exactly why my wife always moans and groans about her yearly exam. The OB's office is a very, very scary place. It's bad enough that it's full of cranky pregnant woman, but you'll also come face to face with unsettling things like stirrups, vaginal ultrasound machines and (perhaps worst of all) women who have just been weighed by the infamous OB scale.

As much as you're tempted to feign illness and stay far, far away from the OB's office, don't! The OB's office may seem scary—and it is—but it's also one of your only sources of good, sound pregnancy information. Guys don't typically call up their other guy friends to chat about pregnancy—so this is your one chance to ask a real, live person your questions, like:

- *What's my job during labor and delivery?*
  (Being as supportive as possible without being (a) annoying, (b) irritating or (c) nauseating—all things that you'll probably manage to do just by standing there.)
- *Is sympathy weight a real phenomenon or have I been eating too many cheeseburgers?*
  (It's the cheeseburgers. Oh, and the ice cream. And the fries.)

- *What if I have to go to the bathroom while my wife is in labor?*
  (Go. Just know you'll pay the price later.)
- *Will my wife's breasts ever return to their normal prepregnancy size?*
  (Yes. About two weeks after she weans your baby. Unless, of course, you manage to impregnate her again before she weans. Something to think about.)
- *Does it really cost $280,000 to raise a child?*
  (Of course not. You forgot to account for inflation.)

Lesson learned: Unnerving as it may sound, go to the OB's office. Not only will you look like the loving, supportive husband that you are, but you'll also glean the pregnancy information that you need to make it through your wife's pregnancy, labor and beyond.

Troy on Cravings

Lesson 1,924
If your wife is craving asparagus dipped in mustard, go get her some asparagus dipped in mustard.

My wife's pregnancy cravings are not of the "I must have this certain food right this instant" variety; they're more the "I'm starving and the only thing in the world that sounds good right now is doughnut holes dipped in ranch dressing" variety. There have been many occasions that I have driven to the grocery store at 11:00 PM and wandered up and down the aisles naming food items to her over the phone:

Ice cream? "Ugh! Gross!"

Pickles? "Don't even talk about it."

Potato chips? "*Eww.* Why did you have to say that?"

A banana? "Troy! You know I hate bananas!"

Finally, I'll stumble across something that might work. And usually it's the weirdest thing possible. Cheese and olive sandwiches. Pickled eggs dipped in ketchup. White bread with mustard and tomato slices. There was a time when I questioned her, but not anymore. I just happily load the items into the cart and head home, where my wife devours whatever delicious (read: crazy) combo I set in front of her.

Lesson learned: Pickled eggs dipped in ketchup may sound disgusting to you, but when your pregnant wife has a craving, she has a craving. Head to the minimart and spoon a giant pickled egg out of the jar. No questions asked.

Peter on the Infamous Push Present

Lesson #6,234
Your wife has carried your child for nine months and will soon push said child out of her body. She deserves a present.

Ever heard of a push present? Neither had I until about three weeks before my wife was due to give birth to our daughter. Apparently, some schmuck somewhere decided that it would be a good idea to give his wife some fancy bauble as a reward for having his baby. His wife was so smitten by his thoughtfulness that she told all of her friends, who in turn told all of their friends, and suddenly every woman in America (a) knows what a push present is and (b) hopes that their husband will follow along in the footsteps of Mr. Romantical and buy them a push present as well.

With this in mind, you might want to hop on the push present bandwagon and pick something up for your wife. And just to be superduper clear, your wife does not want you to buy her a new changing pad for the baby, a shirt that she can't fit into or a new blender. All of those things are great, but when it comes to push presents, you need to pick something sweet, sentimental and just-for-her. I recommend jewelry.

When I was picking out a push present, I didn't have a ton of money. My wife (of course) deserved a twenty-karat diamond necklace, but I had about fifty dollars to spend, so that wasn't really in the budget. Instead, I enlisted the help of my sister-in-law and picked her up a really fun pair of silver earrings. About an hour after my daughter was born, the baby fell asleep on my wife's chest. My wife was stroking her head all dewy-eyed and I felt like it was the perfect moment. I pulled out the earrings and opened the box. My wife started to cry. And at that moment, I realized that the schmuck who came up with the idea of a push present was a genius. A bona fide genius.

Lesson learned: You'll never regret finding the time and money to make your wife feel special—even if it means spending a few hours in a stuffy jewelry store.

Michael on the Trials of Pregnancy

Lesson #7,234
Pregnancy is your wife's permanent
(and well-deserved) trump card.

I wouldn't have dared say this out loud when my wife was pregnant, but there were times that her pregnancy was pretty rough on me. I mean, I did enough cooking, cleaning and foot massaging to last me a lifetime—and that doesn't even address the emotional energy it took to deal with pregnancy mood swings. But when I start to compare my role to my wife's role, I realize that she had it worse. No doubt about it.

She had to deal with morning sickness and weight gain and contractions and—here's the kicker—pushing an eight-pound baby out of her body. There is absolutely nothing in a man's world, hypothetical or real, that is equivalent to the labor and delivery process.

Nothing. I know you're tempted to argue with me that having to have a conversation with your mother-in-law when you're trying to watch a football game compares, but it doesn't. I've seen labor and delivery. And I will attest to the fact that pregnancy is my wife's ultimate trump card.

Lesson learned: Accept the reality that being pregnant is harder than being married to a pregnant woman. Be aware of the fact that you will be reminded of this often.

Peter on the Onset of Labor

Lesson #3,459
If there is any chance at all that your wife is in labor or close to being in labor, you probably shouldn't request her help installing a water softener.

Just before my daughter was born, I had the splendid idea to install a water softener in our garage. I wanted to be sure that the water our baby would eventually drink was pure and free from minerals and chemicals. Noble, right? The problem was that the task ended up being a bit more extensive than I had imagined. And to make matters worse, I had to shut off the water supply to the house the entire time I was installing the thing.

One night, I was tinkering around in the garage, and my wife suddenly seemed very insistent that I get it done. And by insistent, I mean she came into the garage and told me that I had better get the thing installed and the water back on in the next thirty minutes or she was going to call a plumber. I, of course, did what any handyman would do and told her if she wanted it done, she could come on out and hold pipes for me while I screwed things into the wall.

Let's just say that when you're trying to screw pipes into the wall and the pipe keeps getting jerked around every three minutes or so, it's really frustrating. And every time the pipe got jerked, I (very nicely) told my wife to hold it still. And every time I (very nicely) told her to hold still, she grunted something through her teeth about doing her best.

Just as I got the pipes screwed in and the water turned on, my wife turned to me and said, "Now pack your bag. We're going to the hospital." Turns out, she had started having fairly strong contractions, but her fear of not having running water when she came home from the hospital outweighed her fear of having the baby on the side of the road on the way to the hospital. And she knew that once I found out she was in labor, I'd be useless as a water softener installer. So she didn't tell me about the whole contractions thing—and braved her way through thirty minutes of pipe-holding in order to make sure I got the thing installed.

Later, she told me that the entire time she was holding pipes, she was thinking, *Oh man, Peter is going to feel so bad when he realizes I'm having contractions right now!* And she was right—I felt awful! But (top secret information that she can never, ever know) I blame her for at least 50 percent of this. I mean, had she told me, I wouldn't have ever made her hold that pipe. Of course, she's probably right that I would've been useless as a water softener installer, but still…

Lesson learned: Next time I shut the water off in the entire house when my wife is nine months pregnant, I'm calling my neighbor for help. Or just doing it myself.

Cameron on Labor and Delivery Entertainment

Lesson #4,234
Your job during labor and delivery is to stand there and support your wife—no matter how long it takes or how boring standing at your wife's side for twenty-seven hours may sound.

One of my friends advised me to bring along some "while you wait" entertainment since labor can be a long and drawn-out process. This is a true statement. Labor and delivery can take a long time. But it's also a very misguided statement. Because no matter how long labor takes—or how bored you get—your wife will get very, very angry if you decide to watch *Pirates of the Caribbean* on your portable DVD player instead of standing next to her bed and subjecting yourself to hours of hand-squeezing and angry tirades.

I valiantly stood by my wife as they inserted her IV and broke her water—and I even held her hand when the contractions began. But after a while, we got into a rhythm. The line on the contraction monitor would start to rise, my wife would start to yell and scream at me, the line would sink down and my wife would smile at me oh-so-sweetly and we'd both watch the machine in dread of the next bump. After about an hour of this monotony, I figured a little labor entertainment couldn't hurt. I waited until a dip and got out my DVD player. Big (BIG) mistake.

Lesson learned: Even if your wife happens to go into labor during the NCAA Championship game, your job is to stand by her bed, hold her hand and smile while she yells at you. Even if it takes twenty-nine hours, and you don't get to find out the score until the day after the trophy has been handed out.

Michael on Planning for the Unplanned

Lesson #5,789
Plan for a change of plans.

Your wife has been thinking about (read: obsessing about) pregnancy for months now, and she probably has a very specific, very detailed and very *rigid* plan in place for how the rest of her pregnancy will transpire. My wife knew *exactly* what she wanted—from the way she wanted the nursery to look, to the route she wanted to take to the hospital, to the way she wanted to deliver (vaginally, of course, without drugs, if possible). The problem here is that she was so dead set on what she wanted that she spent very little time preparing herself for the unexpected.

So when the argyle pattern on her nursery wall didn't turn out exactly as expected, my job was to convince her that the new (and improved) argyle pattern was better than the one in her head. And in reality, it was. And when our favored route to the hospital got bogged down in a road construction nightmare, I showed her on Google maps how our new (and improved) route was actually *faster* at certain times of the day.

And when things didn't go as planned for my wife during labor and delivery, I was the one to help her readjust her expectations. When she got an epidural, I was there cheering her on, explaining to her why it would make the next few hours way more tolerable for her. When she was rushed for an emergency C-section, I rushed with her, explaining the whole way why this was the best option for us and our baby. And when she started to feel guilty that things hadn't worked out as she had planned, I held up our son and told her exactly how proud I was of her for being such a trouper through a difficult birthing process.

Lesson learned: Your birth plan should look like a tree of possibilities rather than a timeline of events—and when something happens that causes you to branch off of your chosen path, your job is to make your wife believe that the new branch is even better than the old one.

Peter on Breast-Feeding

Lesson #6,234
Breast-feeding is harder than it looks.

The mechanics of breast-feeding seem so simple. Breast makes milk. Baby wants milk. Place breast in baby's mouth and baby gets milk. Happy mommy and full baby fall into a deep and peaceful sleep that lasts through the entire Patriots game. Easy and straightforward, right? Not so much. Apparently there's something about the mechanics of breast-feeding that is too complex for the male mind to comprehend. Because what seems like it would be a simple point-and-shoot maneuver ends up being a weeks-long learning process fraught with angry outbursts and middle-of-the-night crying sessions—by both your wife and your baby.

When my daughter was born, I expected long, sleepless nights and dirty diapers, but I never expected the weeks-long process of learning to breast-feed. I learned about things like "latch" (the way your baby's mouth connects to the breast makes a difference...who knew?), "lactation consultant" (yes, they actually have a degree in breast-feeding) and "lanolin" (a wonder cream that apparently makes your wife's breasts touchable again). And I also learned that it's completely normal for women and babies to struggle with breast-feeding for days—or even weeks—before getting it down to a science.

With this in mind, your job is to give your wife (and your new baby) all of the support they need to get the process down, without giving your wife any of your I-know-a-lot-about-breasts expertise. You may think you understand the complexities of breast-feeding, but trust me, you don't. So thoughts like "just put it in there and let the baby suck" or "latch, schmatch" or "any position should be fine" should probably be kept to yourself. Really. Do *not* voice those thoughts.

So how can you support your wife? Be her breast-feeding champion. Your wife wants to call the lactation consultant for advice? Get her the phone. She wants to try scary-sounding things like "nipple shields" or "supplemental nursing systems"? Get out Mr. Google and see if you can order some on Amazon. She needs you to run to the store for a box of "breast pads" and "lanolin"? Of course. (FYI: They're in the baby section, not the dairy section.) And if she needs a shoulder to cry on about the mangled appendages that were once her breasts, get her best friend on the phone. Trust me, you do not need *that* image in your mind for the rest of the day.

Lesson learned: Keep your mouth shut. Breast-feeding is harder than it looks—and just because you think you understand the anatomy of the human breast does not mean you understand the technicalities of breast-feeding.

The Christian Daddy's Guide in Summary (for Those Daddies Who Only Have Time to Read One Page)

- No whining. No complaining. And no buying chicken potpies in bulk at Costco.
- Keep your mouth shut when it comes to morning sickness. And breast-feeding. And pain relief in labor. And in general when you're talking about pregnancy.
- Pregnancy tests are a justifiable expense—even if your wife goes through them quicker than she goes through toilet paper.
- Expect the unexpected—even if the unexpected involves peanut-butter-and-mustard sandwiches.
- Lanolin cream may soothe your wife's tender breasts enough so that she'll let your baby touch them—but that doesn't mean *you* should try to touch them.
- There is absolutely nothing—real or imagined—in a guy's life that compares to pregnancy. It is *not* just as hard on you. You do not know how she's feeling. And yes, she's going to bring it up every day for the rest of your lives.

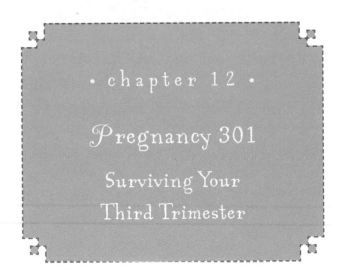

• chapter 12 •

Pregnancy 301

Surviving Your
Third Trimester

Remember your second trimester? Back when you had energy and were still skinny enough to fit into regular clothes? You were probably feeling pretty chipper about the idea of being pregnant. But not anymore. I have yet to meet a third trimester woman who isn't begging God to speed things up a little and get that baby *out*. And really, who can blame a pregnant mama?

You're huge. You can't breathe. And you haven't been able to shave your legs above your knees in seven weeks. If that's not enough to make you crazy, you've suddenly come down with a bad case of pregnancy insomnia that's left you tired and cranky. The only thing that is keeping you sane right now is knowing, for a fact, that your baby will arrive sometime in the next three months. That's right, you have three—okay, maybe three and a half—months *max* right now. You're in the homestretch.

But this homestretch is a long one. And a lot has to happen before you hop in the car and head to the hospital. So while you're sprinting (okay, waddling) toward the finish line, here are a few tidbits of advice to get you through.

The Third Trimester Freak-Out

With motherhood just around the corner, you might start to worry that having a baby will transform you from a perfectly normal, U2-listening, jeans-wearing woman to a sorta-crazy wee-sing-silly-songer who hasn't changed out of her ratty sweats in weeks. It's a bit nerve-racking. You're about to be a mom—like a real, live mom with a real, live baby. And that's certainly going to bring about some changes in your life.

The really crazy part about this whole baby thing is that there's no gradual phasing-in process. It'd be nice if you got a month or two to transition—but at most, you'll get two or three days in the hospital and then suddenly be sent home with this child who needs you twenty-four hours a day, seven days a week, 365 days a year. That means you'll have very little time left to obsess over Jim and Pam or cook gourmet cheese quesadillas anytime in the foreseeable future. Hence, the third-trimester freak-out.

My third trimester freak-out was actually triggered when my friend innocently called me up and asked me if my husband and I wanted to meet them at a favorite restaurant for a spur-of-the-moment dinner. She added, emphatically, that I wouldn't be able to do things like that, well, ever again, so I might as well get it out of my system before my baby was born. Cue panicked breathing and frantic carbo-loading. No. Spur. Of. The. Moment. Dinners. Ever. Again.

As I devoured an entire box of Wheat Thins, I realized all of the things I'd miss out on once my baby was born. I imagined a life chained to my house—unable to grab lunch with friends, go to concerts and—perhaps most frightening of all—unable to head to Target whenever they changed their seasonal offerings. Suddenly I wasn't as excited about the whole baby thing as I had been before.

Now, before you run to the kitchen to search for CheezDoodles and a paper bag, let me assure you that the whole baby thing isn't as drastic as it sounds. You will not be chained to your house watching Barney for the next four years of your life. They actually let moms—even moms who are covered in spit-up and haven't slept in a week—leave the house. And you can still even go to fun, adult places like restaurants, malls and Target. No, you won't be able to hop in the car and run to the Spaghetti Factory for a spur-of-the-moment dinner. But you will be able to toss a few diapers, a Costco-sized box of wipes, three toys, a nursing cover-up, a change of clothes, four receiving blankets, six burp cloths and a box of Nutter Butters (for you) into a diaper bag and head to the Spaghetti Factory for a somewhat spur-of-the-moment dinner.

I was actually pleasantly surprised at the portability of my baby. Sure, it took a bit of planning—and I had to lug around a diaper bag the size of a hiking backpack—but I was actually able to get out of the house quite often. We even brought our baby along when we went out to dinner with friends. It's definitely different. I'm guessing you've never exposed your breast in a crowded restaurant before—but it's not impossible.

Trying to Sleep

Early in your third trimester, you're going to develop a bad case of "crazy eyes." You may not notice them at first (you'll be too tired to pay much attention to the mirror), but you'll know you have them when people start giving you pitying looks and saying things like, "Sweetie, you really need to get some rest, don't you?" And you'll (of course) respond by saying, "Listen here, Missy, you try sleeping with a giant bowling ball attached to your belly and we'll talk."

It seems a little unfair that third trimester mamas get pregnancy insomnia when they are just weeks away from having new-baby insomnia. Logically, it would make sense that a third trimester mama would be able to doze the day away without a care in the world. But as you well know, the world doesn't run on logic. Instead, third trimester mamas spend their nights tossing, turning and resenting their husbands for being able to rest comfortably.

How to Sleep When You're Huge, Hungry and Have to Pee

- **Two words: silky pajamas.** They're slippery—which means you'll be able to ease yourself from an uncomfortable position to a sort-of-more-comfortable position without hoisting, grabbing, tugging and ripping your already stretched-to-the-max pj's.
- **Make a megabed.** When I was in the middle of my third trimester tossing-and-turning insanity, I started sneaking into the guest room so that I could toss and turn in peace without waking up my (cranky) husband. He, sweet guy that he is, objected to my sleeping in the guest room, so he moved the old twin bed we had in storage right up next to the king bed in our master bedroom. We called our new invention "megabed" and we loved it so much that megabed became a permanent fixture in our house until my son moved out of his crib and we had to give him the twin. Anyway, if you're keeping your husband awake, and you don't want to start sleeping in separate rooms, try pushing two beds together or blowing up an air mattress on the floor (for your hubby, of course).
- **Sleep on your left side.** Apparently, when you lie on your back (or on your right side), a major artery in your back gets squashed, which can (a) decrease blood flow to both you and your baby and (b) wake you up from even the deepest sleep. Since both of these are bad things, it's a good idea to position your Snoogle Maternity

Total Body Pillow to keep you propped on your left side. (Side note: Don't freak if you accidentally roll onto your back or right side while you're sleeping. My doctor told me that your body will wake you up long before the crimped blood flow will cause any problem for you or your baby.)

- **Eat a midnight snack.** Here's the *problemo*: If you eat too close to bedtime, your heartburn will probably flare up, but if you don't eat too close to bedtime, you may wake up with your tummy grumbling at four in the morning. The old wives say that if you drink a glass of milk with a bit of honey, it'll keep your tummy full and your heartburn down. My sister Alisa—the one with the degree in nutrition—says that milk doesn't really stop heartburn, but drinking a glass of milk (perhaps to wash down a few chocolate chip cookies?) at night is not a bad idea, especially because it can help you get a little extra calcium.

- **Don't drink any liquids for a few hours before bed.** I know, I'm contradicting myself, but this is one of those pick-your-poison types of things. If you're waking up with middle-of-the-night starvation pangs, have a snack and maybe even drink some milk. If you're waking up because you have to pee, don't.

- **Try to sleep sitting up.** If your husband somehow managed to convince you to let him keep the recliner that he has been hoarding from his bachelor days, this is the time to put that bad boy to use. If you can manage to fall asleep in a somewhat upright position, then you probably won't be woken up with a heartburn flare-up.

- **Get out of bed.** If the fact that you're thinking about not falling asleep is making it impossible for you to fall asleep, get out of bed and do something else for a while. Watch TV, read a book or, heck, paint flowers on your baby's nursery wall.

- **Ask your doctor about sleeping pills.** I know that the thought of taking a sleeping pill while you're pregnant scares the tar out of you—but what's scarier: entering mommyhood as a sleep-deprived zombie or taking a medication that is generally considered to be (a) safe, and (b) effective for pregnant moms? My sister-in-law Annie's doctor finally prescribed (non-habit-forming, of course) sleeping pills for her after she had gone three entire nights without a wink. She said she took it and slept peacefully for the first time in weeks—and delivered a healthy baby boy a month later.

- **Have a cup of tea.** While herbal teas can get a bad rap because certain rare herbs can induce contractions—most common teas like chamomile or peppermint are considered safe and great for helping pregnant mamas relax.
- **Pray.** If your mind is spinning, pray. Ask and thou shalt receive, right?

How to Have Sex When You're Huge, Hungry and Have to Pee

Since we're talking about sleep, I figure it's a good time to talk about third trimester sex. (You know, because if you are in bed and not sleeping, you might as well have *something* to do.) Yes, you're huge and tired and you have to pee every fourteen seconds, but underneath all those layers of fat (*er,* skin), you're still the same old sexy gal that you were in your prepregnancy days.

The good news is that for most gals, sex is completely safe all the way until the end of your pregnancy. There are (of course) a few caveats: If you have placenta previa or any bleeding, you should definitely talk to your doctor before having sex. Same thing goes if you're carrying multiples, have a history of preterm labor or miscarriage, or if it's painful to have sex. And if you have any questions about the safety of sex for you, ask your doctor. Otherwise, unless your water has broken or you're having contractions, you have the medical community's blessing to have sex whenever (and wherever) you please. Here's what you need to know.

Sex 301 for Third Trimester Mamas

- **Try (even more) new positions.** Missionary was probably given the heave-ho from your bedroom about midway through your first trimester. Girl on top survived through your second trimester, but by your third trimester, that will probably get a bit cumbersome (not to mention exhausting). Try "spooning," where you lie side by side and he penetrates from behind.
- **Rev up the foreplay.** Foreplay is always fun, but during your third trimester, it's a necessity. Third trimester hormones (yes, the hormones *again*) can really mess with your libido, making it harder to get into the mood and harder to stay in the mood. Annoying, but nothing that a little make-out session can't remedy.
- **Stretch a little.** Okay, sorry to sound like your high school track coach, but if you try to get too athletic without warming up, you're going to pull something. And trust me, rather than have to explain to your OB that you strained your back/thigh/calf/shoulder having sex, you might want to spend a few minutes presex warming up your legs, back and arms. Sexy, no. Essential, yes.
- **Don't worry about going into labor because you're having sex.** Countless studies have shown that having sex in your third trimester isn't going to cause preterm contractions. The only way sex can kick-start labor is if your cervix is already ripe and labor is imminent (and even *that* is considered an unproven old wive's tale). That said, if you're at that point where you want to have your baby, it can't hurt to try. My friend Karen swears that having sex jump-started labor with her son.

• **Don't be afraid to laugh a little (or a lot).** Trying to have sex with a blossoming—wait, make that *blossomed*—belly is a bit, well, awkward. And if you find yourself in an ungainly position doing unwieldly things with your uncoordinated and überbulky body, don't be afraid to laugh. It is funny, after all, and there's nothing like roll-on-the-floor hysterics to make you feel closer to your man.

Fear of Labor and Delivery

There were times in my first pregnancy when the fear of labor and delivery was almost crippling to me. There were nights when I'd wake up in the middle of the night trembling in fear—terrified of the pain and the unknown. I had heard countless times that God's "grace is sufficient" and that His "power is made perfect in weakness" (2 Corinthians 12:9). Yet there were many times in the dark of the night that those truths were lost in a wave of fear that left me out of breath.

There is a distinct difference between godly fear and ungodly fear. There are countless times in the Bible where godly men and women allowed their fear of the Lord to influence their decisions. During the Israelite's captivity in Egypt, there was a time when Pharaoh asked the midwives who delivered Israel's babies to throw all male children into the Nile. Instead of fearing Pharaoh, these midwives feared the Lord and chose to let these babies live. As a result, God's people were spared great anguish and sorrow. The midwives' godly fear led to good—and God chose to bless them for allowing their fear of the Lord to guide them (Exodus 1).

In stark contrast to a godly fear of the Lord is the crippling, worldly fear that many of us allow to influence our decisions. Crippling fear is not from the Lord. Instead, it's a tool that Satan uses to pull us away from God's grace. So when you find yourself overtaken by a bout of crippling, ungodly fear, your only recourse is to turn to the Lord and ask Him to fill you with His grace.

My middle-of-the-night fear sessions really started having an effect on me during my third trimester. I'd wake up fearful and, instead of turning to God, I'd allow the fear and worry and doubt to work its way into my heart. I'd spend hours wrestling with the fear—unable to sleep, unable to trust and unable to pray. After a few sleepless nights, I realized that this was clearly not from God and I immediately turned to the Lord in prayer. When my heart was too heavy to pray, I read 2 Corinthians 2:9 over and over: "My grace is sufficient for you, for My power is made perfect in weakness.... My grace is sufficient for you, for My power is made perfect in weakness....My grace is sufficient for you, for My power is made perfect in weakness...."

Eventually those words sank in and my fears eased into trust. God's grace truly is sufficient—even when you're facing a daunting task like labor and delivery. When your fear and doubt have taken your legs out from under you, God's grace is sufficient. When your heart is heavy and your body is weak, God's grace is sufficient. When you are in pain, God's grace is sufficient. He is all you need—so turn to Him.

The Third Trimester Nine-Fecta

Remember the First Trimester Trifecta: fatigue, bloating and morning sickness? (How could you forget, right?) Well, as luck would have it, by the time you reach your third trimester, your pregnancy ailments have multiplied and you're faced with what I oh-so-fondly call the Third Trimester Nine-Fecta. Here's what to expect:

1. **Swelling.** You expected to gain a few pant sizes during your

pregnancy, but did you expect to gain a few shoe sizes as well? Isn't pregnancy great? Extra fluids in your body often result in edema, a fun (and common) pregnancy complaint that causes your arms, legs, ankles, feet and (get this) *face* to swell up. This isn't dangerous (unless, of course, you count being unable to wear your favorite boots dangerous) but it is annoying. So if you want to reduce the puffiness, try to limit the sodium in your diet and elevate your legs whenever possible.

2. **Pregnancy Waddle.** You're well aware that you're a walking, talking hormone factory at this point in your life, so it probably doesn't surprise you that during pregnancy, your body will start producing a bunch of the aptly named hormones, one of which is relaxin. Relaxin's job is to help relax your pelvic ligaments so they'll be nice and ready for labor, which also produces the side effect of making you waddle when you walk. Sometime during your third trimester, you'll develop the very noticeable—and admittedly hilarious—pregnancy waddle.

3. **Weight Gain.** You've been gaining weight (very steadily, *thankyouverymuch*) for your entire pregnancy, so it's probably no surprise that you'll continue to do so during your third trimester. The difference between regular pregnancy weight gain and third trimester weight gain is the remarkable speed at which a third trimester mama can pack on the pounds. It's mind-boggling, really, to imagine being able to gain two pounds and five ounces in a week. I learned from experience that it's entirely possible—*er,* make that *probable.*

4. **Heartburn.** As your stomach squishes into your lungs and your lungs squish up into your throat, there are fewer and fewer places for food to go once it's chewed up and swallowed. As you certainly already know, this results in heartburn. The best way to avoid heartburn is to avoid eating anything that's remotely flavorful for the last three months of your pregnancy. If you're un-

able to manage that, you can try to stay upright for about an hour after you eat or ask your doctor if you can load up on TUMS.

5. *Obsessivitis.* This malady is often caused by a third trimester mama's longing (okay, obsessing) to make sure everything in her life is perfectly in order before she reaches motherhood. This often results in sleepless nights spent organizing baby socks and extra trips to the doctor's office "just to make sure the strange twinge in my right breast isn't going to affect my future as a breast-feeder."

6. **Stretch Marks.** As your stomach stretches, your stomach skin starts to revolt—resulting in a parade of grayish jagged stretch marks on your stomach. And let me assure you, they will never, ever go away. (Don't freak. They *will* fade over time!) According to the grapevine, you can avoid stretch marks by slathering loads of cocoa butter cream onto your belly to help it stretch—but the grapevine also says that pregnancy is nine months long and we all know that forty weeks is nowhere near nine months. So it's still to be determined if the grapevine is trustworthy.

7. **Light-headedness.** This has something to do with extra blood volume and the fact that your heart has to work extra hard to keep up with all of that extra blood. However, sometimes your heart just can't do it, which means you may experience a bit of light-headedness, especially when you leap up from your cozy spot on the couch with a sudden urge to, say, get a sandwich.

8. **Squashed Stomach Syndrome.** Sometime during your third trimester, your body will start to develop a love-hate relationship with food. I know what you're thinking: Food is my friend! I will never abandon it! But just wait. Here's what happens: As your baby grows, your uterus expands—as you well know. Unfortunately, your uterus doesn't just expand out—it also expands up, squishing your stomach into a space the size of a golf ball. At this point, no matter how hungry you are, you will get full and

crampy after a few bites. After full and crampy comes belchy and heartburny, which quickly turns to whiney and moany. It's a horrible cycle because as soon as the full, crampy, heartburny pain goes away, you'll be hungry again and quickly devour four bites of pizza before the whole thing starts again. Hence, the love-hate relationship. What's a pregnant mama to do? Make sure every bite you take is packed with nutrition for your baby. Add a slice of turkey to your whole wheat crackers. Smear peanut butter onto your bagel. Sprinkle almonds on your hot fudge sundae.

9. **Incontinence.** Ah, talk about saving the best for last. By the time you're in your third trimester, your baby has been camping out on your bladder for months and your pelvic floor pretty much gives up the fight. This means you might want to head to the supermarket and buy yourself some Poise Pads. Either that or get in the habit of carrying a change of pants with you wherever you go.

Pregnancy Gear That Doesn't Exist— So Stop Looking

Pregnant mamas have to put up with a lot of misery—you'd think there'd be someone out there who could help a pregnant mama out and invent a magic morning sickness cure-all. Oh, and while they're at it, here are a few other things that would really make life with a bun in the oven a whole lot easier:

• **Shaving Extendo-arm.** Remember how I told you that pregnancy can make your hair grow faster than Chewbacca's? I neglected to inform you that said hair growth will quickly become unruly, and shaving will become nearly impossible midway through your second trimester when your belly gets too big to navigate around. The simple solution would be a robotic extendo-arm that gracefully moves around said belly and carefully lathers, shaves and lotions your legs and bikini zones with ease.

- **Midnight Pee Extractor.** Technically, they have these—they're called catheters. But since catheters are both unpleasant and require a hospital stay, you might be on the lookout for a nonmedical pee extractor. I'm thinking along the lines of a pill that makes it so all of the water you drink goes straight to nourishing your baby's brain so you never, ever have to get up in the middle of the night to pee. That would work, right?

- **Gender Double-checker.** This could take the form of a pregnancy test—except that after you pee on it, it tells you whether your baby is a girl or a boy. This would be useful for women who don't want to wait for their ultrasound, but it would also help women like me who weren't 100 percent sure they could trust their ultrasound results—and worry that they'll end up bringing a surprise baby boy home from the hospital wearing a pink flowered nightie.

- **Push-in Bra** You certainly don't need a push-up bra anymore, and the last thing you need is a push-down bra. But a sturdy cleavage-reducing contraption would really come in handy for next weekend's dinner with the in-laws.

- **Baby Namer.** This computerlike device automatically sorts through your favorite names and selects the ideal one. Even better, the baby namer has a mechanism that somehow convinces skeptical husbands that your baby names are the best choices and makes said husbands completely forget any notion that the name Gert is cute.

- **Hip-hider.** No, I'm not talking about that awful drapery-like maternity dress your grandma picked up at a garage sale, but instead, a cute little black dress that can make your pregnancy hips, arms and legs all but disappear, leaving only a cute baby bump—and perhaps some fabulous pregnancy tresses—as your only outward signs of pregnancy.

- **Baby Remover.** This handy tool would somehow help you by-pass the entire labor and delivery process and deliver your baby through a different—and hopefully much larger—hole. Like a C-section without the surgery part, the six-week recovery part or the abdominal scar part.
- **Sleep Inducer.** Conceivably, this could take the form of an extra-large-sized baby-swing apparatus that slowly lulls a pregnant mama to sleep.

Third Trimester Friendships

Late in your pregnancy, you may notice an abundance of friends, co-workers and obscure relatives calling "just to chat." Let me assure you—they aren't calling because you're a hoot to talk to—they have an ulterior motive. They want to know if you've gone into labor. And since your answering the phone makes it clear that you are not in labor, they have to quickly make up an excuse for their seemingly random call.

I'll be the first to admit that I'm the queen of "just to chat" phone calls. When my sister-in-law was pregnant, I thought of a reason to call every day. One day, I wanted the recipe for her famous Tangy Taco Salad. The next day, I wondered if she had seen the new George Clooney movie. On the next, I was suddenly curious about her plans for enrolling my nephew in a Music & Me class. But what my sister-in-law can never know (and certainly couldn't have guessed) is that I was really calling just to see if she was showing any signs of labor. Sneaky, right?

If you're enjoying the chance to catch up with people that you haven't spoken to since your last family reunion, then by all means, answer the phone and learn all about your Uncle Ed's new hearing aid. But if you want to spend your last few months of pregnancy in peace, I want to remind you that there's no rule that says you have to answer your phone all the time. Feel free to let calls go to voice mail and return calls when you're feeling up to it. Or, even better, put a message on your voice mail that says "Nope! Not in labor yet...but I'll make sure to text everyone in my phone book the instant something changes!"

Third Trimester To-Do List

You have a lot on your plate right now—literally and figuratively—and there's nothing like a checklist to help keep you organized and on top of things. So here you go, your very own third trimester to-do list, complete with handy boxes where you can check off your to-dos as you get them done.

❑ Remind your husband to install the car seat.

❑ Return all fourteen wipe warmers that you got at your baby shower and proceed to obsess over whether you're going to exchange them for the truck crib bedding or the purple plaid high chair.

❑ Decide on your baby's name.

❑ Convince your mother-in-law that naming your baby after her distant cousin Moltov would only serve to make her other distant cousin Joltov jealous.

❑ Pick up a nursing bra or two (*Pssst.* You can find supercute, very un-grandmotherish, hot pink and lacey nursing bras at cakelingerie.com.)

❑ Preregister at the hospital.

❑ Remind your husband that even though your nursing bra is supercute, un-grandmotherish, pink and lacey, he still won't be able to touch it for at least six weeks after the baby is born.

❑ Order personalized towels, bibs and onesies with your baby's initials. You know, just in case you forget whether the tiny blue hooded towel belongs to you or your baby.

❑ Remind your husband (again) to install the car seat.

❑ Explain to your mom that your baby probably only needs four hand-knitted sweaters for his or her first winter—but if she's just dying to knit something else, you wouldn't mind a new beanie cap.

❑ Wash a few day's worth of baby clothes and all of your baby's bedding. (Don't wash all of the newborn clothes—if your baby turns out to be a Goliath, you can swap them out for bigger sizes!)

❑ Make and freeze meals to reheat when the baby arrives—that or put the pizza delivery company on your speed dial.

❑ Threaten to install the car seat yourself if it's not done in a week.

❑ Figure out how to assemble—and use—your breast pump. And, yes, this is probably something you should do while your husband isn't home.

❑ Figure out what your baby's name means, how it trends on the popularity charts and which famous people have shared the same name.

❑ Let your husband off the hook and go to the local fire station and have them install your still uninstalled car seat.

There will come a point in your pregnancy that your prayers will shift from "Please, God, help my labor to be easy and short" to "Please, God, GET THIS BABY OUT OF ME RIGHT NOW!" That prayer usually proceeds a long, drawn-out rant where couch cushions are thrown at husbands, husbands calmly rub pregnant mamas' shoulders, and pregnant mamas are eventually given a nice hot cup of tea and told that they need to relax or they might go into premature labor.

It doesn't matter how scared you are of labor early in your pregnancy—by the time labor is actually close, you won't care how painful it is or how long it takes, you'll just want the baby out. I was absolutely terrified of labor early in my pregnancy. I literally refused to watch *A Baby Story* because it gave me nightmares. But by the time I reached the last few weeks of my pregnancy, I was singing a different tune. I spent my days begging and pleading with God to *get that baby out.* And I didn't care what it took.

The good news is that all babies eventually come out—even if they're a few days late like my son. It's guaranteed. So no matter how miserable you are and no matter how much you don't think you can make it another day, you can. And eventually the day will come when your baby *will* be out. Until then, here's what you need to do to prep for that glorious day.

Birth Plans

The idea of writing out a birth plan so that your midwife or doctor and nurses will know exactly what you want for your labor and delivery is a great idea. Theoretically. Realistically, it's probably a waste of time. I'm not saying you shouldn't write one, but simply that you shouldn't become superattached to it. I have yet to meet a woman whose birth plan was followed without a hitch.

My birth plan was this: Go into labor at home (preferably three weeks early), arrive at the hospital just as I reach eight centimeters, try to use a variety of breathing and nonmedical techniques to deal with the pain and deliver the baby with a maximum of two pushes within an hour of entering the hospital. Sounds like a nice plan, *eh?*

This is what really happened: I was induced a few days *after* my due date and after four hours of nonproductive contractions, my son's heartbeat started to drop. The surgical team rushed in and within thirty minutes, my son was delivered by emergency C-section.

My point? Do plan. It can't hurt—because when you're in the throes of a contraction, you won't be thinking clearly enough to decide whether you want to try a bath or a birthing ball. But write your birth plan in pencil instead of in permanent marker—because things are sure to change when you get to the hospital.

God Knows More than Google

I'm sure you've already spent a ton of time reading about all of options that are available to you for your labor and delivery. You probably know all about epidurals and Lamaze and birthing balls (and if you don't, turn ahead to Chapter 14 and I'll fill you in!). But it's easy to get so caught up in your research that you forget about the fact that God knows more about *your* labor and delivery needs than Google does.

My friend Carrie decided early on in her first pregnancy that she was going to get an epidural. But God had other plans. When she started praying about her labor and delivery, she felt a strong sense that God was telling her to go for a natural childbirth. Of course, her first instinct was to argue with God—why would she go through that pain if she didn't have to?—but she felt God really clearly telling her to go natural. After her baby was born, the doctors told her that had she had an epidural, she would've probably ended up having an emergency C-section. There was something about the way her baby was positioned and her need to feel each push that made it healthier for her—and her baby—to have a natural birth.

Interestingly, on her second baby, she just assumed that since God didn't want her to have an epidural the first time, He wouldn't want her to have one the second time. In the middle of her long and painful labor, however, she realized that she had never even asked God about it—and *that* time, she didn't feel any conviction on the topic. It was too late to have an epidural—but Carrie vowed that on any subsequent pregnancies, she'd pray and ask for God's guidance instead of assuming she knew His will.

When she got pregnant for a third time (she has *four* kids!), she prayed about her labor and delivery and didn't feel God urging her to have a natural childbirth. She got an epidural that time— and didn't regret the pain relief at all when she delivered another healthy baby. She realized then that her early conviction to have natural childbirth wasn't that God was telling her to never have an epidural or that natural childbirth was *always* the way to go, but simply that God knew on her first delivery that a natural childbirth would be better.

It's easy to rely on our own research to determine what is best for our babies and our deliveries instead of praying and trusting that God knows. So before you make any major decisions about your labor and delivery, remember to turn to God and pray that He'll make it clear what is best for you and your baby. And if you hear God strongly telling you to go one way or another, trust Him. Proverbs 3:5–6 says it best: "Trust in the Lord with all your heart and lean not on your own understanding; in all your ways acknowledge him, and he will make your paths straight."

Taking a Childbirth Class

I operate under the philosophy that there are some things that you're just better off not knowing. And after reading the pamphlet on the childbirth class offered at my hospital, I decided that childbirth is one of those things that I'd rather not know about—at least until I'd experienced it myself. So I never took a childbirth class. I took the fifty dollars I would've spent on it and got a relaxing pregnancy massage instead. I chose to go into labor and delivery completely oblivious about what would happen.

But since most women want to be at least somewhat aware of what to expect—and because childbirth classes are the thing to do when you're pregnant—most women do take a class of some sort. Since I'm not an expert on childbirth classes (seeing as how I've never been to one), I'm going to have to defer to someone who has a bit more experience. My sister-in-law Stevi thought her childbirth class was great. Not great *great* like a lazy Saturday at home, but she felt that it was really informative and that it helped her to prepare for labor and delivery. She learned how to tell if she was going into labor—which made it so she only made one false labor trip to the hospital instead of the usual seven. She also learned about breathing techniques and pain management options and got a tour of the maternity ward at the hospital to ooh and aah over all the newborn babies in the nursery.

Plus, at childbirth class, you'll get to meet all sorts of other pregnant mamas and daddies—which means you'll have all sorts of new just-as-excited-as-you-are people to chat with about baby names and breast pumps. You might even make a few friends. At the very least you'll realize that (last week's bout of mommy madness notwithstanding) you're actually pretty normal compared to some of the other expectant parents out there.

Types of People You May Encounter at Childbirth Class

- **Wheatgrass-fed Organimommy.** This is the woman who shows up at the class munching on blanched asparagus wearing a maternity T-shirt that says "Organic All the Way Bay-Bee." She'll probably ask important hypothetical questions like "If you exercise for fourteen hours a day, will your labor be quicker?" and "If you eat a purely vegan diet, will you lose your pregnancy weight in four months instead of nine?" Word to the wise: You might want to avoid sitting by Organimommy—she might try to offer you kale chips and quinoa bars and then try to convince you that "they're really quite delicious if you plug your nose while eating them" when you politely decline.

- **Frat Guy.** This is the guy who shouts "*Groooossss!*" when they show a picture of a newborn covered in "some sort of disgusting birth juice" and who asks the question about "extensive vaginal stretching" when they show a birthing video. Warning: Laughing at this guy will only add more uncomfortable moments, so do his mortified wife a favor and keep a straight face.

- **Type-A Supermommy.** This soon-to-be-mom shows up at childbirth class when she's seven weeks pregnant because she "figured it was a great day to slot it in since the nursery was being painted and she wanted to stay away from the fumes." If you happen to be sitting next to Type-A Supermommy, try to swipe her already prepared (and indexed) hospital packing list or her birth plan—no need to reinvent the wheel if Supermommy has already done it for you.

- **Scared-to-Death-of-Needles Mommy.** This poor girl is so frightened of blood and needles and hospitals and pain that she hyperventilates every time she sees anything remotely reminiscent of a hospital. Her husband will eventually have to take her into the hallway to calm her down and to "protect her from the scary parts."

- **"I'm SO excited and I just can't hide it" Mommy.** This is the woman who shows up at childbirth class pushing a stroller with a life-sized doll in it. This woman may even "step out" for a minute to "feed her baby" and will probably spend most of the class telling everyone else all the "superexciting" things she's learned about childcare, including the fact that "babies wake up at least four times every night so—*squeal*—you won't even have to wait until morning to snuggle your little schnookums."

- **"How did I get myself into this?" Mommy.** This is the woman who shouts "WHAT?! I didn't know about that!?" when the nurse explains that babies descend through the birth canal. No, this woman hasn't been living in the dark ages—instead, she's probably more like me and has chosen to remain completely oblivious to the childbirth process. Go easy on her. She's probably in a bit of shock.

- **Public Displays of Adoration Couple.** These people probably won't say much during childbirth class. They'll be too busy gazing into each other's eyes while adoringly whispering sweet nothings to each other. Every time a video or picture is displayed, the husband will kiss his wife tenderly and say something like "I'm so proud of you, baby." This couple is sweet—if you like watching syrupy sweet love dramas play out in real life—but if you start to feel jealous about their überromantic relationship, just remember that labor has a way of making even the most loving wives scream at their husbands. His day is coming.

- **"Busy" Executive.** Every few minutes, this otherwise doting husband will excuse himself to the hall for an "important work call." His call volume will significantly increase when videos of natural childbirth are shown or when the instructor discusses breast pump usage.

The Three Stages of (Pre)Labor

I know you've heard a lot about what's going to happen when you get to the hospital (for the fourth time) and are actually in labor. That's important. But for me, I was more concerned about what would happen *before* I got to the hospital—when I was at home fending for myself without immediate access to a gaggle of medical professionals. With that in mind, I've decided to help a pregnant mama out and give you a clear outline of the stages of prelabor. This way, you'll know exactly what you're getting into and be able to gauge how far along you are in the prelabor process. Yes, you have to go through stages one and two to get to stage three, but you can rest assured that by the time you're in stage three, your baby will arrive shortly. So here they are—my very own (and *very* medically qualified) stages of prelabor.

Symptoms of Stage One Prelabor

- An irresistible urge to go to the hospital every couple of days, just to check and see how much you've dilated. This symptom can last weeks and only goes away once actual labor begins.

- A middle-of-the-night fascination with timing Braxton Hicks contractions (just to make sure they don't magically turn into real contractions without your knowing it).
- The ability to simultaneously read a baby names book, clean baseboards in the nursery and eat a hot fudge sundae.
- An inability to keep your maternity jeans up at waist-level, resulting in a semipermanent plumber's crack.
- Nagging worry that you will not recognize true contractions coupled by a fear that you will be fully dilated (see #1) and ready to push without knowing it.
- Spending large amounts of time walking around the block, eating spicy food and drinking castor oil.
- Constant packing and unpacking of the hospital bag, paired with an ongoing mental debate on whether to pack the pink slipper socks or the purple ones with flowers.

Symptoms of Stage Two Prelabor

- Angry tirades pointed at anyone who asks your due date.
- Complete obsession with walking around the block, eating spicy food and drinking castor oil all while bemoaning the old wives for not figuring out a real way to induce labor.
- Adamant insistence that Braxton Hicks contractions feel *exactly* like real contractions.
- Inability to figure out how to install the car seat correctly and subsequent panic about going into labor without the car seat installed.
- Making constant calls to your doctor's nurse "just to check and make sure the protocol for going to the hospital hasn't changed."
- Seething anger at your husband for having the nerve to impregnate you.
- Bargaining with God that if He'll just get the baby out in the

next few minutes, you'll volunteer in the church nursery every Sunday for a year. No, wait, make that two years.

Symptoms of Stage 3 Prelabor

- Furious diatribes aimed at your husband for not being a labor-inducing expert and knowing exactly how to get the baby out.
- Careful examination of the toilet's contents—in search of a mucus plug—every time you go to the bathroom.
- Inability to walk around the block (too far), eat spicy food (too much heartburn) and drink castor oil (it's all gone).
- Absolute certainty that your husband's contraction-timing stopwatch has somehow broken and that when it says ten minutes, it really means three.
- Inability to sleep more than ten minutes without shaking your husband awake to let him know that the last contraction *might* have been a real one. Maybe.
- Fear that you may be the first and only woman in the world who ends up being pregnant forever.
- Weeping uncontrollably because the baseboards in the nursery look a little dirty, even after you've scrubbed them twenty-nine times.

What to Pack in Your Hospital Bag

You know how it takes weeks of planning and packing and organizing to go on a vacation? Going to the hospital is kind of like going on vacation (*ha!*), so you're going to need to spend some time packing, sorting and getting yourself organized for the big day. (Unless, of course, you plan on wearing a bottom-revealing hospital gown and washing your hair with hand soap the entire time—then you can just carry on as usual without worrying about a thing.)

You will not need an entire jumbo-sized steamer trunk full of things for your hospital stay—you just won't be staying that long. If you delivery vaginally, you'll stay two days max. If you have a C-section, that bumps your stay up to three or four days, but either way, your entire stay will be less than a week. With that in mind, you won't need coordinated outfits and matching shoes to last you for the next month. And since we're talking about cute outfits, let's just say that it's probably best to keep your good clothes as far away as possible from the gunk and goo that will certainly surround you during your entire hospital stay.

Here's another helpful piece of advice: Pack your bag yourself. I have a friend whose water broke and she didn't have time to pack her hospital bag. After she had the baby, she sent her husband home to get supplies. He came back with a flowery sundress (it was December), a gray hoodie, socks, tennis shoes, a comb and a bar of soap. Great as our husbands are, it's probably best to leave the hospital bag packing to someone more qualified (read: a woman). And if you do end up in a pinch and have to send your husband home for supplies, write a very specific list about what you want or risk going home from the hospital in the button-down blouse your mother-in-law got you last Christmas.

My Hospital Bag Must-Haves

- **Paperwork.** Let's get the boring stuff out of the way first. You're going to need a lot of boring paperwork like insurance cards and medical records. Might as well take care of that right now—get up right now and go slip all that stuff into the front pocket of your suitcase. There. Done. Now we can move on to the fun stuff.
- **Toiletries.** Unlike your favorite hotel, the hospital will probably not provide you with a tiny bottle of Pert Plus and a complimen-

tary toothbrush. So pack a few essentials so that you'll at least be presentable (and have good breath) when visitors come to ogle your baby.

- **Chapstick.** I know that lip balm is technically a toiletry but it's so important in the child birthing process that I feel it deserves its own mention. Something about the sweating, moaning, groaning and screaming of childbirth has a tendency to make lips so dry that they crack—so play it safe and pack a couple of tubes of Carmex.

- **Massage Oil or Lotion.** Your hubby is going to need something to do while you're at the hospital, right? Get a bottle of yummy smelling massage oil and pack it along just in case he gets bored— or in case you start yelling at him that if he doesn't start massaging your back in the next twelve seconds you're going to go ballistic. Either way.

- **Phone Charger.** You won't be able to send a mass text with oh-so-adorable baby photos to everyone in your phone book if your cell phone runs out of batteries after you make fifteen calls to your doctor on your way to the hospital and seventy calls to your mother once you get there.

- **Socks or Slippers.** I chose to wear thick socks and slippers whenever I left the comfort of my hospital bed for two reasons: (1) The floors were supercold and I wasn't about to risk frostbite just because I had to get up to pee, and (2) despite the hospital's claim that the floors were sterilized, I just didn't 100 percent trust them. I've seen what goes on in those rooms—and it's in your best interest to keep a thick layer of fabric between your feet and those supposedly hygienic floors.

- **Nursing Pads.** Nursing pads are tiny little maxi pads that you stuff into your bra to prevent you from leaking milk all over your shirt. These things that you probably didn't know even existed until thirty seconds ago will soon become *an essential part of your* *daily hygienic routine.* If you don't believe me, ask one of your girl-friends. Then go buy a jumbo-sized box and practice inserting them into your bra quickly and discreetly.

- **Your Camera.** Every little move your new baby makes will be photo-worthy, so make sure you charge every camera battery, erase every memory card, and make sure that your camera, your video camera and your computer all have enough juice to load (and e-mail) a minimum of a trillion new pictures for each day you will be in the hospital.

- **Receiving Blankets.** The receiving blankets that they give you at the hospital are a different size than the ones you'll probably use at home. And if you go through Swaddling 101 with a blanket that's different than the one you'll use at home, you're going to have to relearn your whole swaddling technique on your first night home when you have a screaming newborn in your arms. It's better to just bring your own.

- **Boppy or Nursing Pillow.** If you have any intention of nursing your baby, you'll want a nursing pillow at the hospital. Boppys (and other nursing pillows) prop your baby up so you don't have to hold them in your exhausted arms while they eat. Trust me, this is a *very* good thing.

- **Your Laptop.** This may sound a bit extreme to some of you—but I'm an e-mail addict so this was a given for me. Many hospitals have Wi-Fi these days—and if you have your laptop with you, you'll be able to send out mass e-mails with pictures of your baby from your hospital bed. Plus, if you have any downtime—say, at three in the morning when your baby wants to nurse for two hours straight—you can head to your favorite parenting sites and chat about your wonderful and adorable baby.

- **A Going-home Outfit for the Baby.** As much as it would delight your mother to see her new grandchild come home in a fancy white lace Christening dress or three-piece suit—don't do it! This is partly because the hospital is no place for anything white, delicate or lacey, but also because it will take you more than an hour to finagle your tiny newborn into anything with buttons, snaps or a collar. Since you'll be new at the whole parenting thing—and your baby will be new at the whole getting dressed thing—it's best to keep your baby's going-home outfit as simple as possible. After a couple of mishaps, both of my kids went home in tiny, one-piece cotton jammies with matching hats—and they looked adorable.

- **Clothes for You.** This is a tough one. As much as you'd love to leave the hospital in your favorite prepregnancy outfit, it's not going to happen. Let me be blunt: *You will still be too fat.* And since I'm guessing you'd rather not be forever commemorated in your baby's first photos as the "woman in the giant muumuu," you're going to have to bring *something* cute(ish) to wear. Maternity clothes are the obvious (though revolting) solution, but I have yet to meet a woman who didn't break down in tears at the mere thought of wearing maternity clothes postpartum. So if that option is out, try going for a sporty chic vibe and wearing sweats and a hoodie. Another option is *lounge pants,* which is really just a fancy name for elastic-wasted pants that look good enough to wear in public. I bought a pair of corduroy lounge pants at the Gap and wore them for almost a month straight after my daughter was born—and I looked pretty cute, if I do say so myself.

Things NOT to Bring to the Hospital

- **Anything White, Silky, Soft or Expensive.** Let's just say that your supernice things will be exposed to a supermessy and superbloody scene at the hospital—and that anything you don't want to get stained should probably stay far, far away. That means no pretty silk nightgowns and no soft, snuggly hotel robes.
- **Your Underwear.** Here's the thing. The hospital actually pro-

vides you with special postpartum underwear that has been specially designed for postpartum moms. I'm not going to lie to you: This underwear (if you can call them that) are *not* nice. In fact, it is made out of jumbo-sized fishing nets and is scratchy, itchy and awful. But let me give it to you straight: The aftermath of childbirth is bloody. And not heavy-day-of-your-period bloody, but I-need-to-change-my-jumbo-maxi-every-hour bloody. Needless to say, you're going to be wearing a ginormous pad inside said hideous underwear and since you are still probably going to leak through (sorry), it's in your best interest to just leave your undies at home. You'll thank me when you don't have to spend your first few days at home Oxi-soaking your stained drawers.

- **A Book.** You may mistakenly believe that all that time you have while cooped up in the hospital will lend itself to you finally being able to read that dissertation: "The Qualitative Impact of the Pythagorean Theorem." Guess again. Your brain will be fried. There's a chance you will have the thinking power to thumb through *Redbook*'s latest beauty finds, but you will certainly not be able to concentrate enough to read anything longer than a paragraph.

- **Snacks.** Every other pregnancy book on the planet is going to tell you to bring snacks, but I'm recommending that you don't. When you're in labor, they won't let you eat anything except for ice chips. After you've had your baby, you're probably going to have something *very* specific and *very* delicious in mind. No use packing a healthy whole-grain veggie bar when all you're going to want to do is send your hubby out to get you a big carb-laden bagel smothered in cream cheese.

- **Snacks for Your Husband.** It's in your husband's best interest not to be downing handfuls of M&M trail mix when you're in the throes of a contraction, so save him the trouble and let him starve. Trust me, with all that sympathy weight he's gained, he'll survive a few hours without a snack.

Prepping for Your Arrival Home

I am a planner, so when I went to the hospital to have my son, his nursery was stocked with every possible baby item he could want or need. I had everything—diapers, wipes, clothes, sheets and sleep-inducing baby soap that was guaranteed to make my baby sleepy at night. I had washed (and rewashed) his clothes, double-made his bed so I could quickly change it in the middle of the night, and I had even set up a cute parade of stuffed animals on his bookshelf to welcome him home.

But in the midst of baby fever, I completely forgot to prep and plan for *my* arrival home. It never even crossed my mind that I would need things—until I arrived home from the hospital and had to send my oh-so-willing husband to the store for maxi pads and lanolin. And FYI, even the most excited new dads will probably balk when you send them to the store for "the biggest maxi pads you can find"—and even the most savvy new dads will not be able to find the kind you want in the panic of trying to get out of the feminine products aisle as quickly as possible. My husband came back with panty liners. Anyway, here are the things you should make sure you have on hand *before* you have your baby:

Things to Have on Hand at Home

- **Maxi (MAXI) Pads.** Just in case no one has warned you about the "period" you'll get after childbirth (technically called lochia), let me fill you in: The bleeding will start out heavy (think: the heaviest period you've ever had) and will last for about four to six weeks (I kid you not). You will definitely need some ginormous, extra-strength maxi pads when you get home. Buy the ones with wings. The silver lining here (yes, there is one) is that once the lochia is over, there's a good chance you won't get your period back for months (or even years if you breast-feed).

- **Nursing Bra.** If you plan on nursing, you're going to need to give your baby easy access to the coffee bar. But before you go out and buy a bunch of new bras, remember that your boobs are going to get even bigger—it's true, I wouldn't lie about something like this—after you start breast-feeding. So when you buy a nursing bra, buy one that's about one size too big.
- **Nursing Pads.** I know I already told you to bring a box to the hospital, but you'll run out of those. So buy another box for at home.
- **Breast Care Gear.** Your breasts are going to be used and abused in ways you never thought possible in the weeks after you have your baby. If you plan on breast-feeding, you'll need to plan ahead to deal with the soreness that comes from the constant sucking. I suggest picking up a tube of lanolin cream (from the drugstore)—it's spendy, but it's a real lifesaver. You can also buy some fancy lanolin gel pads to pop into your bra between feedings to soothe the chafe. Whether you breast-feed or not, you might want to pick up something to help deal with engorgement. Stuffing cabbage leaves in my bra seemed to do the trick for me. (It has something to do with the anti-inflammatory properties of cabbage—who knew?) My sister got Booby Tubes (Earth Mama Angel Baby Organics: earthmamaangelbaby.com) from a friend at one of her baby showers. Booby Tubes are basically beanbag-like compresses that you stuff into your bra to help relieve engorgement. My sister said they were wonderful.
- **Clean Nonmaternity Clothes.** Your old prepregnancy clothes are probably collecting dust in the attic—and it's fine to leave them there for a while as you won't fit into them anyway. But you will need *something* to wear. I recommend washing a few pairs of your husband's sweats before you go to the hospital so you have something to slip on during those first few days home.
- **Chocolate.** So there's a chance I'm an eat-away-my-pain type of girl, but having a baby can sometimes make a gal feel pretty down—and having a chocolate pick-me-up on hand can't hurt!

All Packed and Nowhere to Go

You're packed. Your house is stocked up. Your nursery is decorated. And now you wait. And wait. And unless you happen to go into labor early, you wait some more. And while you wait, you might as well have something to do. Here are my top nine suggestions for ways to pass the time while you wait for that first (real) contraction to come:

1. Address your baby's birth announcements. Many stationery stores (try tinyprints.com) will preship your birth announcement envelopes early so you can get them addressed before your baby arrives.
2. Plan a family trip to Disneyland. (So what if you don't actually go until your baby is seven?)
3. Find supercool nonmaternity clothes online and dream about the day you'll be able to wear them again.
4. Organize your closet, or your pantry or your junk drawer or any other nook in your house that hasn't been cleaned in years and certainly won't be cleaned again for years after your baby is born.
5. Learn to cook a new recipe. Husbands seem to be much more tolerant to hormonal pregnant women when the hormonal pregnant woman is keeping the fridge stocked with banana pudding, enchilada casserole and peanut butter pie.
6. See how many labor-inducing tricks you can try at once. For example, try to eat spicy food while walking around the block. Or, drink raspberry tea while doing acupressure. Or, if you're feeling really daring, have sex while drinking castor oil.
7. Watch *A Baby Story* marathon on TLC (if you can stomach it).
8. Make something crafty for your baby. Even if you're the least

crafty mama on Earth—and your project turns out looking like something your kid brother made in the fourth grade—your baby won't notice. Try your hand at a no-sew baby hat, a picture frame or—if you're really feeling motivated—handmade baby announcements. (By the way, if you need some inspiration, I love the book *Crafty Mama: Makes 49 Fast, Fabulous, Foolproof (Baby & Toddler) Projects*. It's full of supereasy and supercute projects that are unmess-upable.)

9. Pace the house ranting about how long you've been pregnant, glaring at any nonpregnant human being who dares to cross your path.

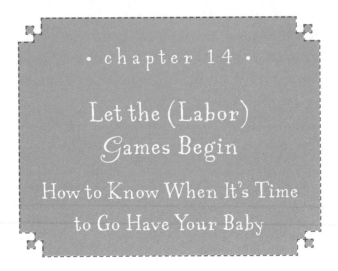

• chapter 14 •

Let the (Labor) Games Begin

How to Know When It's Time to Go Have Your Baby

You're probably past the point of worrying as to whether your baby will come out early (he or she probably won't). And you're past worrying as to whether you'll have time to paint your toenails before the labor pains begin (you won't and you won't care). You're probably even past the point of stressing about how much labor is going to hurt (it will, but you won't care because your baby will *finally* be coming). At this point, your number one concern is how you will know that you are actually in labor.

The answer? You will just know. Okay, I take that back. You will *probably* know. I do have one friend who didn't recognize her labor pains and ended up delivering her baby on the side of the road on the way to the hospital. (Both mama and baby were fine!) But that's a rarity. The vast majority of women deliver their babies hours after they arrive in the hospital—and most make at least three trips to the hospital in false labor before that.

Here's the thing: You're nine months pregnant. The very fact that you have been pregnant for nine-ish months pretty much guarantees that labor is about to begin. Your condition isn't infinite—as much as it feels like it is right now. And while you wait, there's nothing like obsessing over every little sign, symptom and detail of labor just to make sure you're adequately prepared. Let me help feed the obsession.

Signs That Labor Is About to Begin

Just to ease your worries about missing the onset of labor altogether and delivering your baby in the hospital elevator because you arrive too late, I want to assure you (again) that most women have plenty of warning that labor is coming. This will not be anything like the time that your long-lost Aunt Tilda showed up at your door unannounced (surprise!) and stayed for a week. You'll know Aunt Tilda is coming long, long (and did I mention long?) before Aunt Tilda actually arrives. Here are your warning signs:

The Nesting Instinct

If you find yourself suddenly wanting—no, I take that back—*needing* to dust the ceiling fan or arrange the clothes in your baby's closet by color, it might be a sign that labor is about to begin. This is called the nesting instinct—and it's God's way of making sure your house will be properly sanitized, organized and alphabetized before your baby arrives.

I'm a pretty anal person when I'm not pregnant, so when I had a sudden irresistible urge to puts the cans in my pantry in alphabetical order—you know, so I'd be able to quickly find the beans after the baby arrived—it didn't really seem out of the ordinary. But most women can probably chalk unusual cleaning and organizing behavior up to the fact that labor is impending. My friend Sarah started to suspect something was about to happen when she found herself on the bathroom floor scrubbing the grout lines behind the toilet with a toothbrush. Sure enough, contractions started in earnest about six hours later.

Sometimes, the nesting instinct involves paint instead of Pine-Sol. I remember waking up one night about a week before my daughter was born and feeling the sudden (and compelling) urge to paint flowers on her nursery wall. I was certain that if she came home from the hospital without a garden mural on her wall, it would somehow scar her for life. So, naturally, I did what any mother would do and got up, got out a paintbrush and started painting (don't worry, I used low-VOC paint just to make sure I didn't expose my baby to any fumes). When my husband caught me frantically mixing paint at three o'clock in the morning, he immediately knew what was happening—after all, this was my second pregnancy and he had seen the frantic, obsessive nesting instinct before. He just went back to bed and made a mental note that I would probably have my baby within the week.

Since the compulsive urge to clean, organize and sanitize is probably a fleeting sentiment, you need to take full advantage while you can. I guarantee that after your baby is born, you will never, ever feel the need to scrub your baseboards again so look at this as an opportunity to get your life in order. My sister Alisa capitalized on her nesting instinct by cooking several frozen meals that she could defrost for easy dinners after the baby arrived. My friend Jen stocked up on—and organized—scrapbooking supplies so she could easily make a baby book once the baby was born.

Also, I need to point out that not all nesting compulsions are safe. Yes, the fact that there is dust on the blades of the ceiling fan is probably driving you nuts—but you're going to have to wait until your husband gets home to clean it off. A high ladder is no place for a nine-months-pregnant woman. Similarly, sanitize away, but stay away from harsh, fumy cleaning supplies like oven cleaners that can be dangerous for your baby. Leave the oven cleaning to your oven's self-clean setting and do something less dangerous like scrubbing your closet shelves with a Brillo pad.

Dilation and Effacement

Sometime around thirty-six weeks, your doctor or midwife may start checking you for dilation and effacement. This involves putting your feet in those awful stirrups and allowing your doctor to check out what's going on with your cervix. Effacement refers to the thinning of the cervix and dilation refers to the widening of the cervix. Unless your cervix has gotten paper-thin (i.e., 100 percent effaced) and really, really wide (i.e., 10 centimeters dilated), your baby isn't going anywhere.

Here's the thing: You can walk around 100 percent effaced and 3 centimeters dilated for weeks without having your baby. I know this because I've been there. I was given the 100 percent effaced and 3 centimeters diagnoses at about thirty-seven weeks and left the office feeling pretty smug that my baby would arrive within the next few hours. I was induced a few days after my due date—so being 3 centimeters dilated and fully effaced did me absolutely no good at all. Likewise, you can also be closed tight as a drum and have your baby an hour later. My sister-in-law Annie was told she was 0 percent effaced and 0 centimeters dilated at her forty-week appointment and went into labor *that* evening. She had her baby early the next morning. Dilation and effacement are kind of like all of the other signs of labor and delivery. They tell you that something is happening—but don't tell you how soon it's going to happen.

Your Baby Drops

Sometime in the weeks before your baby is born, your baby will "drop" (technical term: lightening) or descend into your pelvis to prepare for birth. Like all other labor signs, this means that labor is coming (*duh*) but will probably give you no clue as to when. My son dropped about a month before he was born—but my friend Emily's baby dropped about two hours before she went into labor.

Regardless of the timing, your baby dropping is a good thing—not only because it means labor is coming—but also because some of the pressure on your stomach and lungs will be relieved, and it'll be easier to do things like eat and breathe. Of course, as with everything pregnancy-related, there's a stipulation. Yes, no more stomach squishing or lung kicking, but now your baby is camped out on your bladder. Good luck making it through a twenty-minute car ride without having to pee.

Losing Your Mucus Plug

A mucus plug is exactly what it sounds like: a thick, mucusy plug that's about the size of two or three quarters piled on top of each other. It serves the purpose of blocking off the opening of your cervix during pregnancy. When your cervix starts to dilate, the mucus plug has nothing to hold it in place anymore so it falls out—splash!—directly into the toilet. Completely gross, right?

I had been on the lookout for my mucus plug for a few weeks when I excitedly (okay, ecstatically)—what could be more exciting than a mucus plug?—noticed it floating in the toilet after I peed one morning. I, of course, screamed for my husband to come up and see—and he proceeded to stare disgustingly into the toilet as if I was showing him some alien life form that had somehow made it into the bathroom. When I explained what it was, he grimaced and then asked me why I had felt the need to show him *that*. Apparently he would've believed me sight unseen.

Anyway, losing your mucus plug is a sign that your cervix is dilating—which means labor can't be too far away. Like dilation and effacement, losing your mucus plug means one thing: Something is happening. But again with the speed thing—there are absolutely no guarantees as to how fast. I also want to be sure to point out that you may never have the privilege of actually seeing your mucus plug. My sister-in-law Stevi never saw hers and her doctor said that sometimes mucus plugs come out slowly over time as they loosen and dissolve.

Extreme Irritability

As we've already established, pregnancy has a way of making sure that everyone else in the world is completely irritating, insane and obnoxious. And when you're nine months pregnant and about to go into labor, you'll find that the fact that you're the only rational person left on earth will really start to grate on you. It's like everyone in your life seems to be on a mission to annoy you. Where does everyone else get off acting so crazy?

Insert deep breath here. I don't know how to say this—especially because my saying this will most likely result in you throwing the book across the room—*you're* the crazy one right now. I really don't blame you. You have lots of reasons to be feeling irritable. You're probably weighing in at about fifty pounds over your ideal weight—and your unseen ankles are probably swollen to double their normal size. Every ten minutes your body is wracked with a painful—but possibly unproductive—contraction. And to top that all off, you're sick of being kicked in the ribs by a baby who clearly wants to get *out*. No wonder you're acting a bit nuts.

You may notice that where before, you were cranky, irritable and moody, you now snap at your husband for rubbing your shoulders, are furious at your doctor for not inducing you and any conversation can turn from playful banter to an angry tirade in seconds.

Relax! The fact that you're completely off of your rocker is a good thing. It just means labor is on the way!

When I was 38 weeks, 6 days, 2 hours and 49 minutes pregnant (not that I was counting), I got sick and was admitted into the hospital for dehydration. In my mind, the obvious solution would be to *just get the baby out*—but my doctor had the gall to refuse to induce me because the hospital had a firm policy against inducing women before 39 weeks. I was furious. And since I was 38 weeks, 6 days, 2 hours and 49 minutes pregnant, I had a bit of a hard time controlling my emotions. I let the doctors...and the nurses...and the orderlies...and the nice woman in the room next door to me who was actually in labor know exactly what I thought of their decision.

I'm not saying that it's okay to act nasty just because you're days away from giving birth—it's not. But if you notice that people—especially your husband—are really starting to annoy the tar out of you, you might want to make a mental note that labor may be just around the corner. And with that in mind, withdrawing to a quiet place to read the Bible—or sort baby clothes—might not be a bad idea. At the very least, you can spare the ones you love from the mommy madness.

Diarrhea and Vomiting

For some reason as your body ramps up for labor and delivery, it also decides to clear itself out. So if you start puking your guts out like you did during your first trimester, labor might be about to start. Of course, you also could just have the stomach flu. Like I said, I was admitted into the hospital when I was almost thirty-nine weeks along because I was dehydrated from vomiting too much—but it was the flu, not labor. Bummer.

Your Water Breaking

For some (lucky) women, the first—and very obvious—sign of labor is their water breaking. My sister-in-law Stevi's water broke when she was about thirty-eight weeks along. She had some friends over to watch a game on TV and suddenly noticed that she was sitting in a pool of water on the leather couch. She stood up and the "water" continued to dribble down her legs and onto the floor—and before her husband could grab a towel, the "water" had pooled around her ankles and was starting to trickle across the hardwood floor.

If your water breaks, it will probably feel like you're peeing and just can't stop. The nonstop trickle of "water" pouring out of you, soaking your clothes and anything else you come in contact with, may seem relentless—and that's because it *is* relentless. As the amniotic fluid gushes out of your body and onto the floor, your body becomes an amniotic-fluid-making machine and literally starts pumping the stuff into your uterus at an astonishing rate. This is a good thing—because amniotic fluid protects your baby from infection—but it also means that once your water breaks, you're going to leak like a faucet until your baby arrives.

If you're concerned about your water breaking in public—say, while you're sitting in church or standing in line at the grocery store—you may want to take some precautions like wearing a super-duper maxi pad and carrying a small towel in your purse. While neither of these items will do a thing to stop the flow once your water has broken, they may buy you a few minutes to get to the bathroom before you soak the floor in front of a crowd of people.

If your water does break—you need to head to the hospital right away. Once your water has broken, it's pretty much a guarantee that you'll have that baby within twenty-four hours (*yay!*). This is because it would not only be pretty uncomfortable walking around town while gushing amniotic fluid, but also because after your water breaks, the membranes that prevent infection are no longer intact so your baby needs to come out.

Contractions

In my very official opinion, there are at least twenty-three different types of contractions—and since all of them pretty much feel (a) painful, (b) uncomfortable, and (c) annoying, sometimes it's hard to tell the difference between the type that mean you need to go to the hospital right away and the kind that mean nothing at all. Study up, my friend. You're going to be experiencing all sorts of contractions in the weeks to come—so you need to get in the know. Here's my primer on contractions:

- **Braxton Hicks.** If your belly is suddenly harder than your husband's presympathy-weight abs, then you're probably having a Braxton Hicks contraction. Braxton Hicks contractions are completely painless—and completely unproductive—so I tend to consider them noncontractions. At the very least, having Braxton Hicks will serve to remind you that your belly does at least have the potential to be rock-hard.
- **Maybe-Real Contractions.** These maybe-so, maybe-not contractions are actually superstrong Braxton Hicks contractions that trick some pregnant women into thinking they are in labor. Of course, once you have experienced a real contraction (think: lots more pain), you'll fondly look back upon your experiences with maybe-real contractions and see them for what they really were.
- **Walkable Contractions.** You may hear people say that a contraction is only real if you can't walk or talk when you're having it. Don't believe these people. I've had plenty of superpainful—and if you ask me, *undoubtedly* real contractions that I could walk and talk through. Even if the nurse at the hospital tells you otherwise,

you're definitely having real contractions in my book. But real doesn't mean you're progressing. So go home, kick your feet up and wait for the real not-walking, not-talking fun to begin.

- **Taunting Contractions.** Taunting contractions happen when you have walkable contractions that continuously grow closer and closer together until they are five minutes apart—and just as you toss your hospital bag in the trunk and buckle up, they subside as if they had been simply a figment of your imagination.

- **Dehydrated Contractions.** Dehydrated contractions happen when you're having walkable contractions that are five minutes apart and you call your doctor and she says to go drink a glass of water and call her in ten minutes. So you do as she says and by the time you call her back, the contractions have all but disappeared and she acts as if she knew that was going to happen.

- **Really (Really) Real Contractions.** These are strong, consistent, throbbing contractions that will make you absolutely certain that this time it's really (really) *for sure* the real deal. You'll be so insistent at the hospital this time that they'll rush you back and check you immediately—only to tell you that yes, you're progressing—but that you're still hours away from delivery so why don't you head home, put your feet up and come back in twelve hours or so once the contractions pick up their pace.

- **Actual Contractions.** Actual contractions are the contractions that make you realize that all of the other types of contractions really weren't real. And yes, this time, you can stay at the hospital.

Timing Your Contractions

Your doctor will probably tell you to head to the hospital when your actual contractions are about five minutes apart—and unlike taunting contractions—they stay five minutes apart for about an hour. With this in mind, you'll probably spend a lot of time in the weeks leading up to your delivery trying to figure out when it's actually time and when it's a false alarm.

Back in the day (like pre-1998), women had to time their contractions by hand—often assigning their husband the duty of manning a stopwatch, a pencil and a note pad. This method, while barbaric, was usually fairly accurate at determining when a woman could hop in the car and head to the hospital.

Of course, now that we're in the Google era, technology has advanced us far beyond archaic implements like pencils and paper. Now we use things like contractionmaster.com—a site specifically designed to help you time your contractions so you know exactly when to head to the hospital. Once you're signed into contractionmaster.com, you simply hit the spacebar on your computer every time a contraction starts—and then hit it again when the contraction stops. It'll keep a long, running list of your contractions and warn you once you win the contraction lottery and hit the five-minutes-apart mark.

For fancy mamas who have iPhones, you can also download a Contraction Master iPhone app—which means you'll have the ability to time your contractions anytime, anywhere. This could be very helpful if you find yourself stuck at, say, the mall while having unwalkable and untalkable contractions every six minutes. You never know, right?

Going to the Hospital or Birthing Center

Once you get to that magic five-minute mark, it's finally (maybe) time to go. So grab your (hopefully already packed) bag and your keys, get into your car with the (hopefully already installed) car seat, and go! Wait—one more thing—grab your husband or a friend or someone else to drive. You should never, ever (ever) try to drive to the hospital alone when you're in labor. Talk about being a distracted driver!

When you arrive at the hospital, you'll be shuffled into the ER waiting room or intake room and asked to fill out a bazillion pieces of paperwork and provide a thousand different ID cards and insurance cards. Most hospitals and birthing centers will actually let you preregister and get this paperwork out of the way beforehand, which is probably something to think about, considering the fact that filling in medical paperwork isn't the most fun thing to do while you're having contractions. Of course, you can also have your husband do it while you stand behind him screaming and moaning that he's the slowest person ever. Your choice.

When you're done with the paperwork, a nurse will probably bring you into the maternity ward or birthing room and hook you up to a contraction-tracking machine. If the thing starts going wild with beeps and mountains and valleys, it's a good sign! If the machine flatlines, it probably means you just have gas. Either way, once they've hooked you up to the machine to determine that you're actually having contractions (as if you couldn't tell), an OB—possibly yours, possibly the one on call—will come and check to see how far you're effaced and dilated. This is the moment of truth.

If the OB or midwife says that you're adequately dilated and effaced, you'll probably be admitted. *Yay!* You're going to have a baby! But here's the kicker—if your contractions aren't very strong—or they haven't done much to dilate and efface you, they'll probably send you home. That's right. You could've made that frantic, swerving and pothole-ridden trip to the hospital for nothing.

This actually happened to my sister. After a long, miserable middle-of-the-night trip to the hospital, the nurses hooked her up to the monitor, checked her for dilation and sent her home. She was having contractions—hard, strong and fast ones—but at that point, she was only dilated to two centimeters and the doctor felt she still had several hours before having the baby. They told her to try to get some sleep because it looked like it was false labor and would go away.

Naturally, she wasn't thrilled with that idea. She knew it wasn't false labor and wanted to stay as close to the hospital—and the epidural—as possible. She decided to go to my mom's house because it was closer to the hospital and spent a miserable couple of hours in the bathtub trying to get comfortable before making her husband drive her back to the hospital. This time, she had progressed enough to be admitted. She had her baby the next morning.

Labor can be a bit elusive—I know many a mama who was sent home from the hospital after timing taunting contractions that were strong and persistent enough to convince them that they were real. And that's okay. If you suspect you might be in labor, GO TO THE HOSPITAL OR BIRTHING CENTER. It can't ever hurt to get checked out, and even if they send you home, they'll probably at least give you a timeline about how close you are to the real deal. At the very least, you'll get some practice runs so when you really are in labor, you'll know which roads have the worst rush hour traffic and which bagel joints are open in the middle of the night.

I also want to remind you that the nurses and doctors and midwives may have fancy medical degrees, but they are not the ones who know what you feel like. They may not be seeing even a blip of a contraction on the monitor—or say that you're negative twenty centimeters dilated—but if you're feeling like something's not right, trust your instincts! My friend Megan was turned away at the hospital because she was only one centimeter dilated. She knew how she felt, so she just camped out in the hospital parking lot and sure enough, she went back in an hour later and she was already dilated to a six! So if you feel that you're really in labor and the nurses or doctors turn you away, don't be afraid to argue— or camp out in the parking lot until you can go back in and try again.

Getting Induced

When you're nine months pregnant and miserable, you're astutely aware that the only cure for your condition is giving birth. And since none of the old wives' methods of inducing labor tend to work, many pregnant mamas turn to labor induction as their method-of-choice for curing their late pregnancy woes.

I was induced with my son. I was miserable—utterly miserable—and after weeks of begging my doctor to do something, he finally agreed that if I went past my Christmas Day due date, he'd induce me. I, of course, sailed past my due date with nary a *real* contraction, so my doctor (finally) scheduled an induction for a few days after my due date.

Here's how getting induced works: Some doctors will bring you in the night before to give you a drug that will "ripen" your cervix. They may even let you spend the night in the hospital—and give you a nice little sleeping pill to help you get some rest. Sleep well, my dear. It will be your last peaceful night—if you consider being awakened every two hours by a nurse taking your blood pressure peaceful—for at least a decade. My doctor didn't see the need to ripen my cervix as it was already ripe (remember how I was dilated to three centimeters weeks before my due date?), so I was just asked to arrive at the hospital at the wicked hour of 5:00 AM.

After getting checked in, the nurses hooked me up to a machine to monitor my (non) contractions and put an IV line into my arm. Then, my doctor came in and broke my water "just to get things moving." (If you must know, he used a long, knitting-needle-like instrument to break my water, and it was slightly painful but nothing to write home about. The only really annoying thing was that the constant leaking of amniotic fluid created a cold, icky wet spot on the bed.) After that, the nurse added Pitocin—a contraction-starting drug—to my IV line and told me to watch the screen for the fire-works to begin.

At first, my contractions felt like really bad, really achy menstrual cramps. But within minutes, they came on fast and strong. My husband—who had the ill-advised idea to bring a movie to watch "while we waited"—realized fairly quickly that movie watching wasn't going to happen and instead, he was going to need to come stand by me so that I'd have something to squeeze during the contractions and someone to yell at when the pain got unbearable. Of course, as soon as each contraction finished, I was all sugar and sweet nothings until the next contraction started.

The good thing about an induction is that you're pretty much guaranteed that you'll start having contractions once the Pitocin starts to take effect. The bad thing about inductions is that you're pretty much guaranteed that you'll start having strong and fast contractions once the Pitocin starts to take effect. I can attest to that. I went from never having experienced a real, actual contraction to having hard, fast contractions one on top of another in a matter of an hour. And while I was glad to (finally) be having the baby, I wasn't exactly thrilled with the speed at which he was coming.

With this all in mind, you're probably wondering whether or not I would recommend that you get an induction. My answer: Maybe. I'm glad I was induced—I had been miserable for weeks and I'm not sure I could've handled much more time being nine months pregnant. But with that said, I'm certain that being induced made my labor come on much stronger and harder than it would have had I let nature take its course. So my recommendation to you if you're considering an induction is to (a) pray and (b) try to go until at least your due date before getting induced, just to see if your body will go into labor naturally.

Labor's a-Comin'

You will go into labor soon. It's guaranteed. Whether you've been dilated and effaced for weeks or you haven't started to progress at all, whether you've been scrubbing behind your bathroom mirror or haven't cleaned—or even thought about cleaning—in nine months, whether you've felt your baby drop or your baby is still kicking you in the lungs every ten minutes, you will go into labor soon. I promise. You will not be waddling around the house scrubbing baseboards and screaming at your husband forever.

Labor day is a-comin'. Are you ready to find out exactly what's going to happen?

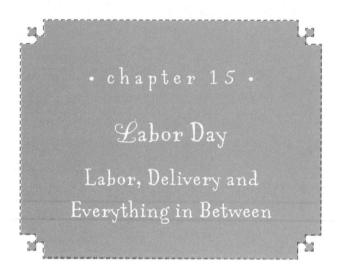

*W*hether you're induced or you go into labor naturally, there will (I promise) be a moment in time that you'll be told "Yes! It's go time!" and suddenly, in one exhilarating moment, your entire world will shift. When my *actual* contractions began in earnest, my first thought was *Finally!* and my next thought was *Is this really happening to me? I'm soooo not ready!* But ready or not, I didn't have a choice. That baby was coming!

While I was (patiently) waiting for labor, I had this idea in my mind that once labor actually began in earnest, it would actually *begin* in earnest and that things would be nonstop action until my baby was born. Instead, there were hours and hours of humdrum involved. Most first-time moms will be in labor for an average of sixteen hours. Just to put that in perspective, in sixteen hours, you could drive to the airport in rush hour traffic, hop on a plane, fly to Paris, order crepes for breakfast and still have time to go see the Eiffel Tower. It's going to take a while. And while some of the time will be action-packed, there will also be a lot of waiting—and a lot of contracting.

Labor day will probably be one of the best, worst, longest, shortest, craziest, most boring and most stressful days of your entire life. And at the end of the wild, messy and amazing journey, your precious baby will enter the world. That's the thing to focus on. That and a few other things—like contracting and pushing and squeezing your husband's hand until he thinks it's going to fall off.

Will It Hurt?

Yes. It's going to hurt.

I don't know anyone who entered labor day fully prepared for the amount of contracting it takes to fully dilate a cervix. When people refer to the pain of labor, they aren't usually referring to the pain of a single contraction or even to the moment of crowning. They are usually referring to the epic length of pain and exertion. It's easy to tolerate a painful contraction—or even a hundred if the end is in sight—but the not knowing how long it's going to take and having to face hours and hours of indefinite contractions is the hardest part. That's when women start to get discouraged.

But now that I've sufficiently terrified you, I also want to assure you that most girls I know have also told me that while the marathon of pain took them by surprise, the incredible feeling they felt when their baby arrived made all of that pain worth it in an instant. I'm not saying you'll forget the pain—you won't—but simply that when they place your tiny newborn on your chest for the first time, you will be so happy (and so relieved that it's over) that you won't care.

Turning to God in the Midst of It All

There will probably be a time during your labor and delivery that you will decide that you have changed your mind and you don't want to have the baby right now after all. You may even turn to the nurse and say something like, "Yeah, I think I've had a change of heart. Let's do this another day, when I'm more prepared and have had time to paint my toenails!" I don't have to tell you that labor doesn't work that way. There's no going back. Once contractions have begun, the only way to stop them is to deliver the baby.

Labor is long—and painful and exhausting and frustrating and trying. It takes a lot of perseverance on your part—and there will be times when you feel like you just want to give up and go home. When you feel that way, ask God to give you grace and strength. After all, Jesus himself had to persevere through some pretty painful moments (to say the least!). And while your trial of labor and delivery doesn't even compare to Jesus' trial on the cross, we can glean some wisdom from how He responded. Jesus turned to the father in the midst of His anguish—and God the father gave Him the grace He needed to persevere. God will do the same for you.

I want to encourage you to pray and turn your thoughts to God every time you start to feel hopeless, discouraged or crippled by fear during your labor and delivery. Instead of snapping at your husband (your first inclination) or begging the nurses for morphine (your second inclination), choose to turn to the Lord. He will grant you the grace you need to get through labor and delivery (and even your baby's not-sleeping, always-crying newborn phase).

The Spirit's Intercession

There may even be a point in your labor and delivery that you lose the ability to pray. I had an emergency C-section with my son, and there was a moment after they wheeled me into the operating room that my blood pressure dropped and my entire world seemed to tilt. I actually thought I was dying—I can't describe the feeling—but it was a terrifying, inexpressible moment where I was unable to speak, unable to move and unable to even comprehend what was happening. At the same moment, my baby's heart rate was floundering, so every doctor and nurse in the entire room was hyperfocused on getting my baby *out*.

At that moment, I couldn't even pray—no words would come to me. But I felt my spirit crying out to the Lord saying "God, God, please...." In Romans 8:26, we are told that "the Spirit himself intercedes for us with groans that words cannot express." When I was lying on the operating table—with machines whirring, doctors scrambling, nurses trying to bring my blood pressure up and my OB frantically trying to save my baby—I'm certain that the Spirit of the Lord was sitting next to the throne of God interceding for me. He knew what I needed—even though the most I could get out was a groan.

During your labor and delivery, there may be times when you feel the same way. Times when you want to turn to the Lord but you don't have the words to express what you need. That's okay. Just turn your thoughts toward Him. While your spirit is screaming "Oh, Lord, please..." His Holy Spirit will be putting those groans and moans into action and intervening on your behalf. That is very comforting when you don't have the words to express what you need.

The Epidural

I'm going to go ahead and get this out in the open right from the start: I am a big (big) fan of the epidural. So if you're looking for someone to convince you about the evils of pregnancy pain relief, this is *not* the place to be looking. I liked my epidural—a lot. As I said earlier, after they gave me Pitocin, my labor came on hard and strong. And after a couple of miserable hours, I was ready for some relief.

Here's how an epidural works: An anesthesiologist will roll a cart of supplies into a room and read you a bunch of legal disclaimers—basically that epidurals are generally considered safe for both you and your baby but as with any medical anesthetic procedure, they do carry some risk. You, of course, won't hear any of what he's saying because you'll be too busy having contractions, but your husband will probably be asked to sign off on some forms. Once all the legal mumbo jumbo is taken care of, they'll finally get to the good stuff.

At this point, it's probably in your best interest to close your eyes and go to a happy place. Getting an epidural involves the anesthesiologist sticking a fairly large needle into the center of your spinal cord, effectively dulling any sensation that you could possible feel down there. Any sane noncontracting person would probably opt out the second they spotted the giant needle—but when you're in the throes of labor and having contractions every three minutes, the needle will suddenly be very, very appealing. After the anesthesiologist preps the site (aka rubs a bunch of orange iodine onto your back), he'll ask you to curl into a ball on your side (as best you can when you have a giant belly) and he'll pop the needle right into the small of your back. When the needle goes into your spine, you probably won't feel much pain, but you may feel a somewhat disconcerting jolt down both of your legs. This means the epidural went in and your legs are getting prepped to stop feeling everything for the next ten hours. Once your epidural is securely in place, the nurse will probably put a catheter in. The catheter serves the very, very important purpose of making sure you don't pee your bed because your bladder sensation has also been dulled along with the pain.

Within minutes, you'll notice that your contractions have become a dull tightening in your abdomen—and suddenly the entire world will be a much, much better place. No more contractions. No more pain. And no more having to get up every five minutes to pee. It's wonderful. The nurse might suggest at this point that you take a nap—but you might be too giddy about the impending arrival of your baby to sleep. I was so excited about my epidural that I spent my last peaceful hours reading a parenting magazine and gushing to my mom on my cell phone about the wonders of modern medicine. I even allowed my husband to go down to the cafeteria to get himself a sandwich. Aren't I nice?

Going Au Natural

Despite my love of epidurals, I need to give proper credit to all of the warrior women who choose to give birth naturally. That sort of thing doesn't appeal to me—I'm not going to lie to you—but that doesn't mean that I don't give major props to those gals who do choose to give birth naturally.

There are actually plenty of compelling reasons for natural birth. My friend Kim didn't want the feeling of losing control of her lower body and felt like she'd be more confident on the delivery table if she didn't have any pain medication. My friend Aimee simply wanted to see if she could do it on her own, and was thrilled to find out that she could. And my friend Brianna, after much prayer and research, realized that a natural birth was simply the best option for her and her baby.

If you do choose to give birth naturally, I have some suggestions for you based on my experiences in an epidural-friendly hospital:

Stick to your guns. If you're dead set on having a natural birth, tell your nurses, doctors and anyone who is wearing scrubs that you're going natural. Don't let anyone try to convince you otherwise. There are lots of epidural pushers (read: me) out there who may try to tell you that an epidural is the way to go—so if you want to go natural, you may have to fight for it. Good thing you're a warrior woman, right?

Be willing to change your mind. I also know several women who changed their mind in the middle of labor. Don't be hard on yourself if you do. Make the decisions that work for you at the moment.

Come prepared with other types of pain relief. Since so many women end up getting epidurals, many hospitals don't have access to other pain relief options. Things like birthing balls (big rubber balls that help you ease into all sorts of laboring positions during labor and delivery) and back massagers aren't often available. So if you want to use those things, bring them with you.

Consider a hospital alternative. If you're absolutely certain you don't want an epidural, consider choosing a midwife, delivering in a birthing center, or even having a home birth. If there's no epidural available, you're not going to have to worry about being convinced to get one.

Natural Labor and Delivery

So I'm sure everyone reading this is wondering what natural labor and delivery feels like? Um, painful, yes, but how bad? I, of course, can't speak much about that considering my far-from-natural childbirth experiences, so I asked my friend Cara—who gave birth naturally in a birthing center—to give you the facts.

Cara said the best part of her birthing center experience was how peaceful and calm the birthing center felt. She had a private room with a big ole queen-sized bed where she could snuggle with her husband. She said for a lot of the labor process, she was able to relax and focus on her breathing techniques because she wasn't constantly inundated with beeping machines and pesky nurses (her words, not mine).

She also said that any time she felt like she couldn't go on any further, her midwives had another suggestion for the pain. They tried a birthing ball. And massage. And breathing methods. And Cara's all-time favorite: a giant whirlpool tub filled with massaging jets. Bet you'll never see one of those at the hospital.

Cara also said that by the time she was in transition and gearing up to push, she had gotten into such a routine with the contractions that it wasn't nearly as bad as she had expected. She claims that pushing and even the dreaded "ring of fire" (read: the moment when the baby crowns and stretches your vaginal muscles to the max) were the least painful part of the entire labor process for a natural mama because she actually got to *do* something with each contraction. Okay, so there's a good chance she was numb by then, but she also said it was nice to feel like there was actually an end in sight—and that her efforts were helping her get to the end more quickly.

Either way, Cara swears by her birthing center experience—and if I'm being honest—it sounds kind of nice. I'm not saying I'm interested—I'm an epidural girl at heart—but I do see the draw.

Home Birth

The idea of having my child at home scares me—not only because of the whole nonmedicated natural childbirth factor but also because I'm a neatnick and the idea of getting all of my sheets and towels stained and dirty really freaks me out. Also, I'd be remiss if I didn't start this section with a warning. Obviously, there are some risks to having a home birth. While the vast majority of home births turn out fine, there have been some recent cases of preventable maternal injuries and even deaths as a result of home births. But more and more mamas are choosing home birth as an option, so I'm going to give you the details—dirty sheets and all.

My friend Beth had her sons at home. (Yes, she did it more than once!) She chose a home birth because she was dead set on having her baby naturally—and she knew that at home, no matter how much she begged, she wasn't getting an epidural. Plus, she wanted to have her baby in a place where she was comfortable, relaxed and totally in her element.

She told me that when her contractions started, she loved the fact that she didn't really need to time them or worry about when to go to the hospital. Instead, she headed to the kitchen and made a pan of enchiladas (crazy, right?) and then relaxed on the couch watching *The Office*. A few hours later when the contractions started to get too strong for her to talk through, she called her midwife and her doula (a woman experienced in childbirth who provides support), who both came over right away and stayed with her for the rest of the process.

Beth said that the best part of giving birth at home (hands down) was soaking in her bathtub. Whenever the pain got really bad, her midwife would draw a nice, warm bath and she'd hop in. Beth says that the warm water relaxed her and brought her pain down at least two notches, which Beth says is quite a nice diversion when your pain levels are at a perfect ten toward the end of labor. Kind of makes you wonder why most hospitals don't have soaking tubs in their labor and delivery suites, doesn't it?

When time came for Beth to push, she moved to her bed to deliver her sons. She said she loved that she could make the birthing room her own. She had her own music playing. She lit candles. She had pictures of her family and friends on the walls. Her husband got to snuggle in bed with her, holding her hand and rubbing her back. It was relaxed and comfortable. Once her sons were born, things were even more relaxed. She was able to snuggle them and breast-feed them without a bunch of doctors scurrying about—and without nurses whisking them away for tests and shots. Plus, right after she delivered her babies, her doula went downstairs and made her a huge plate of fruit salad which she (of course) devoured. Sure beats hospital food.

Oh, and since I know you're wondering (or at least I was wondering), Beth says that she didn't have to throw away her sheets, towels and mattress after the birth. She actually purchased a home birthing kit (yes, they make them...ask Mr. Google) that had tons of absorbent mattress pads, gloves and everything else she needed. Her midwife changed out the pad every time things got dirty and replaced it with a new one and her sheets came through the process without a stain. Pretty smart, eh?

If you choose home birth as an option, make sure to do your homework. Research the risks. Pray about it with your husband. Make a plan on how you're going to get to a hospital if something happens, and most importantly, hire an experienced midwife to help you through the process.

Pooping on the Delivery Table

I know you're nervous that you might poop on the delivery table, and since no one else will talk to you about it, I'm going to cut straight to the chase and give you the dirty details. Yes, a lot of women poop on the delivery table while pushing, and no, you're not the only one who is terrified that you, too, will join the ranks and poop on the table in front of doctors, nurses and worst of all, your husband.

I was so concerned about pooping on the delivery room table that when my doctor told me on Monday morning that he was going to (finally) induce me on Tuesday, I made an inner vow not to eat for the rest of the day. I figured that if there was nothing in there, then nothing could come out. So I discreetly told my husband I wasn't hungry—and he never questioned me. I guess he figured I was just nervous about the impending delivery.

It turns out that my self-imposed fast was unnecessary because I had a C-section. But in the interest of getting you the answers you need—I polled my friends about the poop-on-the-table phenomena. Interestingly, the vast majority of them aren't sure if they pooped on the table or not. They were so involved in the pushing process—and so much was going on around them—that they didn't even notice if they did. The few people I know who did notice said that it wasn't the embarrassing, jaw-dropping moment that they had feared. Instead, the nurses quickly cleaned it away—often before their husbands even noticed.

So as mortifying as it sounds, pooping on the table probably shouldn't be a big concern. Yes, there's a (good) chance you'll do it, but there's also a good chance you'll never know you did. And even if you do know, you'll probably forget about it because pooping on the table probably means you're pushing—and pushing means your baby is just about to enter the world.

Puking During Labor

As if the moaning and groaning and pooping aren't enough, a lot of women also puke during labor. When I had my C-section, I literally threw up all over the lab tech who was monitoring my vitals. My friend Allana said she puked every time she got a contraction for the entire labor process. Evidently, the strain your body is under—you know, with all of that pushing and contracting and deep breathing—causes your stomach to revolt. And you end up puking your guts out.

The good news is that you'll have bigger fish to fry when this happens. Most likely, the nurse will hold one of those puce-pink kidney-shaped buckets in front of your mouth and wipe your chin with a towel and you'll be no worse for wear. And with all of the bloody guck and bodily fluids flying around that room, no one is going to notice a little puke thrown into the mix. So ask for a bucket and a towel and focus on what really matters: Your baby is a-comin'.

Expect the Unexpected

Once my epidural had kicked in, I was feeling pretty confident in my laboring abilities. The handy contraction monitor on my left showed a steady stream of peaks and valleys—meaning my uterus was contracting away. Of course, I wasn't feeling a thing, so I sat and enjoyed my magazine and my ice chips in peace. This had gone on for about four hours when suddenly the monitor at my bedside started beeping like crazy. My husband hopped up from his spot on the couch and within seconds, nurses and doctors swarmed to my bedside.

The nurse quickly explained to me that my baby's heart rate had dropped—and that I was going to need to go for an emergency C-section right away. My doctor rushed in, a nurse threw some scrubs and booties at my husband and they wheeled me into the hall. It was that sudden. Literally, I went from peacefully reading my magazine to preparing for surgery within three minutes. I was absolutely terrified—and absolutely stunned.

Naturally, I didn't relish the idea of surgeons cutting into my abdomen with a knife—and I certainly wasn't keen on living the rest of my life with a big scar etched across my stomach—but the worst part of the C-section to me was the fact that I felt like I was a failure for being unable to give birth vaginally. I was young. I was healthy. I had nice, wide birthing hips. Why couldn't I do this?

In retrospect, I want to encourage you to hope for the best—but to expect the unexpected. You may have a smooth labor and delivery—or you may end up with some complications. You may even end up with a C-section. Or a forceps-assisted delivery. Or having to give birth without an epidural. And just because things don't go how you would've hoped, it doesn't mean you're a failure. In fact, quite the opposite is true—not only did you just birth a baby, but you did it showing great courage and resilience. Go, you! And, really, none of the labor and delivery stuff matters once you have your baby in your arms.

Pushing

Since I have absolutely no experience with pushing—I had C-sections—my telling you about pushing is kind of like your husband telling you about multitasking. You can't explain what you've never done. So in order to give you all of the information you need, I had to call for reinforcements—aka my sisters, whom I begged to let me share their somewhat personal and semi-embarrassing pushing experiences with the entire world. Don't you wish you were related to me? But since I threatened to stop baking my world-famous chocolate chip cookies until I had all of the information that I needed for this chapter, my sisters reluctantly agreed. So here are all the gory pushing details.

My sister Alisa says that one thing that surprised her about pushing is that it isn't as urgent as you think. She had always assumed that once your cervix reached ten centimeters, it was time to push and time to push *now*. Instead, her doctor had her "labor down" for about an hour after she was fully dilated—assumedly so she could get some rest, but possibly because he wasn't quite finished with his morning latte.

But sometime after you've made it through enough contractions to dilate you to ten centimeters, you'll be told that it's time to push. What that means is—it's time to eradicate any semblance of modesty you have left. The nurse or doctor or midwife will ask you to stick your feet in the stirrups, grab your knees with each contraction and push like you've never pushed before.

My sister-in-law Stevi says that pushing is a lot like pooping—gross analogy, I know, but since that's the closest thing in human experience to pushing, that's the comparison you're going to get. So, basically, as each contraction comes on, you pretend like you're having the biggest bowel movement of your life—and keep pushing like that until the nurse tells you to let up and wait for the next contraction.

Depending on whether or not you have an epidural, pushing will rate on the physical exertion scale somewhere between an eleven and a sixteen (on a scale of one to ten). It's not only exhausting—you have to bear down like you're trying to push out a giant poo every minute or so—but it's also painful. I mean, if I tried to tell you that pushing a baby out of a hole the size of your vagina wasn't going to hurt, you'd call me a liar. So let's just be straight: It's going to hurt.

Pushing will take somewhere between the almost unbelievable "five-minutes-and-two-pushes," which my mom claims, to hours and hours and hours. Most women push for about an hour—which is about as long as it takes to pop a bowl of popcorn and watch one episode of *American Idol*. Not too shabby, right? If you can make it through an hour of Idol wannabes, you can make it through anything!

When your baby finally crowns—the fancy word that means his or her head finally emerges from the opening of your vagina—you're almost done. From there, you'll probably use the next few contractions to push your baby's head and then shoulders out, and after that, your baby's slimy arms and legs will probably slide out without much effort on your part.

From there, the doctor will announce "It's a boy!" or "It's a girl"—something that you most likely already know—and then lay your baby on your chest so you two can get acquainted for a few minutes. This moment is utterly indescribable. You've made it— and the reward for your trials will be better than you can even imagine. I promise you that no matter how wrinkled or cone-headed or prune-skinned your baby is—you will be absolutely awestruck by the amazing gift that God has just blessed you with. Absolutely awestruck.

Unfortunately, there's no rest for the weary. Just when you think you're done, the doctor will probably ask you to push some more so you can deliver the placenta. But don't freak—this should be pretty quick and painless considering what you just went through—and as long as you keep your gaze fixed on your baby instead of on what's going on, you probably won't even notice as the medical staff quickly discard the placenta and other gooey birth matter.

Once everything has been adequately cleared out, your doctor will start attending to the damage that has been inflicted on your nether regions. You may have an episiotomy—a small snip where the doctor cut your vaginal opening to make it a bit bigger so the baby could come out. Or your doctor may have just let nature take its course and let you tear naturally. Isn't that a pleasant thought? Either way, you'll most likely need some stitches. It will take quite a while for your doctor to stitch you up down there, but the good news is that it probably won't hurt—especially in comparison to what you just went through. You might be tempted to close shop and go play with the baby, but it's in your best interest to let your doctor do his work. Childbirth can be quite brutal on your lady parts, and it's good to let the experts finish their job by putting everything back into its rightful place.

Getting a C-Section

There are lots of reasons that women end up getting C-sections.

Your baby could be breech. Or you could labor for hours without progressing. Or you could push and push only to find out that your pelvic opening isn't wide enough for your big-brained baby's head. Or, if you're like me, your baby's heart rate might drop, causing your doctor to decide to get that baby out fast. Some girls even schedule C-sections. Whatever the reason, you need to prepare yourself for the fact that you ultimately may end up having a C-section—whether you like it or not.

If this happens, it will probably be a pretty quick process. The first thing they'll do is toss your husband some fancy blue scrubs and tell him to get dressed. Then, they'll quickly put the rails up on your bed and move your entire bed—and all of the monitors you're attached to—into the operating room. Let me warn you: The operating room isn't nearly as nice a place as the cute little delivery room you were probably in before. There are no pictures of babies on the walls, there are no windows, and—in case your husband asks—there is no TV where he can watch the "last two minutes of the game" while they prep you for surgery.

Almost as soon as you get in there, an anesthesiologist will administer either an epidural or a spinal. The difference here is fairly minimal—I've had both and really couldn't feel the difference, so I suggest you leave that decision up to the medical professionals and worry about other, more important things like what your baby's going to look like. If your C-section occurs after you've been in labor for a while, you may already have an epidural so you'll get to skip that part.

Once your epidural or spinal takes effect, they'll lay you down on an operating table and put a big screen up between your head and your belly. Up until this point, they've probably had your husband waiting out in the hall, but once everything is set, they'll allow your husband to come join you so that he can hold your hand and whisper sweet nothings into your ear, provided he promises to wear some cool blue sterile shoes and a hairnet. Try not to laugh at your husband and his hairnet when he walks in—I know he looks ridiculous—but if we're being honest, chances are you look even more ridiculous, so don't even go there.

Before you even have the opportunity to adjust to the fact that they're about to cut into your stomach, the doctor will already have cut a nice, long six-inch hole in your belly. You may feel some movement while the doctor digs around in there for your baby and then your doctor will probably warn you that you may lose the ability to breathe for about ten seconds. This is completely normal—well, as normal as having the complete inability to breathe can be. Basically, as your doctor pulls your baby's head out, your baby's feet will give your lungs one last farewell kick that will most likely knock the wind out of you.

Once your baby's head is out, your doctor will pause for a moment to clear the baby's lungs with a snot-sucker. At this point, your husband may want to sneak a camera over the screen to take a supergory picture with your baby half-in, half-out of your body. I don't recommend allowing this. The only thing more disturbing is a picture taken of a baby that's half-in, half-out in a vaginal birth.

A few seconds later, you'll hear your baby's first cries as the doctor pulls him all the way out and shouts "It's a girl!" or "It's a boy!" When my daughter was born, I had been absolutely ecstatic for months to be having a baby girl and so when my doctor pulled her out and said "Wow! What a healthy, beautiful baby," I took that to mean "Oops! I messed up on the ultrasound so now I'm going to conveniently dodge the whole gender thing and let her husband break the news to her." I, of course, being in such a rational mindset immediately started crying and said, "Please, tell me it's still a girl!" She was.

The real bummer about C-sections is that aside from a quick glance when they hold your baby up over the screen, you'll probably have to wait a long time before actually holding your baby. The nurses will whisk your baby—and probably your husband—away to do weighing and measuring and umbilical cord cutting while the doctor stitches you up. This can take quite a while—which is a good thing—because when it comes to closing wounds in your abdomen, you probably want the doctor to take his time.

Your New Baby

Once you're all stitched up, your doctor will bid you adieu and the nurses will finish their cleanup and probably move you to a post-partum recovery room. And then, after a flurry of activity—everything will go quiet. And in one magical moment, you will suddenly find yourself alone—for the first time—as a new family.

You've probably had high expectations about this moment for months—and let me assure you that your expectations are nothing compared to the way that you'll feel the moment that you look into your baby's eyes for the first time and realize that this—this tiny, beautiful person made in God's own image—is the child that God has chosen to trust to your stewardship. What an honor—and what a responsibility. And you're probably wondering *What now?*

· chapter 16 ·

The Christian Mama's
Guide to Your
Baby's First Days

What to Expect from Your
Brand-New Baby

*W*elcome to motherhood! I'm sure you've already realized that (a) your baby is the most beautiful, precious and miraculous gift God has ever given you, and that (b) with your beautiful, precious and miraculous gift comes *great* responsibility. But just in case it hasn't sunk in yet, let me tell it to you straight: That supercute baby in your arms—the one snuggled into a blanket and gazing at you with those big need-you eyes—is *yours*. Like *yours* yours. And he or she is going home with you.

Take a deep breath. Or seven. One thing's for sure: You are not the most unqualified parent to ever be responsible for a baby. I know this because if anyone wins the award for most ill-equipped parent to ever give birth, it's me. When my son was born, I had never changed a diaper in my life. So I had no clue how to wipe my son's cute little tush and put on a clean diaper. And that was just one of the many facets of parenting that I had no clue about. Breast-feeding? Never thought about it. Swaddling? Never even heard the word. Sleep training? Why would you need to train someone to sleep?

But guess what: I figured it out! Sure, I dealt with the occasional diaper leak and there was a time or eighty that my daughter ended up sleeping in my bed because the only way I could get her to fall asleep was to let her sleep next to me. But I figured it out. And you will too. In the meantime, here are the things you need to know to get you through those first few days.

New Baby Definitions You May Want to Know

- **Burrito Wrap [bu***h***-REE-toh rap].** A mysterious technique for wrapping babies in receiving blankets used by highly trained nurses in maternity wards. Babies who have been wrapped in a *burrito wrap* will instantly stop crying, close their eyes and fall asleep. Note to mothers: You will never, ever be able to replicate your nurse's burrito wrap no matter how hard you try, so it's probably in your best interest to buy a dummy-proof Velcro-closure swaddler.
- **Burrito Wrap [bu***rh***-REE-toh rap].** A delicious snack that your husband will rush out to grab you from Mr. Taco at nine o'clock after you realize that all this talk of burrito wraps is making you hungry.
- **Colostrum [*kuh* LOS *truh* m].** The thick, sticky milk that you'll notice leaking out of your breasts (and hopefully going into your baby's mouth) right after your baby is born. After a few days, this thick, superhealthy-for-newborn-baby milk will be replaced by thinner, wetter and equally-healthy-for-baby breast milk.
- **Ice Cushion [ahys K*OO*SH-*uh*n].** The big ole bag of ice that the nurses will plop under your bum—which will probably be sore for a few weeks—in order to make sure that the entire area is numb before the pain medication starts to wear off.

- **Lactation Consultant [lak-TEY-sh*uh*n k*uh*n-SUHL-tnt].** A woman who loves breast-feeding almost as fiercely as you love Ben & Jerry's—and will go to great lengths to make sure your breast-feeding experience is successful. At times—say, when she grabs your boob and squeezes it to demonstrate proper latch—her techniques may be a bit off-putting, but by the time you leave the hospital, you'll be tempted to invite her to come live with you. Just wait.

- **Meconium [mi-KOH-nee-*uh*m].** The black, tarry and sticky stools that will fill your baby's diapers for the first few days. Note: Due to the trauma of recent childbirth, it's probably best to leave the *meconium* diaper changes to Daddy—at least until you recover.

- **Nipple Confusion [nip-*uh*l k*uh*n-FYOO-zh*uh*n].** Only used in hushed tones in hospitals, nipple confusion is the terrifying condition where a baby is unsure which nipple—the bottle, the "paci" or the real one—they like best.

- **Nipple Maxi [nip-*uh*l MAK-see].** A small, thin pad that protects your shirt from the copious amount of milk that will squirt out and soak your shirt every time your baby cries.

- **Nipple Obsession [NIP-*uh*l *uh*b-SESH-*uh*n].** The strange phenomenon where you are suddenly obsessing over the health and well-being of your nipples—a part of your body that you've hardly given a second thought to before.

- **Nursery [NUR-s*uh*-ree].** The place you send your sobbing baby when you're bleary-eyed with exhaustion and are in desperate need of a nap. One caveat: Your nursery at home is not (I repeat *not*) staffed with professional pediatric nurses, so take advantage of the nursery while you're in the hospital. Once you get home, you'll be dealing with the bleary-eyed exhaustion on your own.

- **REM Sleep [r-e-m slee-ep].** By the time you have your next experience with deep, peaceful and refreshing REM sleep, you will not only know what the term *Ferberizing* means but you'll be so desperate that you won't be afraid to give Ferber a whirl.

- **Sucky Thing [SUHK-ee thing].** Contrary to popular nipple-confusion lore, pacifiers (aka "sucky things") are a must-have for any mom who wishes to (a) sleep, (b) nap, or (c) pry her baby off of her boob for five minutes so she can take a shower.
- **Vitals Check [VAHYT-ls chek].** The every-two-hour interruption where the hospital tech wakes you up to check your blood pressure, measure your heart rate and ogle your baby.

Your Baby's First Few Hours

Right after birth, your baby will be given his or her first little test—the Apgar. This serves the sole purpose of getting your baby used to standardized testing from an early age so they're prepped and ready for college entrance exams. Just kidding. The Apgar test is actually a newborn test designed to make sure that baby's basic vital signs like pulse, respiration, movement and reflexes are all functioning at a normal level. The test is administered by an official proctor (read: your baby's nurse) and is completely painless and unobtrusive.

A friend of mine once told me that her daughter had the highest Apgar score ever at the hospital where she was born, which sounded pretty impressive. But, unfortunately for my friend, your child's Apgar score has absolutely nothing at all to do with his or her future intelligence. My daughter had pretty terrible Apgar scores and she's the smartest kid I've ever met—besides maybe my son. Many babies—my daughter included—struggle with their pulse and respiration in the first few minutes of life, so keep in mind that if your baby's doctors and nurses aren't worried, you shouldn't worry either.

Once your baby's Apgar results are in, the nurses will whisk him or her away for some other new-baby formalities. First, the nurse will probably sponge-bathe off all of the childbirth goo and then she'll put your baby on a scale to be weighed and measured. This is really important so you can have something to write on your birth announcements besides baby's name and birthday.

Sometime during the weighing and measuring and cleaning, you may notice the nurse smearing some greasy eyedrops into your baby's eyes. This is not because he or she has dry eyes. These eyedrops are given to most babies (worldwide) at birth in order to prevent an easily treatable eye infection caused by bacteria that can live in the birth canal. This eye infection used to be a leading cause of childhood blindness and since hospitals made it standard to use goop at birth, infant blindness rates have dropped significantly.

Here's the scoop: The first shot your baby will probably get is a vitamin K shot. In the past, a very small number of babies suffered a potentially fatal bleeding disorder due to low vitamin K levels at birth. And since this disorder is hard to spot until it's already causing damage, most states have chosen to require hospitals and birthing centers to give a routine vitamin K shot to all newborns.

The second needle is a heel prick. The nurse will basically quickly stick a needle into your baby's heel and then squeeze enough blood from the tiny wound to test for some (superrare) genetic, metabolic, endocrinologic and hematologic diseases. (Okay, I confess that I have no clue what *endocrinologic* or *hematologic* means—but I Googled the correct terminology for you just so you'd be able to keep up with the nurse-talk at the hospital.) These diseases sound scary—I know—but if your baby does happen to have one of them, the earlier you know and can start figuring out treatments, the better.

Once all of the weighing and measuring and screening and vitamin-K-injecting is done, the doctors will probably have gotten your nether regions (or your abdomen if you had a C-section) stitched up, reassembled and iced down. At this point, they'll hand your now-exhausted baby back to his or her already-exhausted mother for a little bonding session. At this point, you may be able to make your first attempt at breast-feeding (if you haven't tried already) or just lie there and ogle the new addition to your family. You did it!

Moving to the Maternity Ward

Once the hospital staff has managed to get both you and your baby all clean and presentable, you'll get to make a move from the labor and delivery ward to the maternity ward. This is exciting stuff. Not only will you get to move into a nice, big (-ish) room, but you'll also have access to all sorts of maternity ward amenities like lactation consultants, ice bags to sit on and (best of all) an unlimited supply of tiny cups of grape juice and popsicles.

It's vacation time! You made it through months of pregnancy and hours of labor, and now you have earned yourself a couple of days stay at this all-inclusive resort (*er,* hospital). Just think. That means two *whole* days of on-call childcare, personal chef service (if you call the hospital cafeteria workers "chefs") and sleeping in a bed that raises and lowers at the touch of a button. Take advantage! Once you get home, if you want green Jell-O at two in the morning, you're going to have to make it yourself.

Most women I know loved their little vacation at the maternity ward resort. After all, who doesn't want to start every day with oatmeal and Tang hand-delivered to their bed on a brown plastic tray? You'll get your meals cooked for you. Your bandages changed. Your pillows fluffed. And entire days where your only job is to snuggle and coo at that cute little baby of yours. Sounds great, right? Plus, on top of that, the round-the-clock check-ins (read: supervision) by the nurses will probably help you feel more secure about your abilities as a new mother.

Of course, the flip side of all this is that the hospital food tends to be a bit gross (who drinks Tang for breakfast anyway?) and the pillows tend to be a bit flat. Plus, the constant check-ins can be a real drag—especially when check-in time occurs about ten minutes after you (finally) managed to get your baby to sleep. Unlike many women, I hated the hospital for these reasons—and begged my doctor to release me to the comfort of my own home where I could make my own (instant) oatmeal and drink real orange juice for breakfast.

Crying

By the time I had gone through all of the postchildbirth rigmarole, I was definitely ready for a nap. I double- (okay, triple-) checked to make sure my son was sleeping soundly in his little crib and settled in for a little siesta. I zonked—only to be rudely awakened by a baby's crying. Come on. What kind of mother just lets her baby cry and cry and cry? *Helllllooo!* People are trying to sleep!

And then it hit me. That was *my* baby crying. I scrambled out of bed and got to him just as his face turned red and he kicked off his nice little burrito wrap. I picked him up. He kept right on crying. I bounced him. He started screaming. I tried to shove my breast into his mouth. He screamed louder. Nothing seemed to help! And I started to cry right along with my son. My tears jolted my husband into action: He grabbed my son, propped him face-out and let my one-day-old watch Texas Football highlights. My little Longhorn fan quieted down in an instant. Hook 'em, Horns!

My point here isn't that it's imperative to indoctrinate your children to love Texas football from day one (although, that *is* important), but simply to let you know that newborns cry. A lot. And it's easy to get weepy and emotional when you're a new mom and your baby is hysterical and you don't know how to make him or her better. But your baby's tears have nothing to do with *your* parenting skills. So relax. Do your best to soothe him, and if you're getting nowhere, don't be afraid to let Daddy give it a go. He might just know some trick (*ahem,* Sports Center) that'll get your baby calmed down quickly.

The good news is that during your stay in the maternity ward, you'll probably get lots of practice soothing a crying baby. You'll learn what works (your breast), what doesn't (withholding your breast) and what to do in the middle of the night when you're drop-dead exhausted and can't get your baby to stop crying (call the nurse). Practice. Listen to the nurse's advice. And do your best to figure out exactly what makes your baby tick. After all, I don't have to remind you that in a few days, you're going home with your baby. And the nurses are staying at the hospital.

Circumcision

If you're having a girl, go ahead and just skip this section—it (thankfully) doesn't apply to you. If you're having a boy, read on. Sometime in the first few days of life, you're going to have to decide whether or not you want to circumcise your son. This involves a quick surgical procedure—usually performed by your OB or a neonatologist—to snip off the foreskin on your son's penis. This is done under local anesthesia—thank goodness—and barring an infection, the wound will heal completely within a week or so.

There is a lot of controversy as far as the benefits and disadvantages of circumcision. Proponents of circumcision claim that it's more hygienic, decreases the risk of future sexually transmitted disease and increases sexual pleasure. People in opposition to circumcision say it's an unnecessary surgery, can cause infection and that the benefits are unproven. I'm honestly not very opinionated on the subject (shocker!) so I recommend that you and your husband discuss it and pray about it and then do what you feel is best.

You Got Da Blues

About three hours after I had my daughter, I was in my hospital room and my entire family was crowded around me oohing and aahing over my baby. Suddenly, I started to panic. I felt an overwhelming urge to leap out of the bed, tear my IV cords out of my wrist, escape the crowded hospital room and find a quiet, calm place. The nurse walked in and took one look at me and immediately knew what was going on: I was having a postpartum panic attack. She turned the lights down, told everyone to leave the room, turned down the volume on the beeping monitors, and sat by me while I calmed down—explaining to me that moody, panicky, sad and claustrophobic feelings are completely normal in the few hours—and days—after childbirth.

While postpartum depression is a very real illness caused by postpartum hormones, it doesn't typically set in until a few weeks after childbirth. However, many women experience "the baby blues"—a hormone-induced surge of moodiness, sadness or nervousness right away after their baby is born. If you notice yourself feeling panicky, supersad, jittery, nervous or claustrophobic, call your nurse, doctor or midwife right away. They'll probably give you lots of tips, suggestions and even possibly some medication that can calm you down and help you to relax.

Sending Your Baby to the Hospital Nursery

Unless you happen to deliver at a nurseryless hospital (yes, they exist!), you'll probably have the option to send your baby to the nursery for a few hours so that you can grab some desperately needed uninterrupted rest. If you have this opportunity, take it! There is absolutely nothing wrong with sending your baby to the nursery for a few hours while you get some sleep. I repeat: *There is absolutely nothing wrong with sending your baby to the nursery.*

Many new moms worry that a two-hour separation (most of which your baby will sleep through) will somehow damage their newborn's ability to bond—and that this inability to bond will scar the baby's future ability to have productive long-term relationships. The truth is that your baby is tired too and will probably relish a bit of time to chill in the nursery and snooze away from all of the oohing, aahing and cheek pinching. And you need some sleep too. Look at it this way: You'll be a better mother if you're well-rested. Your baby needs you to be a well-rested, well-adjusted mother. So send the little munchkin to the nursery and get yourself some rest while you still have a staffed nursery at your disposal.

Breast-Feeding 101

Here's something the cute moms in your church who discreetly breast-feed their tiny babies beneath modesty nursing covers probably haven't told you: Breast-feeding is hard. Not like labor and delivery hard (*whew*) but it definitely takes more skill than, say, opening a bottle of formula and popping it into your baby's mouth.

I'm not saying this to discourage you from trying—because I'm a huge breast-feeding advocate. I love breast-feeding. So much so, in fact, that I had a hard time stopping breast-feeding—even after my kids were old enough to pull at my shirt and ask for *"mimis"* in public, but I digress. At first, I hated breast-feeding. It was stressful and painful and frustrating—and I was in no state as a brand-new mom to deal with anything remotely stressful, painful or frustrating. But I sucked it up and did it anyway. Girl, if you can survive pregnancy *and* labor *and* delivery *and* a nine-month hiatus from venti mochas with whip, you can survive anything. Breast-feeding included.

Breast-feeding is so great for your baby. Recent research has shown that breast-fed babies have a much lower risk of health problems like ear infections, stomach ailments, leukemia, SIDS and childhood obesity. Plus, breast-feeding is great for you too. Not only will you lose the baby weight faster, but recent studies have shown that breast-feeding moms have a lower incidence of postpartum depression. Talk about a win-win.

Breast-Feeding Tips for the First Three Weeks

- **Get the latch right—right away.** If the baby's getting milk, then it's working, right? Wrong. If your baby is latching on incorrectly, not only will he or she be getting less milk, but it'll also tear up your nipples, creating a ton of pain during breast-feeding. Ask your nurse (or lactation consultant) to check your baby's latch before you leave the hospital and save yourself a lot of pain later when you're trying to feed a starving baby with cracked, bleeding and supersore nipples.
- **Figure out several positions that work.** While you're at the hospital—with access to trained professionals who understand how breast-feeding works—figure out several breast-feeding positions that work for you and your baby. My son loved the "football hold" where he lay on his side and nursed from the crook of my arm. My daughter loved nursing while I was lying down, which came in handy when I was too tired to get up to nurse her.
- **Make a three-week goal.** Of course, you should breast-feed for much longer than three weeks if you can, but in order to get you over the hump, I suggest making it your goal to breast-feed for at least three weeks. Because if you can make it through the first three weeks, you can probably make it much longer. For me, the

first week hurt because of sore nipples, and the second week wasn't fun due to engorgement, but after that, it was smooth sailing.

- **Stock up on lanolin.** You can get all sorts of fancy nipple treatments to soothe sore and cracked nipples. I've seen breast compresses, breast creams and even (get this) breast tea. But I've found that your best bet is plain old lanolin cream. Pick up a couple of bottles and use it liberally until you get into the breast-feeding groove.

- **Give yourself a break.** I know there's a bunch of talk about nipple confusion and how you should probably just breast-feed your baby for the first twenty years just in case, but if you need a break, give yourself a break. Your baby will be just fine if you pump a bottle and have Daddy get up for the 2:00 AM feeding from time to time.

- **Don't overdo the pumping.** Little anatomy lesson here: The more milk your baby takes, the more milk your body makes. So if you're feeding your baby every two hours—and then pumping in between feedings—your body is going to go into milk production overdrive. When milk production is in overdrive, you'll end up with all sorts of fun things like engorged breasts, too-tight bras and milk-soaked shirts. Hold off on filling your freezer with an infinite supply of breast milk for a few months until you've gotten into a routine.

- **Get a good (tight) sports bra.** Your milk will come in a few days after your baby is born, and at this point, your boobs will resemble those small personal watermelons that you see at the grocery store—in size *and* firmness. The only way to ease the pressure (and pain) of engorgement is to nurse your baby—and sometimes, say, when you just spent four hours rocking your baby to sleep—nursing your baby just isn't possible. For those times, get a good, tight sports bra (or an ace bandage) to support your knockers.

- **Don't give up.** There will be a moment (or twelve) that you want to quit breast-feeding. Your nipples will hurt. You'll get tired of having a little leech (*er,* baby) attached to your breast 24-7. You'll want someone else to take some of the feeding load off of your shoulders. It's not easy, but if you can make it through, it'll be worth it. By the time your baby is two or three months old, breast-feeding will seem like the easiest and most natural thing in the world.

Formula Feeding

Even with the best intentions, some mamas just aren't able to breast-feed. And that's okay! If it's not working for you—whether you've tried once or fifteen thousand times—make the switch to formula. Your baby will be fine. Think of it this way—if you put ten two-year-olds in a room and asked someone to guess which toddlers had been breast-fed, I'd be willing to bet my Maclaren that you wouldn't be able to tell the formula-fed babies from the breast-fed ones. I'm not naïve enough to believe that just because breast-feeding was right for me, it's right for everyone or that every mom who wants to breast-feed is able to.

Eight Common Myths about Newborns

- You'll get some sleep in a few days once your baby figures out the whole day/night reversal thing. (*The truth:* You'll get some sleep in a few years once you realize that your four-year-old can figure out how to get his own glass of water in the middle of the night and that the words *bad dream* are not an automatic excuse to spend the rest of the night in mommy's bed.)
- You can spoil your baby if you hold him too much. (*The truth:*

Does your hubby spoil you when he snuggles up and rubs your back? Nuh-uh.)

- If you eat spicy or flavorful food when you're breast-feeding, your baby will get all gassy and cranky on you. (*The truth:* Your baby is going to get gassy and cranky on you no matter what—but if you don't get some pad thai ASAP, you're going to get cranky. And that's avoidable.)

- New babies are adorable. (*The truth:* Your baby will probably come out with a cone head, baby acne and a smooshed face—if you're lucky! But within a week or two, your baby really *will* be adorable.)

- You'll get a good three- to four-hour break between feedings. (*The truth:* If it were up to your baby, she'd camp out on your boob around the clock. But the reality is that newborns can usually go about three hours from the start of one feeding to the start of the next, which means you'll get a two-hour break between feedings max.)

- You can't go outside for the first few months because your baby may get sick. (*The truth:* Yes, it's probably a good idea to limit your baby's exposure to runny-nosed preschoolers and crowded public spaces, but that doesn't mean you have to spend the next two months in the house. Go out on a walk or head to Grandma's house. Just remember to bring along a bottle of Purell and to wash your hands often!)

- You'll want to spend every waking moment with your baby from the moment he or she is born. (*The truth:* You will be physically and emotionally drained after pregnancy, labor and delivery and will probably need a few weeks—or months—to recuperate. It's a good idea—wait, strike that, a *great* idea—to let your husband or your mother-in-law tend to your baby for a few hours a day so you can take a nap and recover.)

- You'll just *naturally* know what to do with your baby. (*The truth:* There will be moments when you have no clue what you're doing. There will be days when your baby spends more time crying than he or she does sleeping. There will even be times when you make mistakes, get frustrated and feel ready to give up. And at those times, your only recourse is to turn to God. He chose to give you stewardship of your baby and He will give you the skills you need to raise your child up. Trust yourself. And more importantly, trust Him.)

Going Home

I was giddy when I (finally) got my discharge papers for my son. Suddenly, everything I had been dreaming about was finally coming to fruition...we were going home! And my supercute baby was coming with me! I was ecstatic—not only because I got to leave the hospital (and the shots and the pain meds and the Jell-O)—but because I felt like for the first time, I was officially a mother. I was on my own. And I was ready.

Okay, I was sort-of ready. Apparently there's a whole lot more to checking out of the hospital than paying your co-pay and dressing your baby in a cute going-home outfit. I needed security checks. And a car seat check. And a wheel chair. And a latte. But eventually—after a quick run-in with too-big car seat straps—I hopped into the backseat (there was no way I was going to let my baby out of my sight) and we were off.

Five minutes later, we had to pull over. My son had gotten hungry in the twenty-nine minutes that had passed between his last feeding and load time. I breast-fed him on the side of the road and then strapped him back in and we were off. Ten minutes later, we had to pull over again. This time it was a dirty diaper. And he was hysterical. We pulled out our newly stocked diaper bag and laid a squeaky-clean changing pad on the front seat and carefully wiped the kid down. We resnapped his pants and restrapped him in and we were off.

When we finally pulled into our driveway fifteen minutes later, we giddily plopped down on the couch and grinned. We had made it—through the morning sickness and weight gain, through the baby naming and labor contractions, through the hospital stay and first sleepless nights. We had survived! And now we were ready to embark on an entire new chapter of our lives—a chapter that would certainly involve a huge learning curve, but that would also involve an indescribable God-given joy. We were a family. A brand-new (and albeit very inexperienced) family, but a family nonetheless. And we were home.

$\mathcal{G}$uess what? I'm pregnant. Again.

I found out this morning. My two-year-old daughter Kate woke up at the crack of dawn (you'll soon find out that toddlers tend to do that) and came to my bedside to tell me that she was tired of sleeping. And that Jesus had told her that it was a new day and time to play even if it was still dark outside. I moaned and groaned and rolled out of bed and headed to the bathroom so that I could at least brush my teeth and pee before the day began.

As I brushed my teeth, my daughter pulled a box of tampons out of the cabinet. And it dawned on me. My period was late. Like really, *really* late. And, of course, with two kids, two dogs, a husband and a partridge in a pear tree to care for, I hadn't even noticed. I grabbed a pregnancy test and ran to the toilet. My daughter took one look at me peeing on the stick and proceeded to run out and tell my husband that "mommy is going potty on her toys." Uh-huh.

Two minutes and one big fat positive test later, I ran out of the bathroom to tell my still-sleepy husband. It took him a minute to figure out what I was saying, but then he started laughing.

He leaped out of bed and bent me backward and kissed me on the lips right in front of our daughter. You see, crazy as it is to be pregnant again (*three* kids...gulp!), it's also superexciting. We're ecstatic.

My kids are thrilled as well. Josiah has already started praying fervently for a brother. He has also suggested that we call his new baby brother either Obi-Wan Kenobe or Spiderman. Kate, on the other hand, wants sisters. Three of them, to be exact. And she thinks I should name all three of them Princess Kayley.

Of course, we have a long road ahead of us—and I know it won't be easy. Pregnancy never is. I fell asleep at seven o'clock last night (before the *American Idol* finale). While I'm not feeling sick yet, I know morning sickness and bloating and weight gain are all around the corner. Yes, it'll be a long road. But a wonderful one—one that we'll survive with a lot of prayer and a freezer full of ice cream.

For now, I'm just reveling in the fact that God has chosen to bless us again. We're going to have another baby.

PS: For more information on this current pregnancy, future books, press appearances and to send me an e-mail—please visit my Web site at christianmamasguide.com.

Index

A Note to the Reader

To my Christian mama friends:

Congrats on your new baby! I'm so glad we were able to take this journey together and I pray that your transition into motherhood is full of tender and sweet moments.

I would love to hear more about you—and of course, your baby. Please drop by my Web site at christianmamasguide.com or e-mail me at erin@christianmamasguide.com. I can't wait to get to know you!

Blessings,

Erin